Paraguay
a country study

Federal Research Division
Library of Congress
Edited by
Dennis M. Hanratty
and Sandra W. Meditz
Research Completed
December 1988

On the cover: Ñandutí lace

Second Edition, 1990; First Printing, 1990

Library of Congress Cataloging-in-Publication Data

Paraguay: A Country Study

  Area Handbook Series (DA Pam. 550-156)
  Research completed December 1988.
  Bibliography: pp. 255-270.
  Includes index.
  1. Paraguay. I. Hanratty, Dennis M., 1950- . II. Meditz, Sandra W., 1950- . III. Library of Congress. Federal Research Division. IV. Series. V. Series: DA Pam. 550-156.

F 2668.P24   1990   989.2-dc20   89-600299

Headquarters, Department of the Army
DA Pam 550-156

For sale by the Superintendent of Documents, U.S. Government Printing Office
Washington, D.C. 20402

Foreword

This volume is one in a continuing series of books now being prepared by the Federal Research Division of the Library of Congress under the Country Studies—Area Handbook Program. The last page of this book lists the other published studies.

Most books in the series deal with a particular foreign country, describing and analyzing its political, economic, social, and national security systems and institutions, and examining the interrelationships of those systems and the ways they are shaped by cultural factors. Each study is written by a multidisciplinary team of social scientists. The authors seek to provide a basic understanding of the observed society, striving for a dynamic rather than a static portrayal. Particular attention is devoted to the people who make up the society, their origins, dominant beliefs and values, their common interests and the issues on which they are divided, the nature and extent of their involvement with national institutions, and their attitudes toward each other and toward their social system and political order.

The books represent the analysis of the authors and should not be construed as an expression of an official United States government position, policy, or decision. The authors have sought to adhere to accepted standards of scholarly objectivity. Corrections, additions, and suggestions for changes from readers will be welcomed for use in future editions.

Louis R. Mortimer
Acting Chief
Federal Research Division
Library of Congress
Washington, D.C. 20540

Acknowledgments

The authors wish to acknowledge the contributions of Thomas E. Weil, Jan Knippers Black, Howard I. Blutstein, David S. McMorris, Frederick P. Munson, and Charles Townsend, who wrote the 1972 edition of the *Area Handbook for Paraguay*. Portions of their work were incorporated into the present volume.

The authors are grateful to individuals in various agencies of the United States government and private institutions who gave their time, research materials, and special knowledge to provide information and perspective. None of these agencies or institutions is in any way responsible for the work of the authors, however.

The authors also wish to thank those who contributed directly to the preparation of the manuscript. These include Richard F. Nyrop, who reviewed all drafts and served as liaison with the sponsoring agency; Barbara Dash, Deanna D'Errico, Vincent Ercolano, Richard Kollodge, and Sharon Schultz, who edited the chapters; Martha E. Hopkins, who managed editing and production; and Barbara Edgerton, Janie L. Gilchrist, and Izella Watson, who did the word processing. Catherine Schwartzstein performed the final prepublication editorial review, and Shirley Kessel of Communicators Connection compiled the index. Linda Peterson and Malinda Neale of the Library of Congress Printing and Processing Section performed phototypesetting, under the supervision of Peggy Pixley.

David P. Cabitto, who was assisted by Sandra K. Cotugno and Kimberly A. Lord, provided invaluable graphics support. Susan M. Lender reviewed the map drafts, which were prepared by Harriett R. Blood, David P. Cabitto, and Sandra K. Cotugno. Sandra K. Cotugno also deserves special thanks for designing the illustrations for the book's cover and the title page of each chapter.

The authors also would like to thank several individuals who provided research support. Arvies J. Staton supplied information on military ranks and insignia, and Karen M. Sturges-Vera wrote the section on geography in Chapter 2.

Finally, the authors acknowledge the generosity of the individuals and the public and private agencies who allowed their photographs to be used in this study. We are indebted especially to those who contributed original work not previously published.

Contents

Chapter 3. The Economy 97
Daniel Seyler

List of Figures

Preface

Like its predecessor, this study is an attempt to treat in a compact and objective manner the dominant social, political, economic, and military aspects of contemporary Paraguay. Sources of information included scholarly books, journals, and monographs; official reports of governments and international organizations; numerous periodicals; and interviews with individuals having special competence in Paraguayan and Latin American affairs. Chapter bibliographies appear at the end of the book; brief comments on sources recommended for further reading appear at the end of each chapter. Measurements are given in the metric system; a conversion table is provided to assist readers unfamiliar with metric measurements (see table 1, Appendix). A glossary is also included.

Although there are numerous variations, Spanish surnames generally consist of two parts: the patronymic name followed by the matronymic. In the instance of Alfredo Stroessner Mattiauda, for example, Stroessner is his father's name, Mattiauda, his mother's maiden name. In informal use, the matronymic is often dropped. Thus, after the first mention, we have usually referred simply to Stroessner. A minority of individuals use only the patronymic. Special rules govern discussion of Francisco Solano López, who is referred to throughout this book as Solano López to differentiate him from his father, Carlos Antonio López.

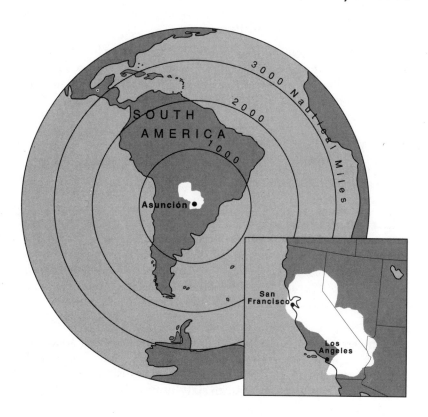

Country

Formal Name: Republic of Paraguay (República de Paraguay).

Short Form: Paraguay.

Term for Citizens: Paraguayan(s).

Capital: Asunción.

Geography

Size: 406,750 square kilometers.

Topography: Divided by Río Paraguay into eastern Paraneña and western Chaco regions. Paraneña landform ranges from lowlands to mountains, highest elevations occurring near border with Brazil.

Chaco's vast low plain—more than 60 percent of Paraguay's total land area—alternately flooded and parched. About 95 percent of population concentrated in Paraneña.

Climate: Subtropical, humid climate in Paraneña with abundant rainfall evenly distributed throughout the year. Tropical climate in Chaco with distinct wet and dry seasons. Modest seasonal variations in temperature in both regions.

Society

Population: 1988 population estimates ranged from 4 to 4.4 million; rate of annual growth estimated at from 2.5 to 2.9 percent in the late 1980s.

Education and Literacy: Compulsory attendance to age fourteen or completion of six-year primary level. Three-year secondary education programs offered in humanities or technical training. University studies available through two institutions, one state-sponsored and the other operated by the Roman Catholic Church. Official literacy rate estimated at over 80 percent in the mid-1980s.

Health: Most people had ready access to medical care of some kind; nonetheless, system's overall effectiveness limited by inadequate funding, supplies, service coordination, and data collection, as well as heavy concentration of medical personnel in urban areas. In the late 1980s, life expectancy at birth sixty-nine for females and sixty-five for males.

Languages: Guaraní recognized as national language and spoken by approximately 90 percent of people in late 1980s. Spanish official language but understood by only 75 percent of the population. Portuguese predominant in area near Brazilian border.

Ethnic Groups: In the late 1980s, approximately 95 percent of population was mestizo; remainder were Indians, Asians, or whites. In 1970s and 1980s, substantial immigration of Brazilians, Koreans, and ethnic Chinese.

Religion: Estimated 92 to 97 percent of the population were Roman Catholics in 1980s; remainder Mennonites or other Protestant groups.

Economy

Gross Domestic Product (GDP): Approximately US$3.4 billion in 1986, roughly US$1,000 per capita. Substantial growth recorded in late 1970s, followed by decline in early 1980s and some recovery in mid- to late 1980s.

Agriculture: About 23 percent of GDP in 1985; also accounted for approximately half of all employment and virtually all export earnings. In 1981 about 7 percent of land dedicated to crop production, 20 percent to forestry, 26 percent to livestock, and 47 percent to other purposes. Main crops—soybeans, cotton, tobacco, coffee, sugarcane, oilseeds, manioc (cassava), corn, beans, peanuts, and wheat. Highly skewed distribution of land.

Industry: About 23 percent of GDP in 1986, including manufacturing (over 16 percent of GDP) and construction (nearly 6 percent of GDP). Manufacturing generally small-scale and focused on consumer goods. Construction activity fluctuated dramatically during the mid- to late 1980s following several years of brisk growth.

Energy: Less than 3 percent of GDP in 1986, but tremendous hydroelectric growth potential. Expected to become world's largest exporter of electricity in 1990s.

Services: About 51 percent of GDP in 1986. Included financial services, transportation and communications, informal services, government services, and tourism.

Imports: Approximately US$898 million in 1986, over 40 percent of which unregistered. Imports mainly manufactured products, capital goods, and fuels.

Exports: Approximately US$371 million in 1986, almost 40 percent of which unregistered. Soybeans and cotton over 60 percent of exports.

Balance of Payments: Acute balance of payments situation in late 1980s, result of an increasing merchandise trade deficit and a decreased level of private capital investment. International reserves equalled less than four months of imports. From 1980 to 1987, indebtedness more than doubled, to roughly US$2 billion. Debt as a percentage of GDP climbed to above 50 percent. Debt restructuring under way in 1989.

Exchange Rate: Guaraní (G) pegged to United States dollar from 1960 to 1982 but devalued numerous times during the mid- to late 1980s. Five exchange rates in use in 1987, reduced to three in mid-1988. Free-market rate exceeded G1,000 = US$1 by early 1989. Multiple exchange-rate system abolished in mid-1989.

Fiscal Year: Calendar year.

Fiscal Policy: Substantial cutbacks in current and capital expenditures in mid-1980s resulted in 1986 budget deficit under 1 percent of GDP. In 1986 public-sector deficit reached 7 percent of GDP because of parastatals' poor financial performance and access to preferential exchange rates.

Transportation and Communications

Roads: In late 1980s, over 15,000 kilometers, 20 percent paved. Most important paved roads linked Asunción to Puerto Presidente Stroessner and Encarnación. Trans-Chaco Highway, 700 kilometers long, under construction.

Railroads: Outdated 367-kilometer passenger and cargo line between Asunción and Encarnación; also small cargo line near Brazilian border.

Ports: Ten ports, the most important being Asunción and Villeta. Brazilian ports of Santos and Paranaguá also handled substantial amount of Paraguayan goods via an overland route from Puerto Presidente Stroessner.

Airports: Only all-weather airports at Asunción, which handled all international flights, and Mariscal Estigarribia.

Telecommunications: Poor communications and domestic telephone services; adequate international service.

Government and Politics

Government: Central government divided into three branches: executive, legislative, and judiciary. Under provisions of Constitution of 1967, chief executive is president of the republic, elected by popular vote for five-year term. Within twenty-four hours of president's resignation, death, or disability, the legislature and an advisory body, the Council of State, designate a provisional president. If at least two years of term have elapsed, provisional president serves out full term. If fewer than two years have elapsed, elections are to be held within ninety days. Legislature consists of Senate with at least thirty members and Chamber of Deputies with at least sixty members, plus alternates. Members popularly elected for five-year terms that run concurrently with presidential term. Highest court in judiciary is Supreme Court of Justice made up of at least five members who serve five-year terms after nomination by president and ratification by legislature. Lower courts include appellate courts, courts of first instance, justice of the peace courts, and military courts. Central government exerts complete control over local administration, which consists of nineteen departments.

Politics: On February 3, 1989, Major General Andrés Rodríguez named provisional president after leading military coup against President Alfredo Stroessner Mattiauda. Rodríguez easily won a presidential election held on May 1, 1989. Military's action consistent with Paraguay's authoritarian style of politics, a tradition that began with dictator José Gaspar Rodríguez de Francia (ruled 1814–40) and continued in an unbroken line to Stroessner himself, who came to power in a 1954 coup. As candidate of the National Republican Association-Colorado Party (Asociación Nacional Republicana-Partido Colorado), Stroessner elected to eight consecutive terms as country's president in elections that observers characterized as fraudulent. Beginning in mid-1980s, Colorado Party broke into militant and traditionalist factions. Stroessner sided with militants and purged traditionalists from government. Rodríguez, an ally of traditionalists, purged militants. In contrast to Stroessner, Rodríguez allowed all noncommunist opposition parties to compete in May 1989 elections.

International Relations: Traditionally dominated by dependence on Argentina to ensure access to the port of Buenos Aires. Stroessner changed course of Paraguayan foreign policy and built close relations with Brazil. Although ties with Stroessner not as close since onset of democratization in Brazil in mid-1980s, massive scale of Brazilian investment in Paraguay precluded significant change in relations. Rodríguez strengthened ties with both Argentina and Brazil. Relations with United States had been strained since early 1980s because of United States concerns over Paraguayan corruption, narcotics trafficking, and human rights abuses; relations improved following Rodríguez's assumption of the presidency.

International Agreements and Memberships: Party to Inter-American Treaty of Reciprocal Assistance (Rio Treaty) and Treaty for the Prohibition of Nuclear Weapons in Latin America (Tlatelolco Treaty). Also a member of Organization of American States, United Nations and its specialized agencies, World Bank, International Monetary Fund, Inter-American Development Bank, and Latin American Integration Association.

National Security

Armed Forces: Includes army, navy, and air force with total strength estimated at 19,500 in 1988. Army organized into three corps (eight infantry divisions and one cavalry division) and combat support, logistical support, and instructional commands. Navy organized into fleet units, naval aviation arm, marine battalion, and coast guard. Air force organized into three squadrons and one paratroop battalion.

Equipment: Ground forces armaments mostly obsolete United States equipment, but also included newer Brazilian armored vehicles and armored personnel carriers. Most of naval fleet antiquated. Air force's only combat airplanes eight Brazilian light counterinsurgency aircraft.

Police: Police force under administration of minister of interior; army officers held many key positions in police hierarchy. In 1988 over half of estimated 0,500 personnel assigned to Asuncion.

Figure 1. Administrative Divisions of Paraguay, 1988

Introduction

ON THE NIGHT OF FEBRUARY 2, 1989, the streets of Asunción became a battleground as forces loyal to First Corps commander Major General Andrés Rodríguez staged a coup d'état against the government of President Alfredo Stroessner Mattiauda. Tank units of the First Cavalry Division left their Ñu Guazú barracks and bombarded the headquarters of the armed forces general staff, the police, and the Presidential Escort Regiment. Elements of the air force's composite squadron also reportedly joined the rebels and carried out aerial attacks. After several hours of heavy fighting, Stroessner surrendered and offered his "irrevocable resignation from the post of president of the Republic of Paraguay and from the post of commander in chief of its armed forces"—positions that he had held since 1954. Typically for Paraguay, the coup was not a bloodless affair; estimates of the number killed ranged from Rodríguez's claim of 27 to Western observers' assertions of up to 300.

During the fighting, the First Cavalry Division seized one of Asunción's radio stations and broadcast an appeal by Rodríguez to the people of Paraguay. The military had left its barracks, the general asserted, "to defend the dignity and honor of the armed forces, for the total and complete unification of the Colorado Party (Asociación Nacional Republicana-Partido Colorado) in government, for the initiation of democratization in Paraguay, for respect for human rights, and for respect for our Christian, apostolic, Roman Catholic religion." In fact, the coup was actually a struggle for political control of a post-Stroessner Paraguay.

Relying on a system of coercion and cooptation, Stroessner had brought remarkable political stability to a nation that experienced over twenty coups between 1870 and 1954 (see Liberals Versus Colorados, ch. 1). Stroessner's skillful use of the ruling Colorado Party as a dispenser of jobs and patronage was a major factor in achieving this stability (see The Twin Pillars of the Stroessner Regime, ch. 4). Political stability also resulted from twenty years of sustained economic growth. This was especially true during the 1970s, when construction of the Itaipú hydroelectric plant, completion of the road from Asunción to Puerto Presidente Stroessner and links to Brazilian Atlantic ports, land colonization along the Brazilian border, and increases in agricultural commodity prices combined to produce gross domestic product (GDP—see Glossary) growth of over 8 percent a year (see Growth and Structure of the Economy, ch. 3).

By the mid-1980s, however, compelling signs pointed to the twilight of the Stronato, as the Stroessner era was called. Real GDP declined in 1982 and 1983 following the completion of most construction at Itaipú and the drop in commodity prices. Foreign governments increasingly condemned and isolated the Stroessner regime for its repression of the political opposition and its reliance on electoral fraud (see Foreign Relations, ch. 4). In addition, Stroessner turned seventy in 1982 and seemed to lose some of his legendary energy and capacity for hard work as he grew older.

It was not surprising, therefore, that leaders of the Colorado Party began to jockey for position. In the mid-1980s, the party's thirty-five-member governing board, the National Committee (Junta de Gobierno), split into rival militant (*militante*) and traditionalist (*tradicionalista*) camps. The militants were led by four key members of Stroessner's inner circle: Sabino Augusto Montanaro, minister of interior; Adán Godoy Jiménez, minister of public health and social welfare; José Eugenio Jacquet, minister of justice and labor; and Mario Abdo Benítez, the president's private secretary. Each of these men had personally profited from the Stronato and felt much more loyalty to Stroessner personally than to the Colorado Party. These militants wanted as little change as possible in any future government. Indeed, many militants promoted air force Lieutenant Colonel Gustavo Stroessner Mora as the ideal successor to his father. Juan Ramón Chaves, the party's president since the early 1960s, headed the traditionalists. Unlike the militants, traditionalist leaders came from distinguished families who had dominated the Colorado Party prior to Stroessner. Although loyal collaborators throughout the Stronato, traditionalists also believed that continued reliance on repression would spell doom for the Colorado Party.

Although the militant-traditionalist split had been brewing since the mid-1980s, it burst into public prominence with the party's National Convention in August 1987. Montanaro employed the police to deny traditionalists access to the convention hall, thus ensuring his election as party president and the elections of Abdo Benítez, Godoy, and Jacquet as the three vice presidents. Stroessner, who had largely remained above the fray, soon endorsed the militants' takeover of the party. The militants continued their purge of the traditionalists over the next year, excluding them from the slate of Colorado Party congressional candidates for the February 1988 election, removing them from key positions within the government, and subjecting them to torrents of abuse in the national media (see Political Developments Since 1986, ch. 4).

Although clearly in control, the militants stumbled badly in late 1988 by becoming embroiled in yet another controversy with the

Roman Catholic Church. In the late 1980s, the church had emerged as Stroessner's most important critic. Its newspaper and radio station broadcast accounts of human rights abuses in Paraguay. The Catholic bishops also issued numerous pastorals condemning government corruption and calling for an end to political violence against regime opponents. The government frequently responded by harassing or deporting priests (see Religion in Society, ch. 2; Interest Groups, ch. 4; Security and Political Offenses, ch. 5). In November 1988, however, the militants overstepped the bounds of propriety in the eyes of many Paraguayans by leveling a personal attack against Aníbal Maricevich Fleitas, the bishop of Concepción and a persistent Stroessner critic. Appearing at a Colorado Party rally, National Committee member Ramón Aquino accused Maricevich of being a communist-follower and a drunkard, and dedicated a bottle of liquor in the name of "Maricewhiskey." Despite widespread outrage within Paraguay, the militant leadership strongly endorsed Aquino's right to free expression. Aquino soon escalated the conflict by accusing the clergy of being beholden to Cuban leader Fidel Castro Ruz and Nicaraguan president Daniel Ortega Saavedra. In response, Ismael Rolón Silvero, the archbishop of Asunción, issued a decree barring Aquino from taking an active part in any religious ceremony, a measure one step short of excommunication. The Aquino episode apparently convinced many among the Paraguayan elites that the militants were too crude and unsophisticated to be trusted with the reins of government.

In addition to the Aquino affair, traditionalists benefited from the emergence of Luis María Argaña as the de facto leader of the movement. In August 1988, Argaña, an urbane, highly respected politician, stepped down from his post as chief justice of the Supreme Court of Justice after completing a five-year term of office. Although Argaña was a known supporter of traditionalism, many recalled his ambiguous stance at the August 1987 party convention and wondered if he would challenge the militants. In speeches in December 1988 and January 1989, however, Argaña dispelled those doubts as he lashed out at the "imposters" who had seized control of the Colorado Party. Accusing the Stroessner government of becoming a police state, Argaña thundered that those who persecute defenseless women or beat priests could not be considered Colorados or even Paraguayans. In response, Aquino accused Argaña of being a traitor with "blue," i.e., Liberal Party (Partido Liberal), blood. Argaña's statements gave new vitality to a movement that had been stagnating under the control of the octogenarian Chaves.

Although the militant-traditionalist battle dominated the headlines, the party's factions tacitly understood that the armed forces remained the ultimate arbiters of Paraguay's future. The armed forces, especially the senior officer corps, allegedly had benefited handsomely during the Stronato from involvement in a variety of legal and illegal businesses. Nonetheless, however, many in the armed forces' upper echelon remained wary of the militants. In the late 1980s, observers felt that the army was particularly opposed to the idea of Stroessner's being succeeded by his son. Selection of an undistinguished air force officer as commander in chief would have challenged the army's status as the preeminent service and also might have necessitated the retirement of many senior officers.

Both sides in the Colorado Party power struggle also knew that General Rodríguez's views would be critical in determining the military's stance. At first glance, Rodríguez seemed an unlikely obstacle in the militants' path. As a young regimental commander in December 1955, Captain Rodríguez defied his immediate superior and supported Stroessner's preemptive purge against the latter's chief rival at the time, Epifanio Méndez Fleitas. In 1961 Stroessner selected his protégé Rodríguez to head the powerful First Cavalry Division. In 1982 Stroessner reorganized the army into three corps and chose Rodríguez to command the First—and most important—Corps. As a result of this promotion, Rodríguez had the best equipped units of the Paraguayan army at his disposal (see The Army, ch. 5). The long-time professional bonds between Stroessner and Rodríguez were also enhanced by the marriage of Stroessner's son Alfredo to Rodríguez's daughter Marta.

But Rodríguez's long period of service on behalf of the Stronato had apparently heightened his interest in the presidency. Rodríguez also had close ties with many traditionalist leaders. Finally, Alfredo and Marta's marital problems reportedly strained the relationship of the two generals.

Stroessner and the militants thus apparently decided that the success of their plan required the neutralization of Rodríguez. On January 12, 1989, two weeks after the promotion of his son to the rank of colonel, Stroessner announced a major reassignment of military commanders. Major General Orlando Machuca Vargas, a key ally of Rodríguez, lost his post as Second Corps commander. The commanders of the Fifth and Seventh Infantry Divisions were sacked and replaced by officers presumed loyal to Stroessner. Stroessner also rotated the commanders of the Third, Fourth, and Sixth Infantry Divisions. The day also saw the swearing in of Stroessner loyalist Brigadier General Alcibiades Ramón Soto Valleau as the new commander of the air force.

*One week after the 1989 coup, workers plaster over bullet holes
and repair the front walls of the Presidential Escort
Regiment headquarters, Asunción.
Courtesy Richard S. Sacks*

Stroessner apparently believed that these reassignments had eliminated Rodríguez's ability to rally his fellow commanders and to stage a coup. Thus, the moment seemed propitious to strike directly against Rodríguez. Citing a purported run on the national currency, the guaraní (see Glossary), Stroessner issued a resolution on January 27, 1989, closing all currency exchange houses in Paraguay. This action reportedly dealt a serious financial blow to Rodríguez, whose Cambios Guaraní was one of Asunción's largest currency traders. On January 30, 1989, Stroessner ordered the replacement of First Corps colonels Mauricio Bartolomé Díaz Delmas and Regis Aníbal Romero Espinola. Finally, on February 2, 1989, Stroessner summoned Rodríguez and ordered him to give up his direct command of units and either accept the much less significant post of minister of national defense or retire. Rodríguez refused and several hours later called out his forces.

As it turned out, Stroessner's concerns were not unwarranted. Two weeks after the coup, Edgar L. Ynsfrán—minister of interior from 1956 to 1966 and leader of the Movement for Colorado Integration (Movimiento de Integración Colorado) faction that was affiliated with the traditionalists—reported that coup preparations had been under way since late December 1988. According to Ynsfrán, Rodríguez ordered Chaves, Argaña, and Ynsfrán to go into hiding immediately prior to the coup. In addition, Ynsfrán claimed that on January 31, 1989, Rodríguez informed key personnel in the First Corps that he would not accept the replacements of Colonels Díaz and Romero. Whether Stroessner was aware of any of this background remains unknown.

In retrospect, Stroessner had overestimated the importance of the earlier command reassignments. The commanders of the Second Corps and Third Corps ignored Rodríguez's appeal for help. But commanders of two of the three major components of the Second Corps—the Second and Fourth Infantry Divisions—and one of the three major units of the Third Corps—the Sixth Infantry Division—pledged loyalty to Rodríguez. In addition, all of Rodríguez's First Corps units—the First Cavalry Division, the First Infantry Division, and the Third Infantry Division—rebelled against Stroessner. Within a week after the coup, Rodríguez promoted the commanders of the six rebellious divisions and purged the armed forces hierarchy of Stroessner loyalists.

Hours after Stroessner's surrender, Rodríguez assumed the presidency. Rodríguez named a nine-member cabinet that had only one Stroessner holdover—the technocratic agriculture and livestock minister Hernando Bertoni Agrón—and included General Machuca as interior minister, Argaña as foreign minister, and Chaves as minister without portfolio. Rodríguez also appointed Chaves and Argaña as president and vice president, respectively, of the Council of State, a body that is primarily advisory in nature but that has the power to issue decrees during the legislature's recess (see The Executive, ch. 4). The traditionalist resurgence was solidified by the selection of Chaves, Argaña, and Ynsfrán as president, first vice president, and second vice president, respectively, of the Colorado Party, and the removal of all militants from the National Committee. Chaves also dissolved all party local committees (*seccionales*) and called for new party elections by March 19, 1989.

The new government went to great lengths to insist that its actions were based on the Constitution of 1967. Because the previous president had "resigned," Rodríguez's title actually was the constitutionally mandated one of provisional president. Rodríguez's call for a new presidential election on May 1, 1989, was consistent with Article 179 of the Constitution, which requires such an election within ninety days upon the resignation of a president who has served fewer than two years of his term. (Stroessner had begun serving his eighth term as president in August 1988.) Again consistent with the Constitution, the winner of the May 1989 election would not serve a five-year term but only the unexpired portion of Stroessner's term. Even Rodríguez's decision on February 6, 1989, to dissolve the National Congress and to call for new elections in May—an action designed to purge the militants—was given a constitutional twist. Argaña informed the media that Article 182 empowers the president to dissolve the legislature if the latter's actions distorted the balance of the three branches of government and adversely affected compliance with the Constitution. Argaña also announced that the Council of State would exercise its constitutional prerogative to issue decrees during the legislature's absence.

In his first three weeks in office, Rodríguez contended that Paraguay had become a much more democratic and open country. Indeed, much that occurred during this period would have been inconceivable under Stroessner's rule. The government announced that all political parties except the Paraguayan Communist Party (Partido Comunista Paraguayo) could complete in the May 1989 elections. This was an extraordinary turn of events for the parties comprising the National Accord (Acuerdo Nacional)—the Authentic Radical Liberal Party (Partido Liberal Radical Auténtico—PLRA), the Christian Democratic Party (Partido Demócrata Cristiano), the Febrerista Revolutionary Party (Partido Revolucionario Febrerista—PRF), and the Colorado Popular Movement (Movimiento Popular Colorado—Mopoco)—all of whose leaders had been repressed by Stroessner (see Toward the 1980s, ch. 1; Opposition Parties, ch. 4). Actually, Mopoco did not even have to plan for the elections because the traditionalists welcomed the movement back into the Colorado fold after thirty years in exile. The government not only authorized a National Accord rally on February 11 but also permitted it to broadcast live on television. For the first time in their history, Colorados opened their party headquarters to the opposition and warmly received an address by PLRA leader Domingo Laíno. A few days after the coup, Humberto Rubín's Radio Ñandutí was back on the air and the PRF's newspaper *El Pueblo* was publishing once again; the police had forced both to close in 1987. The new minister of education and worship stated that teachers need not join the Colorado Party as a condition of employment. Even a rapprochement with the church was in evidence. Rodríguez and Rolón embraced at a special mass to honor those who had died in the coup. In its first public statement, the new Council of State invited Rolón to reoccupy the seat on the council that was reserved under the Constitution for the archbishop of Asunción. Rolón had boycotted council meetings for many years as a protest against Stroessner's repression of the church.

Despite these remarkable developments, some observers remained skeptical concerning the flowering of democracy in Paraguay. From 1954 to 1987, traditionalists served as major collaborators of the Stronato. Positioned at all levels of government, traditionalists helped construct and institutionalize authoritarianism in Paraguay. For example, the Supreme Court rarely issued decisions at odds with the executive branch. Traditionalist legislators routinely enacted laws that served Stroessner's interests. After the coup, traditionalist leaders contended that Stroessner was a great president for thirty-three years but became surrounded by a group of "irresponsible, voracious politicians" in 1987. Such a contention appeared at odds with the structures of authoritarianism that had been in place by the mid-1950s.

Observers also questioned the traditionalist pledge to weed out corruption in government. Following the coup, police arrested over thirty members of Stroessner's government, including Abdo Benítez, Godoy, Aquino, Central Bank director César Romeo Acosta, and Post Office director Modesto Esquivel. (Montanaro avoided arrest by fleeing to the Honduran embassy in Asunción, and Jacquet had the good fortune of being out of the country at the time of the coup.) Interior Minister Machuca announced that those arrested would be tried for corruption. Smuggling and corruption, however, did not begin in 1987 but were endemic throughout the Stronato.

Provisional President Andrés Rodríguez meets with reporters during his first week in office.
Courtesy Richard S. Sacks

Less than a month after the coup, its real significance thus remained unclear. Certainly the new government was much more tolerant of opposition activities than was its predecessor. This tolerance created opportunities by allowing the opposition to organize openly for the first time. But questions remained. Observers awaited future developments to determine if the coup was a breakthrough for democracy or the continuation of authoritarian rule.

February 27, 1989

*   *   *

Presidential and congressional elections dominated the Paraguayan political landscape in the months following completion of research and writing of this book. Rodríguez and the Colorado Party's legislative candidates easily outdistanced their closest challengers, Laíno and the PLRA. The opposition accused the government of numerous electoral irregularities, although it concluded that the Colorados would have won in any event.

Attempting to extract concessions from Rodríguez, the National Accord initially announced that none of its members would participate in the elections unless the government extended the registration period for sixty days; delayed the elections for four months; permitted parties to form coalitions; and determined congressional seats on the basis of proportional representation instead of the constitutional formula of awarding two-thirds to the party garnering the most votes (see The Legislature, ch. 4). The opposition regarded the last issue as particularly important. Many public opinion polls suggested that Rodríguez would capture approximately 70 percent of the vote, but that his congressional running mates would only receive slightly above 50 percent. The government, however, rejected all of the National Accord's demands except for the registration extension. After considerable debate, the PLRA—by far the most important component of the National Accord—decided to participate but adopted a complex formula that would allow it to withdraw prior to the May 1 election date if the government curtailed individual freedoms; to prevent its members from taking their seats in the new congress if fraud occurred on election day; or to remove its representatives from congress if that body did not adopt substantial electoral reforms.

As anticipated, Rodríguez crushed Laíno in the presidential vote by a margin of 74 to 18 percent. But opposition leaders rejected the announcement of election officials that the Colorados had captured almost 73 percent of the congressional vote to only 20 percent by the PLRA. As a result, the Colorados received forty-eight of the seventy-two seats in the Chamber of Deputies and twenty-four of the thirty-six seats in the Senate. The PLRA gained twenty-one and eleven seats, respectively. National Accord leaders charged that the government had tampered with the indelible ink designed to prevent multiple voting; had barred some opposition members and voters from access to the polls; had removed opposition ballots from specific voting stations; and, on occasion, had positioned police or Colorado officials inside the voting booths. Despite these allegations, the opposition occupied its seats in the legislature, contending that to do otherwise would simply perpetuate its marginal role in the political system. Instead of rejecting outright the congressional results, the opposition focused its demands for new elections on specific localities where voting irregularities were the most egregious. International election observers agreed that irregularities had occurred, although not at a level to have affected the eventual outcome.

Although the elections captured the headlines, other important developments also occurred in the months following the February coup. The Rodríguez administration took several steps to restore confidence in the economy. First, the government abolished the multiple exchange-rate system that had severely overvalued the guaraní and allowed the currency to float to its true level (see Exchange-Rate Policy, ch. 3). Second, it announced plans to privatize highly inefficient state enterprises such as the National Cement Industry (Industria Nacional de Cemento—INC) and Paraguayan Steel (see Construction, ch. 3). Third, the government offered five-year tax holidays to new investors, including a total exemption from all financial taxes and a 95-percent exemption from taxes on income and dividends. Finally, the government made considerable progress toward restructuring its substantial foreign debt, which totaled slightly more than US$2 billion in June 1989 (see Balance of Payments and Debt, ch. 3). In April Paraguay received a new twenty-year payment period and new conditions on the US$436 million owed to Brazil. Paraguay's Central Bank also reported in July that it would renegotiate an additional US$811 million in foreign debt.

Considerable information also surfaced detailing the scope of corruption during the Stronato. The former minister of public works and communications reported that from 1984 to January 1989, US$4 million in highway tolls and gasoline taxes were placed in one of Stroessner's personal bank accounts. In May two former senior INC officials were detained on charges of having participated in the embezzlement of US$40 million in government funds. In an ironic twist, the Rodríguez administration announced that several former Stroessner officials would be prosecuted under Law 209, "In Defense of Public Peace and Liberty of Person," for having promoted violence and hatred among Paraguayans. The law, enacted in 1970, had often been used by Stroessner to silence his political opponents (see Security and Political Offenses, ch. 5).

In late 1989, the government indicated that it would accede to opposition demands and would convoke a constituent assembly prior to the 1993 elections. The opposition was determined to use such an assembly to limit the president to one term, to establish proportional representation in congress, and to design a more equitable electoral code. The outcome of that assembly would probably shed considerable light on the future course of democracy in Paraguay.

October 5, 1989   Dennis M. Hanratty

Chapter 1. Historical Setting

Ruins of the Jesuit mission at Trinidad, Itapúa Department

PARAGUAY WAS ONE of the first countries in South America to achieve independence. Its history since the arrival of the Spaniards in 1537 evokes images of tremendous sacrifice and suffering amid lush surroundings. Because of its small population and poverty, however, its weight among the nations of the modern world is small. At the time of the Spanish conquest in the mid-1500s, Paraguay was the second most important of the Spanish dominions in South America after Peru. But its preeminence as a colony did not last because it produced no gold or silver. In the long run, however, the country's lack of precious ores proved to be a blessing because it allowed Paraguay to escape the horrors of slavery that prevailed in the mines of Peru and Mexico. The Spanish conquest and settlement proceeded more humanely in Paraguay than elsewhere in Spanish America.

The country's basic characteristics were determined during the first few decades of European rule and reinforced under the Republic of Paraguay after independence in 1811. The country has a largely egalitarian social structure. Its relatively homogeneous population of mestizos follows Spanish culture and religion but speaks the Indian language, Guaraní, at home. It also has a tradition of authoritarian rule and a concomitant lack of democratic institutions. Finally, Paraguay suffers from a paranoia-inducing isolation, originally because of its location in a wilderness populated by hostile Indians, and later because of its location between powerful neighbors—Brazil and Argentina.

Partly because of its remoteness, Paraguay never had a very large European population. The colony's first governor urged Spanish men to take Indian wives to help them take their minds off returning to Spain, solve the problem of the scarcity of European women, and encourage peaceful relations between the tiny, vulnerable, European colony and its numerous Indian neighbors. Neither Spaniard nor Indian needed any prodding, however, as mixed unions predominated from the start. The Paraguayan republic's first dictator, José Gaspar Rodríguez de Francia, a criollo who distrusted his own criollo upper class, strengthened this pattern of marrying Indians. Francia forced the elite to marry Indian women, confiscated their lands, and broke their power. The disastrous 1865–70 War of the Triple Alliance, which ended with the death of Paraguayan dictator Francisco Solano López, further strengthened the mestizo composition of society. At the end of the war, only 28,000 Spanish males were alive, down from 220,000. Spanish women who wanted to marry had no choice but to accept mestizo suitors.

Dictatorship is to Paraguay what constitutional democracy is to Scandinavia or Britain: it is the norm. Paraguay, a country where power has usually been centered on one man, has a history of domination by authoritarian personalities. Paraguay's authoritarianism derives from Spanish attitudes, isolation amid hostile neighbors, and political inexperience and naiveté among a population that has historically proved willing to abdicate its political rights and responsibilities. Nearly 300 years of Spanish rule rendered many Paraguayans poor, uneducated, unaware of the outside world, and lacking in experience with democracy. Furthermore, the people were nearly always under the threat of attack either from Indians or from raiders from Brazil. Indeed, its three neighbors—Brazil, Argentina, and Bolivia—each went to war with Paraguay at least once since 1810.

Francia, named "dictator for life" in 1816 by a largely uneducated nation grateful for his diplomatic and administrative expertise, set the tone by founding a despotic police state that lasted until his death in 1840. His goal was to keep the country independent at all costs. He succeeded by founding the world's first system of state socialism, sealing off the country's borders, and pouring all available resources into defense. Paraguay was the only major country in Spanish America to undergo a major social revolution as a direct result of independence. Father and son dictators Carlos Antonio López and Francisco Solano López succeeded Francia from 1841 to 1862 and 1862 to 1870, respectively. After the 1865–70 war, military officers began to replace civilians as politicians, but this fact represented no change in the country's pattern of dictatorial rule.

Paraguay's stability diminished after 1904 when the Liberal Party (Partido Liberal—PL) ruled the nation. Paraguay had traded stable dictatorships for unstable ones. Between 1904 and 1954, Paraguay had thirty-one presidents, most of whom were removed from office by force. During the particularly unstable period between 1910 and 1912, seven presidents entered and left office. As political instability grew, so did the importance of the military in politics. Still, military rule did not predominate. Only four of eight presidents who finished their terms were military men.

A 1954 coup ushered in the Stronato, the period of rule of Alfredo Stroessner Mattiauda, who remained in power in late 1988. Few imagined in the 1950s that Stroessner's term of office would become the longest in Paraguay's history. Stroessner effectively combined political skill, hard work, and repression to gain complete control of the National Republican Association-Colorado Party (Asociación Nacional Republicana-Partido Colorado) and eliminate regime opponents. By the early 1960s, all other political parties were either legitimating the political system by participating in fraudulent elections or were effectively isolated.

Although Stroessner clearly represented continuity with Paraguay's authoritarian past, he also dragged the country out of its isolation. A mammoth hydroelectric project at Itaipú on the Río Paraná shattered Paraguay's seclusion forever by injecting billions of dollars into the economy. The project put money into the pockets of previously penniless campesinos and contributed to the emergence of the middle class. Many observers believed that economic growth unleashed demands for democratic reform in Paraguay, and, as the 1980s began, the Stroessner regime seemed increasingly under attack from its critics.

Discovery and Settlement
Early Explorers and Conquistadors

The recorded history of Paraguay began indirectly in 1516 with the failed expedition of Juan Díaz de Solís to the Río de la Plata Estuary, which divides Argentina and Uruguay. After Solís's death at the hands of Indians, the expedition renamed the estuary Río de Solís and sailed back to Spain. On the home voyage, one of the vessels was wrecked off Santa Catarina Island near the Brazilian coast. Among the survivors was Aleixo Garcia, a Portuguese adventurer who had acquired a working knowledge of Guaraní. Garcia was intrigued by reports of "the White King" who, it was said, lived far to the west and governed cities of incomparable wealth and splendor. For nearly eight years, Garcia patiently mustered men and supplies for a trip to the interior and finally left Santa Catarina with several European companions to raid the dominions of "El Rey Blanco."

Marching westward, Garcia's group discovered Iguazú Falls, crossed the Río Paraná, and arrived at the site of Asunción thirteen years before it was founded. There the group gathered a small army of 2,000 Guaraní warriors to assist the invasion and set out boldly across the Chaco, a harsh semidesert. In the Chaco, they faced drought, floods, and cannibal Indian tribes. Garcia became the first European to cross the Chaco and penetrated the outer defenses of the Inca Empire to the foothills of the Andes Mountains in present-day Bolivia, eight years in advance of Francisco Pizarro. The Garcia entourage engaged in plundering and amassed a considerable horde of silver. Only fierce attacks by the reigning Inca, Huayna Cápac, convinced Garcia to withdraw. Indian allies later murdered Garcia and the other Europeans, but news of the raid on the Incas reached the Spanish explorers on the coast and attracted Sebastian Cabot to the Río Paraguay two years later.

The son of the Genoese explorer John Cabot (who had led the first European expedition to North America), Sebastian Cabot was sailing to the Orient in 1526 when he heard of Garcia's exploits. Cabot thought the Río de Solís might provide easier passage to the Pacific and the Orient than the stormy Straits of Magellan where he was bound, and, eager to win the riches of Peru, he became the first European to explore that estuary.

Leaving a small force on the northern shore of the broad estuary, Cabot proceeded up the Río Paraná uneventfully for about 160 kilometers and founded a settlement he named Sancti Spiritu. He continued upstream for another 800 kilometers, past the junction with the Río Paraguay. When navigation became difficult, Cabot turned back, but only after obtaining some silver objects that the Indians said came from a land far to the west. Cabot retraced his route on the Río Paraná and entered the Río Paraguay. Sailing upriver, Cabot and his men traded freely with the Guaraní tribes until a strong force of Agaces Indians attacked them. About forty kilometers below the site of Asunción, Cabot encountered a tribe of Guaraní in possession of silver objects, perhaps some of the spoils of Garcia's treasure. Hoping he had found the route to the riches of Peru, Cabot renamed the river Río de la Plata, although today the name applies only to the estuary as far inland as the city of Buenos Aires.

Cabot returned to Spain in 1530 and informed Emperor Charles V (1519–56) about his discoveries. Charles gave permission to Don Pedro de Mendoza to mount an expedition to the Plata basin. The emperor also named Mendoza governor of Río de la Plata and granted him the right to name his successor. But Mendoza, a sickly, disturbed man, proved to be utterly unsuitable as a leader, and his cruelty nearly undermined the expedition. Choosing what was possibly the continent's worst site for the first Spanish settlement in South America, in February 1536 Mendoza built a fort at a poor anchorage on the southern side of the Plata estuary on an inhospitable, windswept, dead-level plain where not a tree or shrub grew. Dusty in the dry season, a quagmire in the rains, the place was inhabited by the fierce Querandí tribe that resented having the Spaniards as neighbors. The new outpost was named Buenos Aires (Nuestra Señora del Buen Ayre), although it was hardly a place one would visit for the "good air."

Mendoza soon provoked the Querandís into declaring war on the Europeans. Thousands of them and their Timbú and Charrúa allies besieged the miserable company of half-starved soldiers and adventurers. The Spaniards were soon reduced to eating rats and the flesh of their deceased comrades.

Meanwhile, Juan de Ayolas, who was Mendoza's second-in-command and who had been sent upstream to reconnoiter, returned with a welcome load of corn and news that Cabot's fort at Sancti Spiritu had been abandoned. Mendoza promptly dispatched Ayolas to explore a possible route to Peru. Accompanied by Domingo Martínez de Irala, Ayolas again sailed upstream until he reached a small bay on the Río Paraguay, which he named Candelaria, the present-day Fuerte Olimpo. Appointing Irala his lieutenant, Ayolas ventured into the Chaco and was never seen again.

After Mendoza returned unexpectedly to Spain, two other members of the expedition—Juan de Salazar de Espinosa and Gonzalo de Mendoza—explored the Río Paraguay and met up with Irala. Leaving him after a short time, Salazar and Gonzalo de Mendoza descended the river, stopping at a fine anchorage. They commenced building a fort on August 15, 1537, the date of the Feast of the Assumption, and called it Asunción (Nuestra Señora Santa María de la Asunción). Within 20 years, the settlement had a population of about 1,500. Transcontinental shipments of silver passed through Asunción on their way from Peru to Europe. Asunción subsequently became the nucleus of a Spanish province that encompassed a large portion of southern South America—so large, in fact, that it was dubbed "La Provincia Gigante de Indias." Asunción also was the base from which this part of South America was colonized. Spaniards moved northwestward across the Chaco to found Santa Cruz in Bolivia; eastward to occupy the rest of present-day Paraguay; and southward along the river to refound Buenos Aires, which its defenders had abandoned in 1541 to move to Asunción.

The Young Colony

Uncertainties over the departure of Pedro de Mendoza led Charles V to promulgate a *cédula* (decree) that was unique in colonial Latin America. The *cédula* granted colonists the right to elect the governor of Río de la Plata Province either if Mendoza had failed to designate a successor or if a successor had died. Two years later, the colonists elected Irala as governor. His domain included all of present-day Paraguay, Argentina, Uruguay, most of Chile, and large parts of Brazil and Bolivia. In 1542 the province became part of the newly established Viceroyalty of Peru, with its seat in Lima.

*Iguazú Falls at Paraguay's border with Argentina and Brazil.
In 1630 the Jesuits abandoned their* reducciones *north and east
of the falls after attacks by slave traders.
Courtesy Inter-American Development Bank.*

Beginning in 1559, the Audiencia of Charcas (present-day Sucre, Bolivia) controlled the province's legal affairs.

Irala's rule set the pattern for Paraguay's internal affairs until independence. In addition to the Spaniards, Asunción included people—mostly men—from present-day France, Italy, Germany, England, and Portugal. This community of about 350 chose wives and concubines from among the Guaraní women. Irala had several Guaraní concubines, and he encouraged his men to marry Indian women and give up thoughts of returning to Spain. Paraguay soon became a colony of mestizos, and, prompted by Irala's example, the Europeans raised their offspring as Spaniards. Nevertheless, continued arrivals of Europeans allowed for the development of a criollo elite.

The Guaraní, the Cario, Tapé, Itatine, Guarajo, Tupi, and related subgroups, were generous people who inhabited an immense area stretching from the Guyana Highlands in Brazil to the Río Uruguay. Because the Guaraní were surrounded by other hostile tribes, however, they were frequently at war. They believed that permanent wives were inappropriate for warriors, so their marital relations were loose. Some tribes practiced polygamy with the aim of increasing the number of offspring. Chiefs often had twenty or thirty concubines whom they shared freely with visitors, yet they treated their wives well. They often punished adulterers with death. Like the area's other tribes, the Guaraní were cannibals. But they usually ate only their most valiant foes captured in battle in the hope that they would gain the bravery and power of their victims.

In contrast with the hospitable Guaraní, the Chaco tribes, such as the Payaguá (whence the name Paraguay), Guaycurú, M'bayá, Abipón, Mocobí, and Chiriguano, were implacable enemies of the whites. Travelers in the Chaco reported that the Indians there were capable of running with incredible bursts of speed, lassoing and mounting wild horses in full gallop, and catching deer bare-handed. Accordingly, the Guaraní accepted the arrival of the Spaniards and looked to them for protection against fiercer neighboring tribes. The Guaraní also hoped the Spaniards would lead them once more against the Incas.

The peace that had prevailed under Irala broke down in 1542 when Charles V appointed Alvar Núñez Cabeza de Vaca—one of the most renowned conquistadors of his age—as governor of the province. Cabeza de Vaca arrived in Asunción after having lived for ten years among the Indians of Florida. Almost immediately, however, the Río de la Plata Province—now consisting of 800 Europeans—split into 2 warring factions. Cabeza de Vaca's enemies accused him of cronyism and opposed his efforts to protect the interests of the Indians. Cabeza de Vaca tried to placate his enemies by launching an expedition into the Chaco in search of a route to Peru. This move disrupted the Chaco tribes so much that they unleashed a two-year war against the colony, thus threatening its existence. In the colony's first of many revolts against the crown, the settlers seized Cabeza de Vaca, sent him back to Spain in irons, and returned the governorship to Irala.

Irala ruled without further interruption until his death in 1556. In many ways, his governorship was one of the most humane in the Spanish New World at that time, and it marked the transition among the settlers from conquerors to landowners. Irala kept up good relations with the Guaraní, pacified hostile Indians, made further explorations of the Chaco, and began trade relations with Peru. This Basque soldier of fortune saw the beginnings of a textile industry and the introduction of cattle, which flourished in the country's fertile hills and meadows. The arrival of Father Pedro Fernández de la Torre on April 2, 1556, as the first bishop of Asunción marked the establishment of the Roman Catholic Church in Paraguay. Irala presided over the construction of a cathedral, two churches, three convents, and two schools.

Irala eventually antagonized the Indians, however. In the last years of his life, he yielded to pressure from settlers and established the *encomienda*. Under this system, settlers received estates of land along with the right to the labor and produce of the Indians living on those estates. Although *encomenderos* were expected to care for the spiritual and material needs of the Indians, the system quickly degenerated into virtual slavery. In Paraguay 20,000 Indians were divided among 320 *encomenderos*. This action helped spark a full-scale Indian revolt in 1560 and 1561. Political instability began troubling the colony and revolts became commonplace. Also, given his limited resources and manpower, Irala could do little to check the raids of Portuguese marauders along his eastern borders. Still, Irala left Paraguay prosperous and relatively at peace. Although he had found no El Dorado to equal those of Hernán Cortés in Mexico and Pizarro in Peru, he was loved by his people, who lamented his passing.

The Sword of the Word

During the next 200 years, the Roman Catholic Church—especially the ascetic, single-minded members of the Society of Jesus (the Jesuits)—had much more influence on the colony's social and economic life than the feckless governors who succeeded Irala. Three Jesuits—an Irishman, a Catalan, and a Portuguese—arrived in 1588 from Brazil. They promptly moved from Asunción to

11

proselytize among the Indians along the upper Río Paraná. Because they already believed in an impersonal, supreme being, the Guaraní proved to be good pupils of the Jesuits.

In 1610 Philip III (1598–1621) proclaimed that only the "sword of the word" should be used to subdue the Paraguayan Indians, thus making them happy subjects. The church granted extensive powers to Jesuit Father Diego de Torres to implement a new plan, with royal blessings, that foresaw an end to the *encomienda* system. This plan angered the settlers, whose lifestyle depended on a continuing supply of Indian labor and concubines. The settlers' resistance helped convince the Jesuits to move their base of operations farther afield to the province of Guayrá in the distant northeast. After unsuccessful attempts to "civilize" the recalcitrant Guaycurú, the Jesuits eventually put all their efforts into working with the Guaraní. Organizing the Guaraní in *reducciones* (reductions or townships), the hard-working fathers began a system that would last more than a century. In one of history's greatest experiments in communal living, the Jesuits had soon organized about 100,000 Guaraní in about 20 *reducciones*, and they dreamed of a Jesuit empire that would stretch from the Paraguay-Paraná confluence to the coast and back to the Paraná headwaters.

The new Jesuit *reducciones* were unfortunately within striking distance of the *mamelucos*, the slave-raiding, mixed-race descendants of Portuguese and Dutch adventurers. The *mamelucos* were based in São Paulo, Brazil, which had become a haven for freebooters and pirates by the early 1600s because it was beyond the control of the Portuguese colonial governor. The *mamelucos* survived mostly by capturing Indians and selling them as slaves to Brazilian planters. Having depleted the Indian population near São Paulo, they ventured farther afield until they discovered the richly populated *reducciones*. The Spanish authorities chose not to defend the settlements.

Spain and Portugal were united from 1580 to 1640. Although their colonial subjects were at war, the governor of Río de la Plata Province had little incentive to send scarce troops and supplies against an enemy who was nominally of the same nationality. In addition, the Jesuits were not popular in Asunción, where the settlers had the governor's ear. The Jesuits and their thousands of neophytes thus had little means to protect themselves from the depredations of the "Paulistas," as the *mamelucos* also were called (because they came from São Paulo). In one such raid in 1629, about 3,000 Paulistas destroyed the *reducciones* in their path by burning churches, killing old people and infants (who were worthless as slaves), and carrying off to the coast entire human populations, as well as cattle. Their first raids on the *reducciones* netted them at least 15,000 captives.

Faced with the awesome challenge of a virtual holocaust that was frightening away their neophytes and encouraging them to revert to paganism, the Jesuits took drastic measures. Under the leadership of Father Antonio Ruiz de Montoya, as many as 30,000 Indians (2,500 families) retreated by canoe and traveled hundreds of kilometers south to another large concentration of Jesuit *reducciones* near the lower Paraná . About 12,000 people survived. But the retreat failed to deter the Paulistas, who continued to raid and carry off slaves until even the *reducciones* far to the south faced extinction. The Paulista threat ended only after 1639, when the viceroy in Peru agreed to allow Indians to bear arms. Well-trained and highly motivated Indian units, serving under Jesuit officers, bloodied the raiders and drove them off.

Victory over the Paulistas set the stage for the golden age of the Jesuits in Paraguay. The Guaraní were unaccustomed to the discipline and the sedentary life prevalent in the *reducciones,* but adapted to it readily because it offered them higher living standards, protection from settlers, and physical security. By 1700 the Jesuits could again count 100,000 neophytes in about 30 *reducciones*. The *reducciones* exported goods, including cotton and linen cloth, hides, tobacco, lumber, and above all, yerba maté, a plant used to produce a bitter tea that is popular in Paraguay and Argentina. The Jesuits also raised food crops and taught arts and crafts. In addition, they were able to render considerable service to the crown by supplying Indian armies for use against attacks by the Portuguese, English, and French. At the time of the expulsion of the Jesuits from the Spanish Empire in 1767, the *reducciones* were enormously wealthy and comprised more than 21,000 families. Their vast herds included approximately 725,000 head of cattle, 47,000 oxen, 99,000 horses, 230,000 sheep, 14,000 mules, and 8,000 donkeys.

Because of their success, the 14,000 Jesuits who had volunteered over the years to serve in Paraguay gained many enemies. They were a continual goad to the settlers, who viewed them with envy and resentment and spread rumors of hidden gold mines and the threat to the crown from an independent Jesuit republic. To the crown, the *reducciones* seemed like an increasingly ripe plum, ready for picking.

The *reducciones* fell prey to changing times. During the 1720s and 1730s, Paraguayan settlers rebelled against Jesuit privileges and the government that protected them. Although this revolt failed, it was one of the earliest and most serious risings against Spanish authority in the New World and caused the crown to question its continued support for the Jesuits. The Jesuit-inspired War of the Seven Reductions (1750–61), which was fought to prevent the transfer to Portugal of seven missions south of the Río Uruguay, increased sentiment in Madrid for suppressing this "empire within an empire."

In a move to gain the *reducciones'* wealth to help finance a planned reform of Spanish administration in the New World, the Spanish king, Charles III (1759–88), expelled the Jesuits in 1767. Within a few decades of the expulsion, most of what the Jesuits had accomplished was lost. The missions lost their valuables, became mismanaged, and were abandoned by the Guaraní. The Jesuits vanished almost without a trace. Today, a few weed-choked ruins are all that remain of this 160-year period in Paraguayan history.

Independence and Dictatorship

Struggle with the Porteños

The Viceroyalty of Peru and the Audiencia of Charcas had nominal authority over Paraguay, while Madrid largely neglected the colony. Madrid preferred to avoid the intricacies and the expense of governing and defending a remote colony that had shown early promise but ultimately proved to have dubious value. Thus, governors of Paraguay had no royal troops at their disposal and were instead dependent on a militia composed of colonists. Paraguayans took advantage of this situation and claimed that the 1537 *cédula* gave them the right to choose and depose their governors. The colony, and in particular the Asunción municipal council (*cabildo*), earned the reputation of being in continual revolt against the crown.

Tensions between royal authorities and settlers came to a head in 1720 over the status of the Jesuits, whose efforts to organize the Indians had denied the settlers easy access to Indian labor. A full-scale rebellion, known as the Comunero Revolt, broke out when the viceroy in Lima reinstated a pro-Jesuit governor whom the settlers had deposed. The revolt was in many ways a rehearsal for the radical events that began with independence in 1811. The most prosperous families of Asunción (whose yerba maté and tobacco plantations competed directly with the Jesuits) initially led this revolt. But as the movement attracted support from poor farmers in the interior, the rich abandoned it and soon asked the royal authorities to restore order. In response, subsistence farmers began to seize the estates of the upper class and drive them out of the countryside. A radical army nearly captured Asunción and was repulsed, ironically, only with the help of Indian troops from the Jesuit *reducciones*.

14

The revolt was symptomatic of decline. Since the refounding of Buenos Aires in 1580, the steady deterioration in the importance of Asunción contributed to growing political instability within the province. In 1617 the Río de la Plata Province was divided into two smaller provinces: Paraguay, with Asunción as its capital, and Río de la Plata, with headquarters in Buenos Aires. With this action, Asunción lost control of the Río de la Plata Estuary and became dependent on Buenos Aires for maritime shipping. In 1776 the crown created the Viceroyalty of Río de la Plata; Paraguay, which had been subordinate to Lima, now became an outpost of Buenos Aires (see fig. 2). Located at the periphery of the empire, Paraguay served as a buffer state. The Portuguese blocked Paraguayan territorial expansion in the north, the Jesuits—until their expulsion—blocked it in the south, and the Indians blocked it in the west. Paraguayans were forced into the colonial militia to serve extended tours of duty away from their homes, contributing to a severe labor shortage.

Because Paraguay was located far from colonial centers, it had little control over important decisions that affected its economy. Spain appropriated much of Paraguay's wealth through burdensome taxes and regulations. Yerba maté, for instance, was priced practically out of the regional market. At the same time, Spain was using most of its wealth from the New World to import manufactured goods from the more industrialized countries of Europe, notably Britain. Spanish merchants borrowed from British merchants to finance their purchases; merchants in Buenos Aires borrowed from Spain; those in Asunción borrowed from the *porteños* (as residents of Buenos Aires were called); and Paraguayan *peones* (landless peasants in debt to landlords) bought goods on credit. The result was dire poverty in Paraguay and an increasingly impoverished empire.

The French Revolution, the rise of Napoleon Bonaparte, and the subsequent war in Europe inevitably weakened Spain's ability to maintain contact with and defend and control its colonies. When British troops attempted to seize Buenos Aires in 1806, the attack was repulsed by the city's residents, not by Spain. Napoleon's invasion of Spain in 1808, the capture of the Spanish king, Ferdinand VII (ruled 1808, 1814–33), and Napoleon's attempt to put his brother, Joseph Bonaparte, on the Spanish throne, severed the major remaining links between metropolis and satellite. Joseph had no constituency in Spanish America. Without a king, the entire colonial system lost its legitimacy, and the colonists revolted. Buoyed by their recent victory over British troops, the Buenos Aires *cabildo*

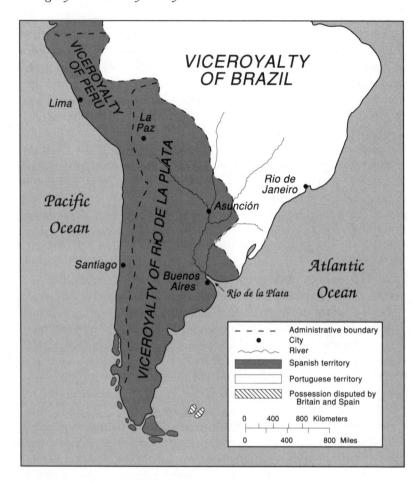

Source: Based on information from A. Curtis Wilgus, *Historical Atlas of Latin America: Political, Geographical, Economic, Cultural,* New York, 1967, 112.

Figure 2. Southern Viceroyalties, 1776

deposed the Spanish viceroy on May 25, 1810, vowing to rule in the name of Ferdinand VII.

The *porteño* action had unforseen consequences for the histories of Argentina and Paraguay. News of the events in Buenos Aires at first stunned the citizens of Asunción, who had largely supported the royalist position. But no matter how grave the offenses of the ancien régime may have been, they were far less rankling to the proud Paraguayans than the indignity of being told to take orders from the *porteños*. After all, Paraguay had been a thriving, established colony when Buenos Aires was only a squalid settlement on the edge of the empty pampas.

The *porteños* bungled their effort to extend control over Paraguay by choosing José Espínola y Peña as their spokesman in Asunción. Espínola was "perhaps the most hated Paraguayan of his era," in the words of historian John Hoyt Williams. Espínola's reception in Asunción was less than cordial, partly because he was closely linked to rapacious policies of the ex-governor, Lázaro de Rivera, who had arbitrarily shot hundreds of his citizens until he was forced from office in 1805. Barely escaping a term of exile in Paraguay's far north, Espínola fled back to Buenos Aires and lied about the extent of *porteño* support in Paraguay, causing the Buenos Aires *cabildo* to make an equally disastrous move. In a bid to settle the issue by force, the *cabildo* sent 1,100 troops under General Manuel Belgrano to subdue Asunción. Paraguayan troops soundly thrashed the *porteños* at Paraguarí and Tacuarí. Officers from both armies, however, fraternized openly during the campaign. From these contacts the Paraguayans came to realize that Spanish dominance in South America was coming to an end, and that they, and not the Spaniards, held the real power.

If the Espínola and Belgrano affairs served to whet nationalist passions in Paraguay, the Paraguayan royalists' ill-conceived actions that followed inflamed them. Believing that the Paraguayan officers who had whipped the *porteños* posed a direct threat to his rule, Governor Bernardo de Velasco dispersed and disarmed the forces under his command and sent most of the soldiers home without paying them for their eight months of service. Velasco previously had lost face when he fled the battlefield at Paraguarí, thinking Belgrano would win. Discontent spread, and the last straw was the request by the Asunción *cabildo* for Portuguese military support against Belgrano's forces, who were encamped just over the border in present-day Argentina. Far from bolstering the *cabildo*'s position, this move instantly ignited an uprising and the overthrow of Spanish authority in Paraguay on May 14 and 15, 1811. Independence was declared on May 17.

The Rise of José Gaspar Rodríguez de Francia

José Gaspar Rodríguez de Francia was one of the greatest figures in Paraguayan history. Ruling from 1814 until his death in 1840, Francia succeeded almost single-handedly in building a strong, prosperous, secure, and independent nation at a time when Paraguay's continued existence as a distinct country seemed unlikely. He left Paraguay at peace, with government coffers full and many infant industries flourishing. Frugal, honest, competent, and diligent, Francia was tremendously popular with the lower classes. But despite his popularity, Francia trampled on human rights, imposing an authoritarian police state based on espionage and coercion. Under Francia, Paraguay underwent a social upheaval that destroyed the old elites.

Paraguay at independence was a relatively undeveloped area. Most residents of Asunción and virtually all rural settlers were illiterate. Urban elites did have access to private schools and tutoring. University education was, however, restricted to the few who could afford studies at the University of Córdoba, in present-day Argentina. Practically no one had any experience in government, finance, or administration. The settlers treated the Indians as little better than slaves, and the paternalistic clergy treated them like children. The country was surrounded by hostile neighbors, including the warlike Chaco tribes. Strong measures were needed to save the country from disintegration.

Francia, born in 1766, spent his student days studying theology at the College of Monserrat at the University of Córdoba. Although he was dogged by suggestions that his father—a Brazilian tobacco expert—was a mulatto, Francia was awarded a coveted chair of theology at the Seminary of San Carlos in Asunción in 1790. His radical views made his position as a teacher there untenable, and he soon gave up theology to study law. A devotee of the Enlightenment and the French Revolution, a keen reader of Voltaire, Jean-Jacques Rousseau, and the French Encyclopedists, Francia had the largest library in Asunción. His interest in astronomy, combined with his knowledge of French and other subjects considered arcane in Asunción, caused some superstitious Paraguayans to regard him as a wizard capable of predicting the future. As a lawyer, he became a social activist and defended the less fortunate against the affluent. He demonstrated an early interest in politics and attained with difficulty the position of *alcalde del primer voto,* or head of the Asunción *cabildo,* by 1809, the highest position he could aspire to as a criollo.

After the *cuartelazo* (coup d'état) of May 14–15, which brought independence, Francia became a member of the ruling junta. Although real power rested with the military, Francia's many talents attracted support from the nation's farmers. Probably the only man in Paraguay with diplomatic, financial, and administrative skills, Francia built his power base on his organizational abilities and his forceful personality. By outwitting *porteño* diplomats in the negotiations that produced the Treaty of October 11, 1811 (in which Argentina implicitly recognized Paraguayan independence in return for vague promises of a military alliance), Francia proved that he possessed skills crucial to the future of the country.

Francia consolidated his power by convincing the insecure Paraguayan elite that he was indispensable. But at the end of 1811, dissatisfied with the political role that military officers were beginning to play, he resigned from the junta. From his retirement in his modest *chacra* (cottage or hut) at Ibaray, near Asunción, he told countless ordinary citizens who came to visit him that their revolution had been betrayed, that the change in government had only traded a Spanish-born elite for a criollo one, and that the present government was incompetent and mismanaged. In fact, the country was rapidly heading for a crisis. Not only were the Portuguese threatening to overrun the northern frontiers, but Argentina had also practically closed the Río de la Plata to Paraguayan commerce by levying taxes and seizing ships. To make matters worse, the *porteño* government agitated for Paraguayan military assistance against the Spanish in Uruguay and, disregarding the Treaty of October 11, for unification of Paraguay with Argentina. The *porteño* government also informed the junta it wanted to reopen talks.

When the junta learned that a *porteño* diplomat was on his way to Asunción, it panicked because it realized it was not competent to negotiate without Francia. In November 1812, the junta members invited Francia to take charge of foreign policy, an offer Francia accepted. In return, the junta agreed to place one-half of the army and half the available munitions under Francia's command. In the absence of anyone equal to him on the junta, Francia now controlled the government. When the Argentine envoy, Nicolás de Herrera, arrived in May 1813, he learned to his dismay that all decisions had to await the meeting of a Paraguayan congress in late September. Meanwhile, Paraguay again declared itself independent of Argentina and expelled two junta members known to be sympathetic to union with Argentina. Under virtual house arrest, Herrera had little scope to build support for unification, even though he resorted to bribery.

The congress, which met on September 30, 1813, was certainly the first of its kind in Latin America. There were more than 1,100 delegates chosen by universal male suffrage, and many of these delegates represented the poor, rural Paraguayan majority. Ironically, the decisions of this democratically elected body would set the stage for a long dictatorship. Herrera was neither allowed to attend the sessions, nor to present his declaration; instead the congress gave overwhelming support to Francia's anti-imperialist foreign policy. The delegates rejected a proposal for Paraguayan attendance at a constitutional congress at Buenos Aires and established a Paraguayan republic—the first in Spanish America—with Francia as first consul. Francia was supposed to trade places every four months with the second consul, Fulgencio Yegros, but Francia's consulship marked the beginning of his direct rule because Yegros was little more than a figurehead. Yegros, a man without political ambitions, represented the nationalist criollo military elite, but Francia was the more powerful because he derived his strength from the nationalist masses.

El Supremo Dictador

Francia, described by a historian as "the frail man in the black frock coat," admired and emulated the most radical elements of the French Revolution. Although he has been compared to the Jacobin leader Maximllien de Robespierre (1758–94), Francia's policies and ideals perhaps most closely resembled those of François-Noël Babeuf, a French utopian who wanted to abolish private property and communalize land as a prelude to founding a "republic of equals." Francia detested the political culture of the old regime and considered himself a "revolutionary."

In essence, the government of Caraí Guazú ("Great Señor," as Francia was called by the poor) was a dictatorship that destroyed the power of the elite and advanced the interests of common Paraguayans. A system of internal espionage destroyed free speech. People were arrested without charge and disappeared without trial. Torture in the so-called Chamber of Truth was applied to those suspected of plotting to overthrow Francia. Francia sent political prisoners—numbering approximately 400 in any given year—to a detention camp where they were shackled in dungeons and denied medical care and even the use of sanitary facilities. In an indirect act of revenge against people who had discriminated against him because of his supposed "impure blood," Francia forbade Europeans from marrying other Europeans, thus forcing the elite to choose spouses from among the local population. Francia tightly sealed Paraguay's borders to the outside world and executed anyone who attempted to leave the country. Foreigners who managed to enter Paraguay had to remain there for the rest of their lives. Paraguayan commerce declined practically to nil. The decline ruined exporters of yerba maté and tobacco. These measures fell most harshly on the members of the former ruling class of Spanish or Spanish-descended church officials, military officers, merchants, and hacendados.

In 1820, four years after a Paraguayan congress had named Francia dictator for life with the title El Supremo Dictador (supreme dictator), Francia's security system uncovered and quickly crushed a plot by the elite to assassinate El Supremo. Francia arrested almost 200 prominent Paraguayans and eventually executed most of them. In 1821 Francia struck again, summoning all of Paraguay's 300 or so *peninsulares* (people born in Spain) to Asunción's main square, where he accused them of treason, had them arrested, and led them off to jail for 18 months. Francia released them only after they agreed to pay an enormous collective indemnity of 150,000 pesos (about 75 percent of the annual state budget), an amount so large that it broke their predominance in the Paraguayan economy.

One of Francia's special targets was the Roman Catholic Church. The church had provided an essential ideological underpinning to Spanish rule by spreading the doctrine of the "divine right of kings" and inculcating the Indian masses with a resigned fatalism about their social status and economic prospects. Francia banned religious orders, closed the country's only seminary, "secularized" monks and priests by forcing them to swear loyalty to the state, abolished the *fuero eclesiástico* (the privilege of clerical immunity from civil courts), confiscated church property, and subordinated church finances to state control.

The common people of Paraguay benefited from the repression of the traditional elites and the expansion of the state. The state took land from the elite and the church and leased it to the poor. About 875 families received homesteads from the lands of the former seminary. The various fines and confiscations levied on the criollos helped reduce taxes for everyone else. As a result, Francia's attacks on the elite and his state socialist policies provoked little popular resistance. The fines, expropriations, and confiscations of foreign-held property meant that the state quickly became the nation's largest landowner, eventually operating forty-five animal-breeding farms. Run by army personnel, the farms were so successful that the surplus animals were given away to the peasants.

In contrast to other states in the region, Paraguay was efficiently and honestly administered, stable, and secure (the army having grown to 1,800 regulars). Crime continued to exist during the Franciata (the period of Francia's rule), but criminals were treated leniently. Murderers, for example, were put to work on public projects. Asylum for political refugees from other countries became a Paraguayan hallmark. An extremely frugal and honest man, Francia left the state treasury with at least twice as much money in it as when he took office, including 36,500 pesos of his unspent salary, or at least several years' salary.

The state soon developed native industries in shipbuilding and textiles, a centrally planned and administered agricultural sector, which was more diversified and productive than the prior export monoculture, and other manufacturing capabilities. These developments supported Francia's policy of virtual economic autarchy.

But Francia's greatest accomplishment—the preservation of Paraguayan independence—resulted directly from a noninterventionist foreign policy. Deciding that Argentina was a potential threat to Paraguay, he shifted his foreign policy toward Brazil by quickly recognizing Brazilian independence in 1821. This move, however, resulted in no special favors for the Brazilians from Francia, who was also on good, if limited, terms with Juan Manuel Rosas, the Argentine dictator. Francia prevented civil war and secured his role as dictator when he cut off his internal enemies from their friends in Buenos Aires. Despite his "isolationist" policies, Francia conducted a profitable but closely supervised import-export trade with both countries to obtain key foreign goods, particularly armaments. A more activist foreign policy than Francia's probably would have made Paraguay a battleground amid the swirl of revolution and war that swept Argentina, Uruguay, and southern Brazil in the decades following independence.

All of these political and economic developments put Paraguay on the path of independent nationhood, yet the country's undoubted progress during the years of the Franciata took place because of complete popular abdication to Francia's will. El Supremo personally controlled every aspect of Paraguayan public life. No decision at the state level, no matter how small, could be made without his approval. All of Paraguay's accomplishments during this period, including its existence as a nation, were attributable almost entirely to Francia. The common people saw these accomplishments as Francia's gifts, but along with these gifts came political passivity and naiveté among most Paraguayans.

Dictatorship and War

Carlos Antonio López

Confusion overtook the state in the aftermath of Francia's death on September 20, 1840, because El Supremo, now El Difunto (the Dead One), had left no successor. After a few days, a junta emerged, freed some political prisoners, and soon proved itself ineffectual at governing. In January 1841, the junta was overthrown. Another coup followed sixteen days later, and chaos continued until in March 1841 congress chose Carlos Antonio López as first consul. In 1844 another congress named López president of the republic, a post he held until his death in 1862. Paraguay had its second dictator.

*Residence of Carlos Antonio López
and Francisco Solano López, Asunción
Courtesy Tim Merrill*

López, a lawyer, was one of the most educated men in the country. Until his elevation to consul, López, born in 1787, had lived in relative obscurity. Although López's government was similar to Francia's system, his appearance, style, and policies were quite different. In contrast to Francia, who was lean, López was obese—a "great tidal wave of human flesh," according to one who knew him. López was a despot who wanted to found a dynasty and run Paraguay like a personal fiefdom. Francia had pictured himself as the first citizen of a revolutionary state, whereas López used the all-powerful state bequeathed by the proverbially honest Francia to enrich himself and his family.

López soon became the largest landowner and cattle rancher in the country, amassing a fortune, which he augmented with the state's monopoly profits from the yerba maté trade. Despite his greed, Paraguay prospered under El Excelentísimo (the Most Excellent One), as López was known. Under López, Paraguay's population increased from about 220,000 in 1840 to about 400,000 in 1860. Several highways and a telegraph system were built. A British firm began building a railroad, one of South America's first, in 1858. During his term of office, López improved national defense, abolished the remnants of the *reducciones,* stimulated economic development, and tried to strengthen relations with foreign

23

countries. He also took measures to reduce the threat to settled Paraguayans from the marauding Indian tribes that still roamed the Chaco. Paraguay also made large strides in education. When López took office, Asunción had only one primary school. During López's reign, more than 400 schools were built for 25,000 primary students, and the state reinstituted secondary education. López's educational development plans progressed with difficulty, however, because Francia had purged the country of the educated elite, which included teachers.

Less rigorous than Francia, López loosened restrictions on foreign intercourse, boosted exports, invited foreign physicians, engineers, and investors to settle in Paraguay, and paid for students to study abroad. He also sent his son Francisco Solano to Europe to buy guns.

Like Francia, López had the overriding aim of defending and preserving Paraguay. He launched reforms with this goal in mind. Trade eased arms acquisitions and increased the state's income. Foreign experts helped build an iron factory and a large armory. The new railroad was to be used to transport troops. López used diplomacy to protect the state's interests abroad. Yet despite his apparent liberality, López was a dictator who held Paraguayans on a tight leash. He allowed Paraguayans no more freedom to oppose the government than they had had under Francia. Congress became his puppet, and the people abdicated their political rights, a situation enshrined in the 1844 constitution, which placed all power in López's hands.

Under López, Paraguay began to tackle the question of slavery, which had existed since early colonial days. Settlers had brought a few slaves to work as domestic servants, but were generally lenient about their bondage. Conditions worsened after 1700, however, with the importation of about 50,000 African slaves to be used as agricultural workers. Under Francia, the state acquired about 1,000 slaves when it confiscated property from the elite. López did not free these slaves; instead, he enacted the 1842 Law of the Free Womb, which ended the slave trade and guaranteed that the children of slaves would be free at age twenty-five. But the new law served only to increase the slave population and depress slave prices as slave birthrates soared.

Foreign relations began to increase in importance under López, who retained Paraguay's traditional mistrust of the surrounding states, yet lacked Francia's diplomatic adroitness. Initially López feared an attack by the Buenos Aires dictator Rosas. With Brazilian encouragement, López had dropped Francia's policy of neutrality and began meddling in Argentine politics. Using the slogan "Independence or Death," López declared war against Rosas in 1845 to support an unsuccessful rebellion in the Argentine province of Corrientes. Although complications with Britain and France prevented him from moving against Paraguay, Rosas quickly established a *porteño* embargo on Paraguayan goods. After Rosas fell in 1852, López signed a treaty with Buenos Aires that recognized Paraguay's independence, although the Argentines never ratified it. In the same year, López signed treaties of friendship, commerce, and navigation with France and the United States. Nonetheless, growing tensions with several countries, including the United States, characterized the second half of López's rule. In 1858 the United States sent a flotilla to Paraguayan waters in a successful action to claim compensation for an American sailor who had been killed three years earlier.

Although he wore his distrust for foreigners like a badge of loyalty to the nation, López was not as cautious as he appeared. López recklessly dropped Francia's key policies of neutrality without making the hard choices and compromises about where his allegiances lay. He allowed unsettled controversies and boundary disputes with Brazil and Argentina to smolder. The two regional giants had tolerated Paraguayan independence, partly because Paraguay served to check the expansionist tendencies of the other. Both were satisfied if the other could not dominate Paraguayan affairs. At the same time, however, a Paraguay that was antagonistic to both Brazil and Argentina would give these countries a reason for uniting.

Francisco Solano López

Born in 1826, Francisco Solano López became the second and final ruler of the López dynasty. He had a pampered childhood. His father raised him to inherit his mantle and made him a brigadier general at the age of eighteen. He was an insatiable womanizer, and stories abound of the cruel excesses he resorted to when a woman had the courage to turn him down. His 1853 trip to Europe to buy arms was undoubtedly the most important experience of his life; his stay in Paris proved to be a turning point for him. There, Solano López admired the trappings and pretensions of the French empire of Napoleon III. He fell in love with an Irish woman named Elisa Alicia Lynch, whom he made his mistress. "La Lynch," as she became known in Paraguay, was a strong-willed, charming, witty, intelligent woman who became a person of enormous influence in Paraguay because of her relationship with Solano López. Lynch's Parisian manners soon made her a trendsetter in the Paraguayan capital, and she made enemies as quickly as she made friends. Lynch bore Solano López five sons, although the two never married. She became the largest landowner in Paraguay after Solano López transferred most of the country and portions of Brazil to her name during the war, yet she retained practically nothing when the war ended. She buried Solano López with her own hands after the last battle in 1870 and died penniless some years later in Europe.

Solano López consolidated his power after his father's death in 1862 by silencing several hundred critics and would-be reformers through imprisonment. Another Paraguayan congress then unanimously elected him president. Yet Solano López would have done well to heed his father's last words to avoid aggressive acts in foreign affairs, especially with Brazil. Francisco's foreign policy vastly underestimated Paraguay's neighbors and overrated Paraguay's potential as a military power.

Observers sharply disagreed about Solano López. George Thompson, an English engineer who worked for the younger López (he distinguished himself as a Paraguayan officer during the War of the Triple Alliance, and later wrote a book about his experience) had harsh words for his ex-employer and commander, calling him ''a monster without parallel.'' Solano López's conduct laid him open to such charges. In the first place, Solano López's miscalculations and ambitions plunged Paraguay into a war with Argentina, Brazil, and Uruguay. The war resulted in the deaths of half of Paraguay's population and almost erased the country from the map. During the war, Solano López ordered the executions of his own brothers and had his mother and sisters tortured when he suspected them of opposition. Thousands of others, including Paraguay's bravest soldiers and generals, also went to their deaths before firing squads or were hacked to pieces on Solano López's orders. Others saw Solano López as a paranoid megalomaniac, a man who wanted to be the ''Napoleon of South America,'' willing to reduce his country to ruin and his countrymen to beggars in his vain quest for glory.

However, sympathetic Paraguayan nationalists and foreign revisionist historians have portrayed Solano López as a patriot who resisted to his last breath Argentine and Brazilian designs on Paraguay. They portrayed him as a tragic figure caught in a web of Argentine and Brazilian duplicity who mobilized the nation to repulse its enemies, holding them off heroically for five bloody, horror-filled years until Paraguay was finally overrun and prostrate. Since the 1930s, Paraguayans have regarded Solano López as the nation's foremost hero.

Solano López's basic failing was that he did not recognize the changes that had occurred in the region since Francia's time. Under his father's rule, the protracted, bloody, and distracting birth pangs of Argentina and Uruguay; the bellicose policies of Brazil; and Francia's noninterventionist policies had worked to preserve Paraguayan independence. Matters had decidedly settled down since then in both Argentina and Brazil, as both countries had become surer of their identities and more united. Argentina, for example, began reacting to foreign challenges more as a nation and less like an assortment of squabbling regions, as Paraguayans had grown to expect. Solano López's attempt to leverage Paraguay's emergence as a regional power equal to Argentina and Brazil had disastrous consequences.

The War of the Triple Alliance

Solano López accurately assessed the September 1864 Brazilian intervention in Uruguay as a slight to the region's lesser powers. He was also correct in his assumption that neither Brazil nor Argentina paid much attention to Paraguay's interests when they formulated their policies. But he concluded incorrectly that preserving Uruguayan ''independence'' was crucial to Paraguay's future as a nation. Consistent with his plans to start a Paraguayan ''third force'' between Argentina and Brazil, Solano López committed the nation to Uruguay's aid. When Argentina failed to react to Brazil's invasion of Uruguay, Solano López seized a Brazilian warship in November 1864. He quickly followed this move with an invasion of Mato Grosso, Brazil, in March 1865, an action that proved to be one of Paraguay's few successes during the war. Solano López then decided to strike at his enemy's main force in Uruguay. But Solano López was unaware that Argentina had acquiesced to Brazil's Uruguay policy and would not support Paraguay against Brazil. When Solano López requested permission for his army to cross Argentine territory to attack the Brazilian province of Rio Grande do Sul, Argentina refused. Undeterred, Solano López sent his forces into Argentina, probably expecting local strongmen to rebel and remove Argentina from the picture. Instead, the action set the stage for the May 1865 signing by Argentina, Brazil, and Uruguay (now reduced to puppet status) of the Treaty of the Triple Alliance. Under the treaty, these nations vowed to destroy Solano López's government.

Paraguay was in no sense prepared for a major war, let alone a war of the scope that Solano López had unleashed. In terms of size, Solano López's 30,000-man army was the most powerful in Latin America. But the army's strength was illusory because it lacked trained leadership, a reliable source of weapons and matériel, and adequate reserves. Since the days of El Supremo, the officer corps had been neglected for political reasons. The army suffered from a critical shortage of key personnel, and many of its fighting units were undermanned. Paraguay lacked the industrial base to replace weapons lost in battle, and the Argentine-Brazilian alliance prevented Solano López from receiving arms from abroad. Paraguay's population was only about 450,000 in 1865—a figure lower than the number of people in the Brazilian National Guard— and amounted to less than one-twentieth of the combined allied population of 11 million. Even after conscripting for the front every able-bodied man—including children as young as ten—and forcing women to perform all nonmilitary labor, Solano López still could not field an army as large as those of his rivals.

Apart from some Paraguayan victories on the northern front, the war was a disaster for Solano López. The core units of the Paraguayan army reached Corrientes in April 1865. By July more than half of Paraguay's 30,000-man invasion force had been killed or captured along with the army's best small arms and artillery. The war quickly became a desperate struggle for Paraguay's survival.

Paraguay's soldiers exhibited suicidal bravery, especially considering that Solano López shot or tortured so many of them for the most trivial offenses. Cavalry units operated on foot for lack of horses. Naval infantry battalions armed only with machetes attacked Brazilian ironclads. The suicide attacks resulted in fields of corpses. Cholera was rampant. By 1867 Paraguay had lost 60,000 men to casualties, disease, or capture, and another 60,000 soldiers were called to duty. Solano López conscripted slaves, and infantry units formed entirely of children appeared. Women were forced to perform support work behind the lines. Matériel shortages were so severe that Paraguayan troops went into battle seminude, and even colonels went barefoot, according to one observer. The defensive nature of the war, combined with Paraguayan tenacity and ingenuity and the difficulty that Brazilians and Argentinians had cooperating with each other, rendered the conflict a war of attrition. In the end, Paraguay lacked the resources to continue waging war against South America's giants.

As the war neared its inevitable denouement, Solano López's grip on reality—never very strong—loosened further. Imagining himself surrounded by a vast conspiracy, he ordered thousands of executions in the military. In addition, he executed 2 brothers and 2 brothers-in-law, scores of top government and military officials, and about 500 foreigners, including many diplomats. He frequently had his victims killed by lance thrusts to save ammunition. The bodies were dumped into mass graves. His cruel treatment of prisoners was proverbial. Solano López condemned troops to death if they failed to carry out his orders to the minutest detail. "Conquer or die" became the order of the day.

Solano López's hostility even extended to United States Ambassador Charles A. Washburn. Only the timely arrival of the United States gunboat *Wasp* saved the diplomat from arrest.

Allied troops entered Asunción in January 1869, but Solano López held out in the northern jungles for another fourteen months until he finally died in battle. The year 1870 marked the lowest point in Paraguayan history. Hundreds and thousands of Paraguayans had died. Destitute and practically destroyed, Paraguay had to endure a lengthy occupation by foreign troops and cede large patches of territory to Brazil and Argentina.

Despite several historians' accounts of what happened between 1865 and 1870, Solano López was not wholly responsible for the war. Its causes were complex and included Argentine anger over Antonio López's meddling in Corrientes. The elder López also had infuriated the Brazilians by not helping to overthrow Rosas in 1852 and by forcing Brazilian garrisons out of territory claimed by Paraguay in 1850 and 1855. Antonio López also resented having been forced to grant Brazil free navigation rights on the Río Paraguay in 1858. Argentina meanwhile disputed ownership of the Misiones district between the Río Paraná and Río Uruguay, and Brazil had its own ideas about the Brazil-Paraguay boundary. To these problems was added the Uruguayan vortex. Carlos Antonio López had survived mainly with caution and a good bit of luck; Solano López had neither.

Liberals Versus Colorados

The Postwar Period

Ruined by war, pestilence, famine, and foreign indemnities (which were never paid), Paraguay was on the verge of disintegration in 1870. But its fertile soil and the country's overall backwardness probably helped it survive. After the war, Paraguay's mostly rural populace continued to subsist as it had done for centuries, eking out a meager existence in the hinterland under unimaginably difficult conditions. The allied occupation of Asunción in 1869 put the victors in direct control of Paraguayan affairs. While Bolivia pressed its nebulous claim to the Chaco, Argentina and Brazil swallowed huge chunks of Paraguayan territory (around 154,000 square kilometers).

Brazil had borne the brunt of the fighting, with perhaps 150,000 dead and 65,000 wounded. It had spent US$200 million, and its troops formed the senior army of occupation in the country, so it was logical that Rio de Janeiro temporarily overshadowed Buenos Aires in Asunción. Sharp disagreements between the two powers prolonged the occupation until 1876. Ownership of the Paraguayan economy quickly passed to foreign speculators and adventurers who rushed to take advantage of the rampant chaos and corruption.

The internal political vacuum was at first dominated by survivors of the Paraguayan Legion. This group of exiles, based in Buenos Aires, had regarded Solano López as a mad tyrant and fought for the allies during the war. The group set up a provisional government in 1869 mainly under Brazilian auspices and signed the 1870 peace accords, which guaranteed Paraguay's independence and free river navigation. A constitution was also promulgated in the same year, but it proved ineffective because of the foreign origin of its liberal, democratic tenets. After the last foreign troops had gone in 1876 and an arbitral award to Paraguay of the area between the Río Verde and Río Pilcomayo by an international commission headed by Rutherford B. Hayes, United States president, the era of party politics in Paraguay was free to begin in earnest. Nonetheless, the evacuation of foreign forces did not mean the end of foreign influence. Both Brazil and Argentina remained deeply involved in Paraguay because of their connections with Paraguay's rival political forces. These forces eventually came to be known as the Colorados and the Liberals.

The political rivalry between Liberals and Colorados was presaged as early as 1869 when the terms Azules (Blues) and Colorados (Reds) first appeared. The National Republican Association-Colorado Party (Asociación Nacional Republicana-Partido Colorado) dominated Paraguayan political life from the late 1880s until Liberals overthrew it in 1904. The Liberal ascent marked the decline of Brazil, which had supported the Colorados as the principal political force in Paraguay, and the rise of Argentine influence.

In the decade following the war, the principal political conflicts within Paraguay reflected the Liberal-Colorado split, with Legionnaires battling Lopiztas (ex-followers of Solano López) for power, while Brazil and Argentina maneuvered in the background. The Legionnaires saw the Lopiztas as reactionaries. The Lopiztas accused the Legionnaires of being traitors and foreign puppets. The situation defied neat categories, since many people constantly changed sides. Opportunism characterized this era, not ideological purity.

The Legionnaires were a motley collection of refugees and exiles who dated from Francia's day. Their opposition to tyranny was sincere, and they gravitated toward democratic ideologies. Coming home to backward, poor, xenophobic Paraguay from cosmopolitan, prosperous Buenos Aires was a big shock for the Legionnaires. Believing that more freedom would cure Paraguay's ills, they abolished slavery and founded a constitutional government as soon as they came to power. They based the new government on the standard liberal prescriptions of free enterprise, free elections, and free trade.

The Legionnaires, however, had no more experience in democracy than other Paraguayans. The 1870 constitution quickly became irrelevant. Politics degenerated into factionalism, and cronyism and intrigue prevailed. Presidents still acted like dictators, elections did not stay free, and the Legionnaires were out of power in less than a decade.

Free elections were a startling, and not altogether welcome, innovation for ordinary Paraguayans, who had always allied themselves with a *patrón* (benefactor) for security and protection. At the same time, Argentina and Brazil were not content to leave Paraguay with a truly free political system. Pro-Argentine militia chief Benigno Ferreira emerged as de facto dictator until his overthrow with Brazilian help in 1874. Ferreira later returned to lead the 1904 Liberal uprising, which ousted the Colorados. Ferreira served as president between 1906 and 1908.

The First Colorado Era

Cándido Bareiro, López's ex-commercial agent in Europe, returned to Paraguay in 1869 and formed a major Lopizta faction. He also recruited General Bernadino Caballero, a war hero with close ties to López. After President Juan Bautista Gil was assassinated in 1877, Caballero used his power as army commander to guarantee Bareiro's election as president in 1878. When Bareiro died in 1880, Caballero seized power in a coup. Caballero dominated Paraguayan politics for most of the next two decades, either as president or through his power in the militia. His accession to power is notable because he brought political stability, founded a ruling party—the Colorados—to regulate the choice of presidents and the distribution of spoils, and began a process of economic reconstruction.

Despite their professed admiration for Francia, the Colorados dismantled Francia's unique system of state socialism. Desperate for cash because of heavy debts incurred in London in the early postwar period, the Colorados lacked a source of funds except through the sale of the state's vast holdings, which comprised more than 95 percent of Paraguay's total land. Caballero's government sold much of this land to foreigners in huge lots. While Colorado politicians raked in the profits and themselves became large land-owners, peasant squatters who had farmed the land for genera-tions were forced to vacate and, in many cases, to emigrate. By 1900 seventy-nine people owned half of the country's land.

Although the Liberals had advocated the same land-sale policy, the unpopularity of the sales and evidence of pervasive government corruption produced a tremendous outcry from the opposition. Liber-als became bitter foes of selling land, especially after Caballero bla-tantly rigged the 1886 election to ensure a victory for General Patricio Escobar. Ex-Legionnaires, idealistic reformers, and former Lopiz-tas joined in July 1887 to form the Centro Democrático (Democratic Center), a precursor of the Liberal party, to demand free elections, an end to land sales, civilian control over the military, and clean government. Caballero responded, along with his principal adviser, José Segundo Decoud, and Escobar, by forming the Colorado Party one month later, thus formalizing the political cleavage.

Both groups were deeply factionalized, however, and very little ideology separated them. Colorado and Liberal partisans changed sides whenever it proved advantageous. While the Colorados re-inforced their monopoly on power and spoils, Liberals called for reform. Frustration provoked an aborted Liberal revolt in 1891 that produced changes in 1893, when war minister General Juan B. Egusquiza overthrew Caballero's chosen president, Juan G. González. Egusquiza startled Colorado stalwarts by sharing power with the Liberals, a move that split both parties. Ex-Legionnaire Ferreira, along with the *cívico* (civic) wing of the Liberals, joined the government of Egusquiza—who left office in 1898—to allow a civilian, Emilio Aceval, to become president. Liberal *radicales* (rad-icals) who opposed compromising with their Colorado enemies boy-cotted the new arrangement. Caballero, also boycotting the alliance, plotted to overthrow civilian rule and succeeded when Colonel Juan Antonio Ezcurra seized power in 1902. This victory was Caballero's last, however. In 1904, General Ferreira, with the support of *cívicos, radicales,* and *egusquistas,* invaded from Argentina. After four months of fighting, Ezcurra signed the Pact of Pilcomayo aboard an Argentine gunboat on December 12, 1904, and handed power to the Liberals.

Liberal Decades

The revolution of August 1904 began as a popular movement, but liberal rule quickly degenerated into factional feuding, military

*Santísima Trinidad Church in Asunción,
the original burial place of Carlos Antonio López
Courtesy Tim Merrill*

coups, and civil war. Political instability was extreme in the Liberal era, which saw twenty-one governments in thirty-six years. During the period 1904 to 1922, Paraguay had fifteen presidents. By 1908 the *radicales* had overthrown General Ferreira and the *cívicos*. The Liberals had disbanded Caballero's army when they came to power and organized a completely new one. Nevertheless, by 1910 army commander Colonel Albino Jara felt strong enough to stage a coup against President Manuel Gondra. Jara's coup backfired as it touched off an anarchic two-year period in which every major political group seized power at least once. The *radicales* again invaded from Argentina, and when the charismatic Eduardo Schaerer became president, Gondra returned as minister of war to reorganize the army once more. Schaerer became the first president since Egusquiza to finish his four-year term.

The new political calm was shattered, however, when the *radicales* split into Schaerer and Gondra factions. Gondra won the presidential election in 1920, but the *schaereristas* successfully undermined him and forced him to resign. Full-scale fighting between the factions broke out in May 1922 and lasted for fourteen months. The *gondristas* beat the *schaereristas* decisively and held on to power until 1936.

Laissez-faire Liberal policies had permitted a handful of hacendados to exercise almost feudal control over the countryside, while peasants had no land and foreign interests manipulated Paraguay's economic fortunes. The Liberals, like the Colorados, were a deeply factionalized political oligarchy. Social conditions—always marginal in Paraguay—deteriorated during the Great Depression of the 1930s. The country clearly needed reforms in working conditions, public services, and education. The stage was set for an anti-Liberal nationalist reaction that would change the direction of Paraguayan history.

Paraguay's dispute with Bolivia over the Chaco, a struggle that had been brewing for decades, finally derailed the Liberals. Wars and poor diplomacy had prevented the settling of boundaries between the two countries during the century following independence. Although Paraguay had held the Chaco for as long as anyone could remember, the country did little to develop the area. Aside from scattered Mennonite colonies and nomadic Indian tribes, few people lived there (see Natural Regions; Minority Groups, ch. 2). Bolivia's claim to the Chaco became more urgent after it lost its seacoast to Chile during the 1879–84 War of the Pacific. Left without any outlet to the sea, Bolivia wanted to absorb the Chaco and expand its territory up to the Río Paraguay in order to gain a river port. In addition, the Chaco's economic potential intrigued the Bolivians. Oil had been discovered there by Standard Oil Company in the 1920s, and people wondered whether an immense pool of oil was lying beneath the entire area. Ironically, South America's two greatest victims of war and annexation in the previous century were ready to face each other in another bout of bloody combat, this time over a piece of apparently desolate wilderness.

While Paraguayans were busy fighting among themselves during the 1920s, Bolivians established a series of forts in the Paraguayan Chaco. In addition, they bought armaments from Germany and hired German military officers to train and lead their forces. Frustration in Paraguay with Liberal inaction boiled over in 1928 when the Bolivian army established a fort on the Río Paraguay called Fortín Vanguardia. In December of that year, Paraguayan major (later colonel) Rafael Franco took matters into his own hands, led a surprise attack on the fort, and succeeded in destroying it. The routed Bolivians responded quickly by seizing two Paraguayan forts. Both sides mobilized, but the Liberal government felt unprepared for war so it agreed to the humiliating condition of rebuilding Fortín Vanguardia for the Bolivians. The Liberal government also provoked criticism when it forced Franco, by then a national hero, to retire from the army.

As diplomats from Argentina, the United States, and the League of Nations conducted fruitless "reconciliation" talks, Colonel José Félix Estigarribia, Paraguay's deputy army commander, ordered his troops into action against Bolivian positions early in 1931. Meanwhile, nationalist agitation led by the National Independent League (Liga Nacional Independiente) increased. Formed in 1928 by a group of intellectuals, the League sought a new era in national life that would witness a great political and social rebirth. Its adherents advocated a "new democracy" that might sweep the country free of petty partisan interests and foreign encroachments. An amalgam of diverse ideologies and interests, the League reflected a genuine popular wish for social change. When government troops in October 1931 fired on a mob of League students demonstrating in front of the Government Palace, the Liberal administration of President José Guggiari lost what little legitimacy it retained. The students and soldiers of the rising "New Paraguay" movement (which wanted to sweep away corrupt party politics and introduce nationalist and socialist reforms) would thereafter always see the Liberals as morally bankrupt.

The Chaco War and the February Revolution

When war finally broke out officially in July 1932, the Bolivians were confident of a rapid victory. Their country was richer and more populous than Paraguay, and their armed forces were larger, had a superior officer corps, and were well-trained and well-equipped. These advantages quickly proved irrelevant in the face of the Paraguayans' zeal to defend their homeland. The highly motivated Paraguayans knew the geography of the Chaco better than the Bolivians and easily infiltrated Bolivian lines, surrounded outposts, and captured supplies. In contrast, Indians from the Bolivian high plateau area, known as the Altiplano, were forced into the Bolivian army, had no real interest in the war, and failed to adapt to the hot Chaco climate. In addition, long supply lines, poor roads, and weak logistics hindered the Bolivian campaign. The Paraguayans proved more united than the Bolivians—at least initially—as President Eusebio Ayala and Colonel (later Marshal) Estigarribia worked well together.

After the December 1933 Paraguayan victory at Campo Vía, Bolivia seemed on the verge of surrendering. At that moment, however, President Ayala agreed to a truce. His decision was greeted with derision in Asunción. Instead of ending the war with a swift victory that might have boosted their political prospects, the Liberals signed a truce that seemed to allow the Bolivians to regroup. The war continued until July 1935. Although the Liberals had successfully led Paraguay's occupation of nearly all the disputed territory and had won the war when the last truce went into effect, they were finished politically.

In many ways, the Chaco War acted as a catalyst to unite the political opposition with workers and peasants, who furnished the raw materials for a social revolution. After the 1935 truce, thousands of soldiers were sent home, leaving the regular army to patrol the front lines. The soldiers who had shared the dangers and trials of the battlefield deeply resented the ineptitude and incompetence they believed the Liberals had shown in failing to prepare the country for war. These soldiers had witnessed the miserable state of the Paraguayan army and were forced in many cases to face the enemy armed only with machetes. After what they had been through, partisan political differences seemed irrelevant. The government offended the army rank-and-file by refusing to fund pensions for disabled war veterans in 1936 while awarding 1,500 gold pesos a year to Estigarribia. Colonel Franco, back on active duty since 1932, became the focus of the nationalist rebels inside and outside the army. The final spark to rebellion came when Franco was exiled for criticizing Ayala. On February 17, 1936, units of the army descended on the Presidential Palace and forced Ayala to resign, ending thirty-two years of Liberal rule.

Outside Paraguay, the February revolt seemed to be a paradox because it overthrew the politicians who had won the war. The soldiers, veterans, students, and others who revolted felt, however, that victory had come despite the Liberal government. Promising a national and social revolution, the Febrerista Revolutionary Party (Partido Revolucionario Febrerista—PRF)—more commonly known as the Febreristas—brought Colonel Franco back from exile in Argentina to be president. The Franco government showed it was serious about social justice by expropriating more than 200,000 hectares of land and distributing it to 10,000 peasant families. In addition, the new government guaranteed workers the right to strike and established an eight-hour work day. Perhaps the government's most lasting contribution affected national consciousness. In a gesture calculated to rewrite history and erase seven decades of national shame, Franco declared Solano López a national hero *sin ejemplar* (without precedent) because he had stood up to foreign threats and sent a team to Cerro Corá to find his unmarked grave. The government interred his remains along with those of his father in a chapel designated the National Pantheon of Heroes, and later erected a monument to him on Asunción's highest hill.

Despite the popular enthusiasm that greeted the February revolution, the new government lacked a clear program. A sign of the times, Franco practiced his Mussolini-style, spellbinding oratory from a balcony. But when he published his distinctly fascist-sounding Decree Law No. 152 promising a "totalitarian transformation" similar to those in Europe, protests erupted. The youthful, idealistic elements that had come together to produce the Febrerista movement were actually a hodgepodge of conflicting political tendencies and social opposites, and Franco was soon in deep political trouble. Franco's cabinet reflected almost every conceivable shade of dissident political opinion, and included socialists, fascist sympathizers, nationalists, Colorados, and Liberal *cívicos*. A new party of regime supporters, the Revolutionary National Union (Unión Nacional Revolucionaria), was founded in November 1936. Although the new party called for representative democracy, rights for peasants and workers, and socialization of key industries, it failed to broaden Franco's political base. In the end, Franco forfeited his popular support because he failed to keep his promises to the poor. He dared not expropriate the properties of foreign landowners, who were mostly Argentines. In addition, the Liberals, who still had influential support in the army, agitated constantly for Franco's overthrow. When Franco ordered Paraguayan troops to abandon the advanced positions in the Chaco that they had held since the 1935 truce, the army revolted in August 1937 and returned the Liberals to power.

The army, however, did not hold a unified opinion about the Febreristas. Several attempted coups served to remind President Félix Pavia (the former dean of law at the National University) that although the February Revolution was out of power, it was far from dead. People who suspected that the Liberals had learned nothing from their term out of office soon had proof: a peace treaty signed with Bolivia on July 21, 1938, fixed the final boundaries behind the Paraguayan battle lines. In 1939 the Liberals, recognizing that they would have to choose someone with national stature to be president if they wanted to hold onto power, picked General Estigarribia, the hero of the Chaco War who had since served as special envoy to the United States. Estigarribia quickly realized that he would have to adopt many Febrerista ideas to avoid anarchy. Circumventing the die-hard Liberals in the National Assembly who opposed him, Estigarribia assumed "temporary" dictatorial powers in February 1940, but promised the dictatorship would end as soon as a workable constitution was written.

Estigarribia vigorously pursued his goals. He began a land reform program that promised a small plot to every Paraguayan family. He reopened the university, balanced the budget, financed the public debt, increased the capital of the Central Bank, implemented monetary and municipal reforms, and drew up plans to build highways and public works. An August 1940 plebiscite endorsed Estigarribia's constitution, which remained in force until 1967. The constitution of 1940 promised a "strong, but not despotic" president and a new state empowered to deal directly with social and economic problems (see Constitutional Development, ch. 4). But by greatly expanding the power of the executive branch, the constitution served to legitimize open dictatorship.

Morínigo and World War II

The era of the New Liberals, as Estigarribia's supporters were called, came to a sudden end in September 1940, when the president died in an airplane crash. Hoping to control the government through a more malleable military man, the "Old Liberal" cabinet named War Minister Higinio Morínigo president. Morínigo had gained fame in Paraguay by heading the 1936 expedition to Cerro Corá to retrieve López's remains. The apparently genial Morínigo soon proved himself a shrewd politician with a mind of his own, and the Liberals resigned within a few weeks when they realized that they would not be able to impose their will on him. Having inherited Estigarribia's dictatorial powers, Morínigo quickly banned both Febreristas and Liberals and clamped down drastically on free speech and individual liberties. A nonparty dictator without a large body of supporters, Morínigo survived politically—despite the numerous plots against him—because of his astute handling of an influential group of young military officers who held key positions of power.

The outbreak of World War II eased Morínigo's task of ruling Paraguay and keeping the army happy because it stimulated demand for Paraguayan export products—such as meat, hides, and cotton—and boosted the country's export earnings. More important, United States policy toward Latin America at this time made Paraguay eligible for major economic assistance. A surge of German influence in the region and Argentina's pro-Axis leanings alarmed the United States, which sought to wean Paraguay away from German and Argentine solicitation. At the same time, the United States sought to enhance its presence in the region and pursued close cooperation with Brazil, Argentina's traditional rival. To this end, the United States provided to Paraguay sizable amounts of funds and supplies under the Lend-Lease Agreement, provided loans for public works, and gave technical assistance in agriculture and health care. The United States Department of State approved of closer ties between Brazil and Paraguay and especially supported Brazil's offer to finance a road project designed to reduce Paraguay's dependence on Argentina.

Much to the displeasure of the United States and Britain, Morínigo refused to act against German economic and diplomatic interests until the end of the war. German agents had successfully converted many Paraguayans to the Axis cause. South America's first Nazi Party branch had been founded in Paraguay in 1931. German immigrant schools, churches, hospitals, farmers' cooperatives, youth groups, and charitable societies became active Axis backers. All of those organizations prominently displayed swastikas and portraits of Adolf Hitler.

It is no exaggeration to say that Morínigo headed a pro-Axis regime. Large numbers of Paraguayan military officers and government officials were openly sympathetic to the Axis. Among these officials was the national police chief, who named his son Adolfo Hirohito after the leading Axis personalities. By 1941 the official newspaper, *El País*, had adopted an overtly pro-German stance. At the same time, the government strictly controlled pro-Allied labor unions. Police cadets wore swastikas and Italian insignia on their uniforms. The December 1941 Japanese attack on Pearl Harbor and Germany's declaration of war against the United States gave the United States the leverage it needed, however, to force Morínigo to commit himself publicly to the Allied cause. Morínigo officially severed diplomatic relations with the Axis countries in 1942, although he did not declare war against Germany until February 1945. Nonetheless, Morínigo continued to maintain close relations with the heavily German-influenced Argentine military throughout the war and provided a haven for Axis spies and agents.

United States protests over German and Argentine activities in Paraguay fell on deaf ears. While the United States defined its interests in terms of resisting the fascist threat, Paraguayan officials believed their interests lay in economic expediency and were reluctant to antagonize Germany until the outcome of the war was no longer in doubt. Many Paraguayans believed Germany was no more of a threat to Paraguay's sovereignty than the United States.

The Allied victory convinced Morínigo to liberalize his regime. Paraguay experienced a brief democratic opening as Morínigo relaxed restrictions on free speech, allowed political exiles to return, and formed a coalition government. Morínigo's intentions about stepping down were murky, however, and his de facto alliance with Colorado Party hardliners and their thuggish Guión Rojo (red script) paramilitary group antagonized the opposition. The result was a failed coup d'état in December 1946 and full-scale civil war in March 1947.

Led by Colonel Rafael Franco, the revolutionaries were an unlikely coalition of Febreristas, Liberals, and communists, united only in their desire to overthrow Morínigo. The Colorados helped Morínigo crush the insurgency, but the man who saved Morínigo's government during crucial battles was the commander of the General Brǧez Artillery Regiment, Lieutenant Colonel Alfredo Stroessner Mattiauda. When a revolt at the Asunción Navy Yard put a strategic working-class neighborhood in rebel hands, Stroessner's regiment quickly reduced the area to rubble. When rebel gunboats threatened to dash upriver from Argentina to bombard the capital into submission, Stroessner's forces battled furiously and knocked them out of commission.

By the end of the rebellion in August, a single party—one that had been out of power since 1904—had almost total control in Paraguay. The fighting had simplified politics by eliminating all parties except the Colorados and by reducing the size of the army. Because nearly four-fifths of the officer corps had joined the rebels, fewer individuals were now in a position to compete for power. As had often happened in the past, however, the Colorados split into rival factions. The hardline *guionistas,* headed by the fiery left-leaning nationalist writer and publisher Natalicio González, opposed democratic practices. The moderate *democráticos,* led by Federico Chaves, favored free elections and a power-sharing arrangement with the other parties. With Morínigo's backing, González used the Guión Rojo to cow the moderates and gain his party's presidential nomination. In the Paraguayan tradition, he ran unopposed in the long-promised 1948 elections. Suspecting that Morínigo would not relinquish power to González, a group of Colorado military officers, including Stroessner, removed Morínigo from office. González joined Morínigo in exile early in 1949, and Chaves became president in 1950 as the military finally allowed power to pass to the *democráticos.*

Paraguayan politics had come full circle in a certain sense. The Chaco War had sparked the February revolution, which, in turn, sounded the death knell of the Liberal state and ushered in a revival of Paraguayan nationalism along with a reverence for the dictatorial past. The result was the constitution of 1940, which returned to the executive the power that the Liberals had stripped away. When a brief flirtation with democracy became a civil war after World War II, the Colorados, the party of the Lopiztas, were again running Paraguay. In the interim, the influence of the armed forces had increased dramatically. Since the end of the Chaco War, no Paraguayan government has held power without the consent of the army. Morínigo maintained order by severely restricting individual liberties but created a political vacuum. When he tried to fill it with the Colorado Party, he split the party in two, and neither faction could establish itself in power without help from the military. The institution of one-party rule, the establishment of order at the expense of political liberty, and the acceptance of the army's role of final political arbiter created the conditions that encouraged the emergence of the Stroessner regime.

The Stronato

The 1954 Coup

Despite his reputation as a democrat, Chaves imposed a state of siege three weeks after he took office, aiming his emergency powers at the supporters of González and ex-President Felipe Molas López. Mounting economic problems immediately confronted the new government. Two decades of extreme political and social unrest—including depression, war, and civil conflicts—had shattered Paraguay's economy. National and per capita income had fallen sharply, the Central Bank's practice of handing out soft loans to regime cronies was spurring inflation and a black market, and Argentina's economic woes were making themselves felt in Paraguay. Still, Chaves stayed in office without mishap; the country simply needed a rest.

By 1953, however, the seventy-three-year-old president's political support began to erode markedly. His decision to run for reelection disappointed younger men who nursed political ambitions, and rumors that Chaves would strengthen the police at the army's expense disappointed the military. Early in 1954, recently fired Central Bank Director Epifanio Méndez Fleitas joined forces with Stroessner—at that time a general and commander in chief of the armed forces—to oust Chaves. Méndez Fleitas was unpopular with Colorado Party stalwarts and the army, who feared that he was trying to build a following as did his hero, Juan Domingo Perón, Argentina's president from 1946 to 1955. In May 1954, Stroessner ordered his troops into action against the government after Chaves had tried to dismiss one of his subordinates. Fierce resistance by police left almost fifty dead.

As the military "strongman" who made the coup, Stroessner was able to provide many of his supporters with positions in the provisional government. About two months later, a divided Colorado Party nominated Stroessner for president. For many party members, he represented an "interim" choice, as Morínigo had been for the Liberals in 1940. When Stroessner took office on August 15, 1954, few people imagined that this circumspect, unassuming forty-one-year-old commander in chief would be a master politician capable of outmaneuvering and outlasting them all. Nor was it apparent that his period of rule, known as the Stronato, would be longer than that of any other ruler in Paraguayan history.

Consolidation of the Stroessner Regime

The son of an immigrant German brewer and a Paraguayan woman, Stroessner was born in Encarnación in 1912. He joined the army when he was sixteen and entered the triservice military academy, the Francisco López Military College. Like Franco and Estigarribia, Stroessner was a hero of the Chaco War. He had gained a reputation for his bravery and his abilities to learn quickly and to command and inspire loyalty in troops. He was also known to be thorough and to have an unusual capacity for hard work. His extremely accurate political sense failed him only once, when he found himself in 1948 on the wrong side of a failed coup attempt and had to be driven to the Brazilian embassy in the trunk of a car, earning him the nickname "Colonel Trunk." Career considerations and an antipathy for communists possibly caused Stroessner to decide against joining the rebels in 1947. Morínigo found his talents indispensable during the civil war and promoted him rapidly. Because he was one of the few officers who had remained loyal to Morínigo, Stroessner became a formidable player once he entered the higher echelons of the armed forces.

Repression was a key factor in Stroessner's longevity (see Opposition Parties, ch. 4; Security and Political Offenses, ch. 5). Stroessner took a hard line from the beginning in his declaration of a state of siege, which he renewed carefully at intervals prescribed by the constitution. Except for a brief period in 1959, Stroessner renewed the state of siege every three months for the interior of the country until 1970 and for Asunción until 1987. He was lucky from the outset; the retirement of González and the death of Molas López had removed two of his most formidable opponents. Another helpful coincidence was the September 1955 Argentine coup that deposed Perón, thus depriving Méndez Fleitas of his main potential source of support. After the coup, Perón fled to Asunción, where his meddling in Paraguayan politics complicated Méndez Fleitas's position further and intensified the political struggle going on behind the scenes. Forced to play his hand after the Argentine junta compelled Perón to depart Asunción for Panama in November, Méndez Fleitas prepared to stage a coup in late December. However, Stroessner purged the military of Méndez Fleitas's supporters and made him go into exile in 1956.

To observers, Stroessner did not seem to be in a particularly strong position. He was hardly in control of the Colorado Party, which was full of competing factions and ambitious politicians, and the army was not a dependable supporter. The economy was in bad shape and deteriorating further. Stroessner's adoption of economic austerity measures proved unpopular with military officers, who had grown used to getting soft loans from the Central Bank; with businessmen, who disliked the severe tightening of credit; and with workers, who went out on strike when they no longer received pay raises. In addition, the new Argentine government, displeased with Stroessner's cordial relations with Perón, cancelled a trade agreement.

A 1958 national plebiscite elected Stroessner to a second term, but dissatisfaction with the regime blossomed into a guerrilla insurgency soon afterward. Sponsored by exiled Liberals and Febreristas, small bands of armed men began to slip across the border from Argentina. Venezuela sent large amounts of aid to these groups starting in 1958. The following year, the new Cuban government under Fidel Castro Ruz also provided assistance.

Stroessner's response was to employ the state's virtually unlimited power by giving a free hand to the military and to Minister of Interior Edgar Ynsfrán, who harassed and allegedly murdered family members of some of the regime's foes. A cycle of terror and counter-terror began to make life in Paraguay precarious.

The guerrillas received little support from Paraguay's conservative peasantry. The Colorado Party's peasant *py nandí* irregulars ("barefoot ones" in Guaraní), who had a well-deserved reputation for ferocity, often tortured and executed their prisoners. Growing numbers of people were interned in jungle concentration camps. Army troops and police smashed striking labor unions by taking over their organizations and arresting their leaders.

In April 1959, however, Stroessner grudgingly decided to heed the growing call for reform within the army and the Colorado Party. He lifted the state of siege, allowed opposition exiles to return, ended press censorship, freed political prisoners, and promised to rewrite the 1940 constitution. After two months of this democratic "spring," the country was on the verge of chaos. In late May, nearly 100 people were injured when a student riot erupted in downtown Asunción over a bus fare increase. The disturbance inspired the legislature to call for Ynsfrán's resignation. Stroessner responded swiftly by reimposing the state of siege and dissolving the legislature.

An upsurge in guerrilla violence followed, but Stroessner once again parried the blow. Several factors strengthened Stroessner's hand. First, United States military aid was helping enhance the army's skills in counterinsurgency warfare. Second, the many purges of the Colorado Party had removed all opposition factions. In addition, Stroessner's economic policies had boosted exports and investment and reduced inflation, and the right-wing military coups in Brazil in 1964 and Argentina in 1966 also improved the international climate for nondemocratic rule in Paraguay.

Another major factor in Stroessner's favor was a change in attitude among his domestic opposition. Demoralized by years of fruitless struggle and exile, the major opposition groups began to sue for peace. A Liberal Party faction, the Renovation Movement, returned to Paraguay to become the "official" opposition, leaving the remainder of the Liberal Party, which renamed itself the Radical Liberal Party (Partido Liberal Radical—PLR), in exile. In return for Renovationist participation in the elections of 1963, Stroessner allotted the new party twenty of Congress's sixty seats. Four years later, PLR members also returned to Paraguay and began participating in the electoral process. By this time, the Febreristas, a sad remnant of the once powerful but never terribly coherent revolutionary coalition, posed no threat to Stroessner and were legalized in 1964. The new Christian Democratic Party (Partido Demócrata Cristiano—PDC) also renounced violence as a means of gaining power. The exhaustion of most opposition forces enabled Stroessner to crush the Paraguayan Communist Party (Partido Comunista Paraguayo—PCP) by mercilessly persecuting its members and their spouses and to isolate the exiled Colorado *epifanistas* (followers of Epifanio Méndez Fleitas) and *democráticos,* who had reorganized themselves as the Colorado Popular Movement (Movimiento Popular Colorado—Mopoco).

Under "liberalization," Ynsfrán, the master of the machinery of terror, began to outlive his usefulness to Stroessner. Ynsfrán opposed political decompression and was unhappy about Stroessner's increasingly clear intention to stay president for life. A May 1966 police corruption scandal gave Stroessner a convenient way to dismiss Ynsfrán in November. In August 1967, a new Constitution created a two-house legislature and formally allowed Stroessner to serve for two more five-year presidential terms (see Constitutional Development, ch. 4).

International Factors and the Economy

During the 1960s and 1970s, the main foreign influences on Paraguay were Brazil and the United States. Both countries aided Paraguay's economic development in ways that enhanced its political stability. A 1956 agreement with Brazil to improve the transport link between the two countries by building roads and a bridge over the Río Paraná broke Paraguay's traditional dependence on Argentine goodwill for the smooth flow of Paraguayan international trade. Brazil's grant of duty-free port facilities on the Atlantic Coast was particularly valuable to Paraguay.

Brazil's financing of the US$19 billion Itaipú Dam on the Río Paraná between Paraguay and Brazil had far-reaching consequences for Paraguay. Paraguay had no means of contributing financially to the construction, but its cooperation—including controversial concessions regarding ownership of the construction site and the rates for which Paraguay agreed to sell its share of the electricity— was essential. Itaipú gave Paraguay's economy a great new source of wealth. The construction produced a tremendous economic boom, as thousands of Paraguayans who had never before held a regular job went to work on the enormous dam. From 1973 (when construction began) until 1982 (when it ended), gross domestic product (GDP—see Glossary) grew more than 8 percent annually, double the rate for the previous decade and higher than growth rates in most other Latin American countries. Foreign exchange earnings from electricity sales to Brazil soared, and the newly employed Paraguayan workforce stimulated domestic demand, bringing about a rapid expansion in the agricultural sector (see Growth and Structure of the Economy, ch. 3).

There were, however, several drawbacks to the construction at Itaipú. The prosperity associated with the major boom raised expectations for long-term growth. An economic downturn in the early 1980s caused discontent, which in turn led to demands for reform. Many Paraguayans, no longer content to eke out a living on a few hectares, had to leave the country to look for work. In the early 1980s, some observers estimated that up to 60 percent of Paraguayans were living outside the country. But even those people who were willing to farm a small patch of ground faced a new threat. Itaipú had prompted a tidal wave of Brazilian migration in the eastern border region of Paraguay. By the mid-1980s, observers estimated there were between 300,000 and 350,000 Brazilians in the eastern border region. With Portuguese the dominant language in the areas of heavy Brazilian migration and Brazilian currency circulating as legal tender, the area became closely integrated with Brazil (see Immigrants, ch. 2). Further, most of Paraguay's increased wealth wound up in the hands of wealthy supporters of the regime. Landowners faced no meaningful land reform, the regime's control of labor organizers aided businessmen, foreign investors benefited from tax exemptions, and foreign creditors experienced a bonanza from heavy Paraguayan borrowing. Although the poorest Paraguayans were somewhat better off in 1982 than they were in the 1960s, they were worse off relative to other sectors of the population.

Closer relations with Brazil paralleled a decline in relations with Argentina. After Perón's expulsion, Paraguay slipped from the orbit of Buenos Aires as Argentina declined politically and economically. Argentina, alarmed by Itaipú and close cooperation between Brazil and Paraguay, pressed Stroessner to agree to participate in hydroelectric projects at Yacyretá and Corpus (see Electricity, ch. 3). By pitting Argentina against Brazil, Stroessner improved Paraguay's diplomatic and economic autonomy and its economic prospects.

Stroessner also benefited from the 1950s and 1960s Cold War ideology in the United States, which favored authoritarian, anticommunist regimes. Upon reaching Asunción during his 1958 tour of Latin America, Vice President Richard M. Nixon praised Stroessner's Paraguay for opposing communism more strongly than any other nation in the world. The main strategic concern of the United States at that time was to avoid at all costs the emergence in Paraguay of a left-wing regime, which would be ideally situated at the heart of the South American continent to provide a haven for radicals and a base for revolutionary activities around the hemisphere. From 1947 until 1977, the United States supplied about US$750,000 worth of military hardware each year and trained more than 2,000 Paraguayan military officers in counterintelligence and counterinsurgency. In 1977 the United States Congress sharply cut military assistance to Paraguay.

Paraguay regularly voted in favor of United States policies in the United Nations (UN) and the Organization of American States (OAS). Stroessner, probably the United States' most dependable ally in Latin America, once remarked that the United States ambassador was like an extra member of his cabinet. Relations faltered somewhat during the administration of President John F. Kennedy, as United States officials began calling for democracy and land reform and threatened to withhold Alliance for Progress funds (an amount equal to about 40 percent of Paraguay's budget) unless Paraguay made progress. Although pressure of this sort no doubt encouraged Stroessner to legalize some internal opposition parties, it failed to make the Paraguayan ruler become any less a personalist dictator. Regime opponents who agreed to play Stroessner's electoral charade received rewards of privileges and official recognition. Other opponents, however, faced detention and exile. Influenced by Paraguay's support for the United States intervention in the Dominican Republic in 1965, the United States

The National Pantheon of Heroes, Asunción
Courtesy United States Department of State

became friendlier to Stroessner in the mid-1960s under President Lyndon B. Johnson. New United States-supported military governments in Brazil and Argentina also improved United States-Paraguay ties.

Relations between Paraguay and the United States changed substantially after the election of President Jimmy Carter in 1976. The appointment of Robert White as United States ambassador in 1977 and the congressional cut-off of military hardware deliveries in the same year reflected increasing concern about the absence of democracy and the presence of human rights violations in Paraguay (see Relations with the United States, ch. 4).

Toward the 1980s

After a period of inactivity, the political opposition became increasingly visible in the late 1970s. In 1977 Domingo Laíno, a PLR congressman during the previous ten years, broke away to form the Authentic Radical Liberal Party (Partido Liberal Radical Auténtico—PLRA). Laíno's charges of government corruption, involvement in narcotics trafficking, human rights violations, and inadequate financial compensation from Brazil under the terms of the Treaty of Itaipú earned him Stroessner's wrath. In 1979 Laíno helped lead the PLRA, the PDC, Mopoco, and the legally recognized Febreristas—the latter angered by the constitutional

47

amendment allowing Stroessner to seek yet another presidential term in 1978—into the National Accord (Acuerdo Nacional). The National Accord served to coordinate the opposition's political strategy (see Opposition Parties, ch. 4).The victim of countless detentions, torture, and persecution, Laíno was forced into exile in 1982 following the publication of a critical book about ex-Nicaraguan dictator Anastasio Somoza Debayle, who was assassinated in Asunción in 1980.

Beginning in the late 1960s, the Roman Catholic Church persistently criticized Stroessner's successive extensions of his stay in office and his treatment of political prisoners. The regime responded by closing Roman Catholic publications and newspapers, expelling non-Paraguayan priests, and harassing the church's attempts to organize the rural poor (see Interest Groups, ch. 4).

The regime also increasingly came under international fire in the 1970s for human rights abuses, including allegations of torture and murder. In 1978 the Inter-American Commission on Human Rights convinced an annual meeting of foreign ministers at the OAS to pass a resolution calling on Paraguay to improve its human rights situation. In 1980 the Ninth OAS General Assembly, meeting in La Paz, Bolivia, condemned human rights violations in Paraguay, describing torture and disappearances as ''an affront to the hemisphere's conscience.'' International groups also charged that the military had killed 30 peasants and arrested 300 others after the peasants had protested against encroachments on their land by government officials.

Paraguay entered the 1980s less isolated, rural, and backward than it had traditionally been. Political and social structures remained inflexible, but Paraguayans had changed their world views and their perceptions of themselves.

By skillfully balancing the military and the Colorado Party, Stroessner remained very much in control. Still, he was increasingly being challenged in ways that showed that his control was not complete. For example, in November 1974, police units captured seven guerrillas in a farmhouse outside of Asunción. When the prisoners were interrogated, it became clear that the information possessed by the guerrillas, who had planned to assassinate Stroessner, could have come only from a high Colorado official. With the party hierarchy suddenly under suspicion, Stroessner ordered the arrest and interrogation of over 1,000 senior officials and party members. He also dispatched agents to Argentina and Brazil to kidnap suspects among the exiled Colorados. A massive purge of the party followed. Although the system survived, it was shaken.

Perhaps the clearest example of cracks in Stroessner's regime was the assassination of Somoza. From Stroessner's standpoint, there were ominous similarities between Somoza and himself. Like Stroessner, Somoza had run a regime based on the military and a political party that had been noted for its stability and its apparent imperviousness to change. Somoza also had brought economic progress to the country and had skillfully kept his internal opposition divided for years. Ultimately, however, the carefully controlled changes he had introduced began subtly to undermine the traditional, authoritarian order. As traditional society broke down in Paraguay, observers saw increasing challenges ahead for the Stroessner regime.

* * *

There are many excellent works in English on Paraguayan history. Two enjoyable accounts are George Pendle's concise overview *Paraguay: A Riverside Nation* and Harris Gaylord Warren's more detailed *Paraguay: An Informal History*. Philip Caraman's *The Lost Paradise* and R.B. Cunninghame Graham's *A Vanished Arcadia* offer valuable information about the colonial period, especially the Jesuit *reducciones*. Another valuable book is Paul H. Lewis's *Socialism, Liberalism, and Dictatorship in Paraguay*. The standard work up to 1870 remains Charles A. Washburn's *The History of Paraguay*.

John Hoyt Williams's *The Rise and Fall of the Paraguayan Republic, 1800–1870* provides a comprehensive look at independence and the Francia and López dictatorships. The War of the Triple Alliance is scrutinized in Pelham Horton Box's *The Origins of the Paraguayan War*. Readers interested in the postwar period may refer to Harris Gaylord Warren's *Rebirth of the Paraguayan Republic, 1878–1904*. David H. Zook, Jr.'s *The Conduct of the Chaco War* focuses on the 1932–35 war with Bolivia. Paul H. Lewis's *The Politics of Exile: Paraguay's Febrerista Party* examines the 1936–40 revolution and the Febreristas, and Michael Grow amply treats Morínigo and World War II in *The Good Neighbor Policy and Authoritarianism in Paraguay*. No full-length biography of Alfredo Stroessner exists; however, Richard Bourne's *Political Leaders of Latin America* contains an insightful chapter on him. (For further information and complete citations, see Bibliography.)

Chapter 2. The Society and Its Environment

Traditional bottle dance

FOR MOST OF ITS HISTORY, a series of dichotomies characterized Paraguayan society. A contrast existed between rural and urban Paraguay and, even more pointedly, between Asunción—where economic, social, and political trends originated—and the rest of Paraguay. In rural Paraguay a divide existed between those holding legal title to land, usually the owners of large estates dedicated to commercial farming, and the mass of peasant squatters growing crops largely for their families' subsistence. Similarly, there was a gulf between the elite—educated, prosperous, city-based and -bred—and the country's poor, whether rural or urban. Finally, although most Paraguayans retained their fluency in Guaraní and this indigenous language continued to play a vital role in public life, there was a continuum of fluency in Spanish that paralleled (and reflected) the social hierarchy. These dichotomies not only continued into the 1980s but were exacerbated by the extensive, dramatic changes that had occurred in Paraguayan society since the 1960s.

Paraguayans of all classes viewed family and kin as the center of the social universe. Anyone not related through blood or marriage was regarded with reserve, if not distrust. People expected to be able to call upon extended kin for assistance as necessary and counted on them for unswerving loyalty. Godparents (whether or not they were kin) were important as well in strengthening social links within the web of kinship.

Migration was a perennial fact of life: peasants changed plots; men worked on plantations, factories, and river boats; women migrated to cities and towns to find employment in domestic service. Since the mid-nineteenth century, there also had been a large contingent of emigré Paraguayans in Argentina.

In the early 1970s, Paraguay's eastern border region—long underpopulated and undeveloped—replaced neighboring Argentina as the major destination of most Paraguayan migrants. Historically, land in the region had been held in immense plantations; the inhabitants were largely tropical forest Indians and mestizo peasant squatters. Beginning in the late 1960s, however, government land reform projects settled as many as 250,000 rural Paraguayans in agricultural colonies in this area. Many others bypassed the government entirely and settled in the region on their own.

Improvements in transportation and the construction of massive hydroelectric projects brought more far-reaching changes in the 1970s and 1980s. Economic growth drew tens of thousands of migrants—immigrants from neighboring Brazil as well as Paraguayan nationals—into the eastern border region. Their sheer numbers transformed the east from a sleepy hinterland into a maelstrom of change. In the process, both Indians and traditional small farmers were dispossessed of their lands and their traditional livelihood. As the construction projects were completed in the early 1980s, the region saw increased rural unrest as the peasants who had temporarily held jobs in construction found that there were no unclaimed agricultural lands for them to occupy.

The pace of urbanization—modest by world and Latin American standards—quickened during the boom years. Economic growth enabled the cities to absorb large numbers of rural Paraguayans who had been displaced by increased population pressures and the country's skewed land distribution. Economic downturns in the 1980s, however, stoked unrest among workers and peasants.

Geography

Although landlocked, Paraguay is bordered and criss-crossed by navigable rivers. The Río Paraguay divides the country into strikingly different eastern and western regions. Both the eastern region—officially called Eastern Paraguay (Paraguay Oriental) and known as the Paraneña region—and the western region—officially Western Paraguay (Paraguay Occidental) and known as the Chaco—gently slope toward and are drained into the Río Paraguay, which thus not only separates the two regions but unifies them. With the Paraneña region reaching southward and the Chaco extending to the north, Paraguay straddles the Tropic of Capricorn and experiences both subtropical and tropical climates.

External Boundaries

Paraguay is bounded by three substantially larger countries: Bolivia, Argentina, and Brazil (see fig. 1). The northwestern boundary with Bolivia, extending through the low hills of the Chaco region, was set in 1938. The boundary between the Chaco and Brazil was defined in 1927; it continues from the confluence of the Río Apa and Río Paraguay northward along the course of the Río Paraguay to the border with Bolivia. The northern border of the Paraneña region, set in 1872, follows the course of the Río Paraná, the ridges of the mountains in the northeast region, and finally the course of the Río Apa until it empties into the Río Paraguay. Paraguay's southern border with Argentina is formed by the

Río Pilcomayo, Río Paraguay, and Río Paraná. These boundaries were agreed to in 1876.

Natural Regions

The two main natural regions in Paraguay are the Paraneña region—a mixture of plateaus, rolling hills, and valleys—and the Chaco region—an immense piedmont plain. About 95 percent of Paraguay's population resides in the Paraneña region, which has all the significant orographic features and the more predictable climate. The Paraneña region can be generally described as consisting of an area of highlands in the east that slopes toward the Río Paraguay and becomes an area of lowlands, subject to floods, along the river. The Chaco is predominantly lowlands, also inclined toward the Río Paraguay, that are alternately flooded and parched (see fig. 3).

The Paraneña Region

The Paraneña region extends from the Río Paraguay eastward to the Río Paraná, which forms the border with Brazil and Argentina. The eastern hills and mountains, an extension of a plateau in southern Brazil, dominate the region, whose highest point is about 700 meters above sea level. The Paraneña region also has spacious plains, broad valleys, and lowlands. About 80 percent of the region is below 300 meters in elevation; the lowest elevation, 55 meters, is found in the extreme south at the confluence of the Río Paraguay and Río Paraná.

The Paraneña region is drained primarily by rivers that flow westward to the Río Paraguay, although some rivers flow eastward to the Río Paraná. Low-lying meadows, subject to floods, separate the eastern mountains from the Río Paraguay.

The Paraneña region as a whole naturally divides into five physiographic subregions: the Paraná Plateau, the Northern Upland, the Central Hill Belt, the Central Lowland, and the Ñeembucú Plain. In the east, the heavily wooded Paraná Plateau occupies one-third of the region and extends its full length from north to south and up to 145 kilometers westward from the Brazilian and Argentine borders. The Paraná Plateau's western edge is defined by an escarpment that descends from an elevation of about 460 meters in the north to about 180 meters at the subregion's southern extremity. The plateau slopes moderately to east and south, its remarkably uniform surface interrupted only by the narrow valleys carved by the westward-flowing tributaries of the Río Paraná.

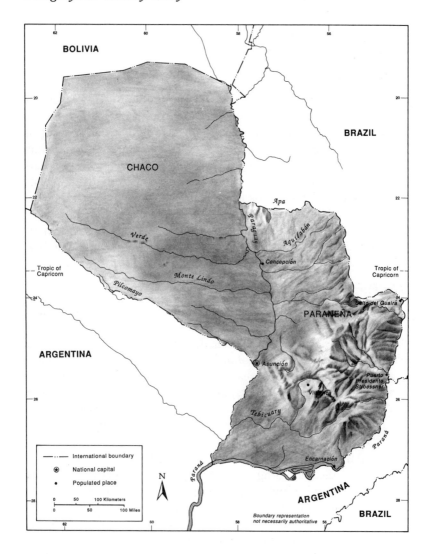

Figure 3. Topography and Drainage

The Northern Upland, the Central Hill Belt, and the Central Lowland constitute the lower terrain lying between the escarpment and the Río Paraguay. The first of these eroded extensions stretching westward of the Paraná Plateau—the Northern Upland—occupies the portion northward from the Río Aquidabán to the Río Apa on the Brazilian border. For the most part it consists of a rolling plateau about 180 meters above sea level and 76 to 90 meters above the plain farther to the south. The Central Hill Belt encompasses the area in the vicinity of Asunción. Although nearly flat surfaces are not lacking in this subregion, the rolling terrain is extremely uneven. Small, isolated peaks are numerous, and it is here that the only lakes of any size are found. Between these two upland subregions is the Central Lowland, an area of low elevation and relief, sloping gently upward from the Río Paraguay toward the Paraná Plateau. The valleys of the Central Lowland's westward-flowing rivers are broad and shallow, and periodic flooding of their courses creates seasonal swamps. This subregion's most conspicuous features are its flat-topped hills, which project six to nine meters from the grassy plain. Thickly forested, these hills cover areas ranging from a hectare to several square kilometers. Apparently the weathered remnants of rock related to geological formations farther to the east, these hills are called *islas de monte* (mountain islands), and their margins are known as *costas* (coasts).

The remaining subregion—the Ñeembucú Plain—is in the southwest corner of the Paraneña region. This alluvial flatland has a slight westerly-southwesterly slope obscured by gentle undulations. The Río Tebicuary—a major tributary of the Río Paraguay— bisects the swampy lowland, which is broken in its central portion by rounded swells of land up to three meters in height.

The main orographic features of the Paraneña region include the Cordillera de Amambay, the Cordillera de Mbaracayú, and the Cordillera de Caaguazú. The Cordillera de Amambay extends from the northeast corner of the region south and slightly east along the Brazilian border. The average height of the mountains is 400 meters above sea level, although the highest point reaches 700 meters. The main chain is 200 kilometers long and has smaller branches that extend to the west and die out along the banks of the Río Paraguay in the Northern Upland.

The Cordillera de Amambay merges with the Cordillera de Mbaracayú, which reaches eastward 120 kilometers to the Río Paraná. The average height of this mountain chain is 200 meters; the highest point of the chain, 500 meters, is within Brazilian territory. The Río Paraná forms the Salto del Guairá waterfall where it cuts through the mountains of the Cordillera de Mbaracayú to enter Paraguayan territory.

The Cordillera de Caaguazú rises where the other two main mountain ranges meet and extends south, with an average height of 400 meters. Its highest point is Cerro de San Joaquín, which reaches 500 meters above sea level. This chain is not a continuous massif but is interrupted by hills and undulations covered with forests and meadows. The Cordillera de Caaguazú reaches westward from the Paraná Plateau into the Central Hill Belt.

A lesser mountain chain, the Serranía de Mbaracayú, also rises at the point where the Cordillera de Amambay and Cordillera de Mbaracayú meet. The Serranía de Mbaracayú extends east and then south to parallel the Río Paraná; the mountain chain has an average height of 500 meters.

The Chaco Region

Separated from the Paraneña region by the Río Paraguay, the Chaco region is a vast plain with elevations reaching no higher than 300 meters and averaging 125 meters. Covering more than 60 percent of Paraguay's total land area, the Chaco plain gently slopes eastward to the Río Paraguay. The Gran Chaco, the entire western portion of the region, is subdivided into the Alto Chaco (Upper Chaco), bordering on Bolivia, and the Bajo Chaco (Lower Chaco), bordering on the Río Paraguay. The low hills in the northwestern part of the Alto Chaco are the highest parts in the Gran Chaco. The main feature of the Bajo Chaco is the Estero Patiño, the largest swamp in the country at 1,500 square kilometers.

Drainage

Rivers have greatly influenced the character of the country. The Río Paraguay and Río Paraná and their tributaries define most of the country's borders, provide all its drainage, and serve as transportation routes. Most of the larger towns of the interior, as well as Asunción, are river ports.

The Río Paraguay has a total course of 2,600 kilometers, 2,300 of which are navigable and 1,200 of which either border on or pass through Paraguay. The head of navigation is located in Brazil, and during most years vessels with twenty-one-meter drafts can reach Concepción without difficulty. Medium-sized ocean vessels can sometimes reach Asunción, but the twisting course and shifting sandbars can make this transit difficult. Although sluggish and shallow, the river sometimes overflows its low banks, forming temporary swamps and flooding villages. River islands, meander scars, and oxbow (U-shaped) lakes attest to frequent changes in course.

The major tributaries entering the Río Paraguay from the Paraneña region—such as the Río Apa, Río Aquidabán, and Río Tebicuary—descend rapidly from their sources in the Paraná Plateau to the lower lands; there they broaden and become sluggish as they meander westward. After heavy rains these rivers sometimes inundate nearby lowlands.

About 4,700 kilometers long, the Río Paraná is the second major river in the country. From Salto del Guairá, where the river enters Paraguay, the Río Paraná flows 800 kilometers to its juncture with the Río Paraguay and then continues southward to the Río de la Plata Estuary at Buenos Aires, Argentina. In general, the Río Paraná is navigable by large ships only up to Encarnación, but smaller boats may go somewhat farther. In summer months the river is deep enough to permit vessels with drafts of up to three meters to reach Salto del Guairá, but seasonal and other occasional conditions severely limit the river's navigational value. On the upper course, sudden floods may raise the water level by as much as five meters in twenty-four hours; west of Encarnación, however, the rocks of the riverbed sometimes come within one meter of the surface during winter and effectively sever communication between the upper river and Buenos Aires.

The rivers flowing eastward across the Paraneña region as tributaries of the Río Paraná are shorter, faster-flowing, and narrower than the tributaries of the Río Paraguay. Sixteen of these rivers and numerous smaller streams enter the Río Paraná above Encarnación.

Paraguay's third largest river, the Río Pilcomayo, flows into the Río Paraguay near Asunción after demarcating the entire border between the Chaco region and Argentina. During most of its course, the river is sluggish and marshy, although small craft can navigate its lower reaches. When the Río Pilcomayo overflows its low banks, it feeds the Estero Patiño.

Drainage in the Chaco region is generally poor because of the flatness of the land and the small number of important streams. In many parts of the region, the water table is only a meter beneath the surface of the ground, and there are numerous small ponds and seasonal marshes. As a consequence of the poor drainage, most of the water is too salty for drinking or irrigation.

Because of the seasonal overflow of the numerous westward-flowing streams, the lowland areas of the Paraneña region also experience poor drainage conditions, particularly in the Ñeembucú Plain in the southwest, where an almost impervious clay subsurface prevents the absorption of excess surface water into the aquifer. About 30 percent of the Paraneña region is flooded from time to time, creating extensive areas of seasonal marshlands. Permanent bogs are found only near the largest geographic depressions, however.

Climate

Paraguay experiences a subtropical climate in the Paraneña region and a tropical climate in the Chaco. The Paraneña region is humid, with abundant precipitation throughout the year and only moderate seasonal changes in temperature. During the Southern Hemisphere's summer, which corresponds to the northern winter, the dominant influence on the climate is the warm sirocco winds blowing out of the northeast. During the winter, the dominant wind is the cold pampero from the South Atlantic, which blows across Argentina and is deflected northeastward by the Andes in the southern part of that country. Because of the lack of topographic barriers within Paraguay, these opposite prevailing winds bring about abrupt and irregular changes in the usually moderate weather. Winds are generally brisk. Velocities of 160 kilometers per hour have been reported in southern locations, and the town of Encarnación was once leveled by a tornado.

The Paraneña region has only two distinct seasons: summer from October to March and winter from May to August. April and September are transitional months in which temperatures are below the midsummer averages and minimums may dip below freezing. Climatically, autumn and spring do not really exist. During the mild winters, July is the coldest month, with a mean temperature of about 18°C in Asunción and 17°C on the Paraná Plateau. There is no significant north-south variation. The number of days with temperatures falling below freezing ranges from as few as three to as many as sixteen yearly, and with even wider variations deep in the interior. Some winters are very mild, with winds blowing constantly from the north, and little frost. During a cold winter, however, tongues of Antarctic air bring subfreezing temperatures to all areas. No part of the Paraneña region is entirely free from the possibility of frost and consequent damage to crops, and snow flurries have been reported in various locations.

Moist tropical air keeps the weather warm in the Paraneña region from October through March. In Asunción the seasonal average is about 24°C, with January—the warmest month—averaging 29°C. Villarrica has a seasonal mean temperature of 21°C and a January mean of 27°C. During the summer, daytime temperatures reaching 38°C are fairly common. Frequent waves of cool air from the south, however, cause weather that alternates between clear, humid conditions and storms. Skies will be almost cloudless for a week to ten days as temperature and humidity rise continually. As the soggy heat nears intolerable limits, thunderstorms preceding a cold front will blow in from the south, and temperatures will drop as much as 15°C in a few minutes.

Rainfall in the Paraneña region is fairly evenly distributed. Although local meteorological conditions play a contributing role, rain usually falls when tropical air masses are dominant. The least rain falls in August, when averages in various parts of the region range from two to ten centimeters. The two periods of maximum precipitation are March through May and October to November.

For the region as a whole, the difference between the driest and the wettest months ranges from ten to eighteen centimeters. The annual average rainfall is 127 centimeters, although the average on the Paraná Plateau is 25 to 38 centimeters greater. All subregions may experience considerable variations from year to year. Asunción has recorded as much as 208 centimeters and as little as 56 centimeters of annual rainfall; Puerto Bertoni on the Paraná Plateau has recorded as much as 330 centimeters and as little as 79 centimeters.

In contrast to the Paraneña region, the Chaco has a tropical wet-and-dry climate bordering on semi-arid. The Chaco experiences seasons that alternately flood and parch the land, yet seasonal variations in temperature are modest. Chaco temperatures are usually high, the averages dropping only slightly in winter. Even at night the air is stifling despite the usually present breezes. Rainfall is light, varying from 50 to 100 centimeters per year, except in the higher land to the northwest where it is somewhat greater. Rainfall is concentrated in the summer months, and extensive areas that are deserts in winter become summer swamps. Rainwater evaporates very rapidly.

Population

The 1982 census enumerated a population of slightly more than 3 million. Demographers suggested annual growth rates from 2.5 to 2.9 percent in the late 1980s. Thus, in mid-1988, estimates of total population ranged from 4 to 4.4 million. Assuming a yearly increase of between 2.5 and 2.9 percent until the end of the century, Paraguay would have a population of 5 to 6 million by the year 2000.

Modern censuses began under the direction of the General Office of Statistics following the War of the Triple Alliance (1865–70). In 1886–87 the census enumerated nearly 330,000 Paraguayans. Beginning with the 1950 census, population counts have been conducted by the General Directorate of Statistics and Census. Censuses were taken in 1886–87, 1889, 1914, 1924, 1936, 1950, 1962, 1972, and 1982. Demographers distrust the 1889 data since the numbers do not follow the generally accepted population growth curve.

After moderate growth in the 1930s and 1940s, the annual intercensal growth rate climbed sharply in the 1950s and 1960s (see table 2, Appendix). Population was concentrated most densely in

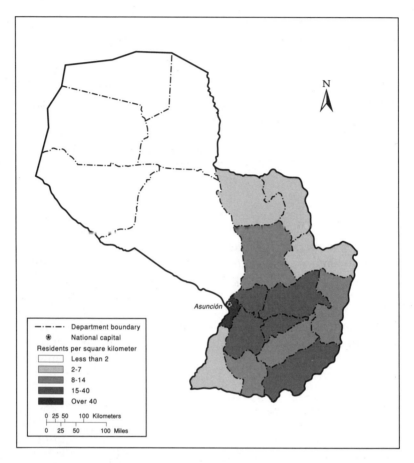

Source: Based on information from Paraguay, Dirección General de Estadística y Censos, *Censo nacional de población y viviendas, 1982: Cifras provisionales,* Asunción, December 1982, 4.

Figure 4. Population Density by Department, 1982

an arc surrounding Asunción east of the Río Paraguay (see fig. 4). The Chaco was the least settled area; the region lost population in the 1970s at an annual rate nearly equal to the national rate of population increase during the same period—a trend that observers believed continued into the 1980s. Settlement along the country's eastern border increased significantly with improvements in transportation and the construction of hydroelectric projects in the region (see Migration and Urbanization, this ch.).

Since the 1950s, the ratio of males to females had increased steadily—an unexpected trend. As a population's general level of living, basic nutrition, and sanitation improve, the proportion of women to men typically tends to rise as degenerative diseases take a greater toll on the male population and women's longevity begins to have a discernible statistical impact. Observers suggested that a partial explanation of Paraguay's unusual pattern might be the decreasing effect of the male emigration that occurred during the decade following the civil war of 1947. The ratio of males to each 100 females was highest in rural areas (107) and lowest in cities (94), reflecting a greater tendency of women to migrate to urban areas.

The 1982 census also revealed a slightly aging population. In 1982 nearly 5 percent of Paraguayans were over sixty-five years old, in contrast to 4 percent for this age-group a decade earlier. Meanwhile, the percentage under age fifteen had dropped 3 percent, to 41.8 percent (see fig. 5).

The average age at which Paraguayan women entered their first marriage or consensual union began to rise in the 1950s. By the late 1970s, women in Asunción averaged 19.7 years of age at their first marriage; those in other cities were about 8 months younger, and those in rural areas were a year younger. The Ministry of Public Health and Social Welfare cooperated in the family-planning efforts of a number of international agencies active in the country and managed several family-planning clinics in Asunción and other parts of the country. Between 1959 and 1978, the total fertility rate—an estimate of the average number of children a woman will bear during her reproductive years—declined by nearly one-third, to 4.97. Estimates put the rate at 4.6 in the mid-1980s, with 3.4 projected by the turn of the century.

Social Relations

Colonial Paraguay (basically, what is now Eastern Paraguay) lacked productive mines, strategic seaports, or lucrative plantation agriculture. Through most of the colonial era, it languished as a backwater of the Spanish Empire in the Americas, a region of small estates with a minimal number of Spanish settlers. The Guaraní-speaking Indians of the region were drawn into colonial society principally through high rates of intermarriage and concubinage with Spanish settlers, a process that created a mestizo society within a few generations (see The Young Colony, ch. 1). In the resulting cultural synthesis, the dominant language remained Guaraní, whereas the rest of the dominant social institutions and culture remained Hispanic.

The few remaining Hispanic overlords were largely eliminated in the upheaval of the War of the Triple Alliance, leaving a homogeneous population of mestizo farmers. Despite far-reaching

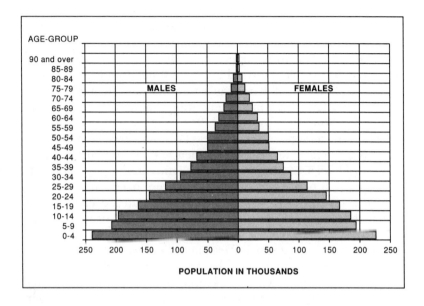

AGE-GROUP

90 and over
85-89
80-84
75-79   MALES   FEMALES
70-74
65-69
60-64
55-59
50-54
45-49
40-44
35-39
30-34
25-29
20-24
15-19
10-14
5-9
0-4

250   200   150   100   50   0   50   100   150   200   250

POPULATION IN THOUSANDS

Source: Based on information from Paraguay, Dirección General de Estadística y Censos,
Censo nacional de población y viviendas, 1982: Muestra del 10%, Asunción, September
1984, 20.

Figure 5. Population by Age and Sex, 1982

changes from the 1960s to the 1980s, Paraguay remained a country of peasants engaged in subsistence farming. The basic social
dichotomy was between small farmers and a narrow stratum of elite
families whose diverse resources included links to industry, commerce, government, the military, and commercial agriculture. The
upper class was centered in the capital and was interlinked by ties
of kinship and marriage. Many, if not most, members of the elite
knew each other from childhood, having grown up in the same
neighborhoods and attended the same schools.

Guaraní—which, unlike many indigenous New World languages,
included a written form after the Jesuits developed an orthography
in the mid-sixteenth century—remained a vital element of Paraguayan national identity. Guaraní had always been one of the principal ways Paraguayans distinguished themselves from the rest of
Latin America, and the 1967 Constitution recognizes Guaraní as
a national language. Guaraní theater, in which both Paraguayan
works and translations of European classics were performed, was
popular with all levels of society. Paraguayan songs were internationally popular; lyrics in Spanish and Guaraní were a hallmark
of Paraguayan culture.

Sociolinguist Joan Rubin characterized Paraguay as ". . . a Guaraní-speaking nation with a heavy incidence of Spanish-Guaraní bilingualism in which each language tends to fulfill distinct functions." Spanish had been the official language since the sixteenth century, and in the late twentieth century it remained the language of government, education, and religion. Nevertheless, Paraguayans of all classes spoke Guaraní much of the time. Language use varied by social context, however. Guaraní was appropriate in more intimate contexts. Spanish was used in more formal situations; it implied respect toward one of higher status. In families, for example, parents might use Guaraní in speaking to one another and require that their children speak to them in Spanish. The upper echelons were distinguished by their relative fluency and ease in using Spanish. By contrast, most rural Paraguayans were monolingual Guaraní speakers until as late as the 1960s.

Family and Kin

For Paraguayans of all social strata and backgrounds, family and kin were the primary focus of an individual's loyalties and identity. In varying degrees of closeness, depending on individual circumstances and social class, the family included godchildren, godparents, and many members of the extended family. Paraguayans felt some reserve toward anyone not able to claim relationship through kinship or marriage. Family and kin—not the community—were the center of the social universe. An individual could expect assistance from extended kin on an ad hoc basis in times of need. Poorer Paraguayans relied particularly on their mother's relatives; the more prosperous were more even-handed in their dealings with extended kin. The country's elite buttressed its economic advantages through a web of far-reaching kinship ties. The truly elite family counted among its kindred large landholders, merchants, intellectuals, and military officers. Political allegiances also reflected family loyalties; all available kin were marshalled in support of the individual's political efforts.

Nonetheless, most people lived in nuclear families consisting of spouses and their unmarried offspring. Most families consisted of a couple and their pre-adult children or a single mother and her children. Individual adults living alone were rare. If a marriage broke up, the mother typically kept the children and home, whereas the father either formed another union or moved in with relatives until he did so. The most typical extension of the nuclear family was a form of "semi-adoption" in which well-to-do townspeople took in a child of poorer rural relatives or adopted (on a more permanent basis) the illegitimate offspring of a female relative. There were few intergenerational households. Adoption conformed to cultural norms favoring assistance to relatives, but intergenerational families were viewed as a source of conflict. This characterization also usually prevented a daughter and her children from moving back home following a divorce or separation.

The nuclear family prevailed, in part, because of the limited economic opportunities available to most families. Few of the traditional enterprises by which most Paraguayans earned a living could support more than the immediate family members.

Surveys in the late 1970s and early 1980s found that nearly 20 percent of all households were headed by a single parent—usually the mother. The incidence was highest in cities outside of Greater Asunción and lowest in rural areas. Households headed by a female generally were poor. Children's fathers might or might not acknowledge their offspring; in either event, admitting paternity did not obligate men to do much in the way of continued support for their children. Most single mothers worked in poorly paying jobs or a variety of cottage industries (see Rural Society, this ch.). In almost all cases, they were consigned to a sector of the economy where competition was intense and earnings low.

Within two-parent families, the male was the formal head of the household. Fathers were treated with respect, but typically had little to do with the daily management of the home. Their contact with children, especially younger ones, was limited. Women maintained ties with extended kin, ran the home, and dealt with finances; they often contributed as well to the family's income. Men spent a good deal of time socializing outside the home.

There were three kinds of marriage: church, civil, and consensual unions. Almost all adults married. Although stable unions were socially esteemed, men's extramarital affairs drew little criticism as long as they did not impinge on the family's subsistence and continued well-being. By contrast, women's sexual behavior reflected on their families and affected family stability; women were expected to be faithful as long as they were involved in a reasonably permanent union. A church wedding represented a major expense for the families involved. The common view held that a fiesta was an essential part of the ceremony and required that it be as large and costly as the two families could possibly afford. The celebrations attendant on a civil marriage or the formation of a consensual union were considerably less elaborate. Typically, the couple's families met for a small party and barbecue. Church weddings were rare among peasants—the expenses were simply beyond

Shoppers on a busy Asunción street
Courtesy Inter-American Development Bank

the reach of the average farm family. Even a civil marriage was a mark of status among peasants.

So-called illegitimacy was neither a stigma nor a particular disadvantage if the child came from a stable consensual union and could assume the father's name. But children of upper-class males and lower-class women suffered because, although their fathers recognized them as offspring, they could not use the paternal family name, nor did they have a claim to the father's inheritance. Children whose fathers were not known or would not acknowledge them lost the most status. They were typically the offspring of single mothers who themselves were very poor.

Reality was often at odds with the Paraguayan ideal of extended kinship ties. Because the poor migrated frequently and often had unstable marital unions, relatives typically were well-known only for a generation preceding and following a given individual. The wealthy were more adept at tracing lines of descent through several generations. This was a function of their greater marital stability and their vested interest in maintaining the links that tied them to potential inheritance. Relatives in prosperous families often were not as close as their less affluent counterparts, however, because the well-to-do relied less on relatives for mutual aid and were potential competitors for inheritance.

Ritual Kinship

Ritual kinship in the form of godparenthood (*compadrazgo*) played an important role in strengthening and extending the ties of kinship, as it did in much of Latin America. Parents selected godparents for a child at his or her baptism, confirmation, and marriage. The godparents were then tied to the parents as co-parents. Those chosen for the child's baptism were considered the most important, and great care was exercised in their selection.

Ideally co-parents should be a married couple; they were preferred because their unions were typically more stable and they were more likely to be able to provide a home for the child should the need arise. In most communities, however, there were not enough couples to serve as godparents for all children, so single women of good reputation were frequently chosen. It was important that the person asked should be of proper character and good standing in the community.

Often parents asked a close, important relative to serve as godparent. The tie between co-parents reinforced that of kinship. The same godparents could serve for the couple's successive children, a practice that further strengthened the ties between the families involved.

A godparent was expected to see to his or her godchild's upbringing, should the parents be unable to do so. In many ways the social link between co-parents was more significant than that between godparents and godchildren. Co-parents were required to treat each other with respect and assist one another in times of need. Marriage or sexual relations between co-parents were considered incestuous; an insult to a co-parent was a grave matter, condemned by the community at large. In the countryside, ties to godparents had daily social significance; children visited their godparents often and were expected to treat them with particular respect. Not even quarrels or the death of the godchildren should break the ties between co-parents.

Compadrazgo served different purposes in rural and urban areas and among different social classes. In cities and among the more prosperous, the institution principally fulfilled the requirements for a Roman Catholic baptism. Godparents assumed the cost of the baptism and were expected to give gifts on a godchild's birthday and other significant occasions. Rarely did they have to assume the responsibility of raising a godchild; if they did, the financial wherewithal was provided through inheritance. In the countryside and among the poor, the responsibility to care for the godchild was taken more literally. If the parents were unable to care for their offspring, a godparent was expected to do so or find someone who could. Godparents should not only give gifts to the godchild on special occasions, but also assist with his or her schooling. Co-parents should come to one another's aid in times of social or economic distress.

The choice of a godparent also varied by social class. The urban and rural upper class and the urban middle class selected friends or relatives. In both groups co-parents were usually social equals. The institution had less practical significance than it had among the poor. For those of limited means, the emphasis was less on the feeling of friendship the co-parents shared and more on the potential economic benefits that the child might enjoy. Among peasants or the urban poor the choice could be either a relative or an influential benefactor (*patrón*) (see Rural Society, this ch.). When a *patrón* agreed to serve as a godparent, the lower-class individual was entitled to more extensive dealings with the higher-status person. He or she could, for example, visit the *patrón*'s house and expect to be received hospitably. The *patrón* expected in return absolute and unquestioning loyalty. In essence, this system satisfied the poor person's need to look above his or her class for protection, while satisfying the desire of the wealthy for a more loyal following. Where the expectations were met on both sides, *compadrazgo* could blunt the obvious economic disparities in small towns and the countryside. It also had important political implications. It was through such traditional kinlike ties that landholders from the ruling National Republican Association-Colorado Party (Asociación Nacional Republicana—Partido Colorado) could mobilize support among the peasantry (see The Twin Pillars of the Stroessner Regime, ch. 4).

Rural Society

Rural life, like much else in Paraguay, was defined by a series of dichotomies: commercial versus subsistence agriculture, large landholdings as opposed to small farms, and landowners in contrast to squatters. Land ownership was highly concentrated, and large-scale enterprises dominated the production of lucrative commercial crops (see Agriculture, ch. 3). Most farms were smaller than ten hectares. In the densely settled central region (comprising the departments of Paraguarí, Cordillera, Guairá, and Caazapá), these small landholdings constituted as much as 80 percent of all landholdings.

Although inequality underlay the system as a whole, the extensive land reserves and low population density that characterized Paraguay until the 1950s softened the impact of the disparities recorded in agricultural surveys and censuses. The largest holdings were vast ranches in the Chaco or along the country's eastern border, regions of low population density. Large estates were typically worked extensively, but custom permitted squatters to occupy the fringes with little interference. The landowner would be either unaware of their presence or undisturbed by it. Even where there were terms of rent for land, they might be as minimal as occasional labor for the landlord or gifts of produce at harvest or on the landlord's birthday. Although surveys showed that few Paraguayans owned land, fewer still paid much for the privilege of using it. Historically, squatters were useful to a landowner in a variety of informal ways. They were a pool of reserve labor, semi-obligated to work for below-average wages during labor shortages. The presence of squatters also was insurance against more serious incursions on one's lands in an environment where clear land titles were not easy to come by. Patterns of land use were deeply ingrained in any event, and they often limited a landowner's options in dealing with tenants.

The relationship between the landowner and squatters was usually transitory, but in some instances it persisted for generations as a *patrón-peón* arrangement. The patrón served as an advocate for his *peones;* they were to him the elements of a loyal following. In essence, the connection was that of client to powerful protector. It implied unquestioning loyalty and respect on the part of the *peón.*

The *patrón-peón* relationship served as a metaphor and model for proper social relations for rural society; indeed, the terms effectively delineated social boundaries. Peasants used *patrón* as a general term of respectful address in speaking to any urban person of obviously higher status. Townspeople generalized *peón* to refer to any

Workers picking strawberries near Paraguarí
Courtesy Inter-American Development Bank

lower-class person—although not in direct address, because to call a person *peón* to his face would be a breach of etiquette. The relationship also colored economic relations between *patrón* and *peón;* anthropologists Elman and Helen Service described contracting wage labor between the two: ''. . . a *patrón* hires a person as though he were asking a personal favor, and the *peón* responds as though he were obliged to grant it.'' Economic relations as a whole were ideally enmeshed in social ties like that of *patrón* to *peón*. Storekeepers each had their loyal followings, and it was considered disloyal to shop at another shop merely to take advantage of better prices. In return, customers expected preferential treatment, small favors, and some credit when they needed it.

Peasant farming was characterized by ''agricultural nomadism''; the search for a better plot or improved circumstances was perennial. Cultivation was slash-and-burn followed by a fallow period of several years. Farmers preferred land on the fringe of primary or dense secondary strands of tropical forests. Agricultural income among small farmers was not particularly tied to land tenure. A successful peasant might own, rent, or simply use the lands he farmed.

Population growth eventually increased pressure on farmland and forest reserves. The pressure was most acute in the arc stretching roughly 100 kilometers north and east of Asunción, where

71

approximately half the farms and half the squatters in the country were found. By the late 1950s, squatters and landowners faced increasingly bitter confrontations over communal grazing rights and land boundaries. Large landholders called for programs to ''decongest'' the central area and move the squatters to less populated regions along the northern and eastern borders.

These calls led to the formation in 1963 of an agrarian reform agency—the Rural Welfare Institute (Instituto de Bienestar Rural—IBR)—charged with the task of resettling peasants in the eastern border region, especially the departments of Alto Paraná, Canendiyú, Amambay, and Caaguazú. Although the program resettled many families in the 1960s and 1970s, critics noted that efforts to improve the farmers' standard of living were hampered by a lack of credit, technical assistance, and infrastructure (see Land Reform and Land Policy, ch. 3).

The eastern region enjoyed an economic boom during the building of the Itaipú hydroelectric power plant (see Electricity, ch. 3). As construction was completed, however, thousands of laborers lost their jobs. In the meantime, the land tenure situation in the region had changed dramatically. Many large landowners sold their properties to Brazilian and other foreign agribusinesses. These new owners, more committed than their predecessors to modern farming techniques, strongly objected to the presence of peasants on their properties. In addition, thousands of Brazilian farmers entered the area to claim properties significantly cheaper than comparable lands in their own country (see Immigrants, this ch.). As a result, the erstwhile Itaipú laborers were unable to resume the practice of occupying plots as squatters. Clashes occurred between squatters and authorities throughout the mid-1980s. During the same period, the demand for farm laborers declined as the large-scale timber and soybean enterprises in the area became more mechanized.

Despite these dramatic changes in land tenure, many other aspects of rural society remained unchanged into the late 1980s. Most farming was subsistence-oriented. Given a holding of some ten hectares, a family might keep four to six hectares under actual cultivation at any given time. The traditional tool kit and technological repertoire reflected the limited economic opportunities the countryside afforded most farmers.

The family was the chief source of farm labor. Men usually cleared the land and prepared the soil; women and children planted, weeded, and harvested the crops. Men were frequently absent in search of wage labor and women were accustomed to manage the farm in their absence. Farms permanently headed by women were

A family with a property deed issued by the Rural Welfare Institute
Courtesy Inter-American Development Bank

rare, however; a woman widowed or deserted by her spouse typically moved to a nearby town.

Neighbors frequently exchanged labor for various agricultural tasks; recipients were obliged to return the assistance when the neighbor needed help, although this arrangement was not formalized. The rate of labor exchange was greater when, as was often the case, neighbors were also relatives. Most crops had a lengthy planting and harvesting season, which spread out the periods of peak labor demand and facilitated the exchange of labor among households.

Wage labor was important to the family's subsistence. In some regions men supplemented agricultural production by gathering the yerba maté bush—the leaves of which produced a bitter tea consumed by Paraguayans—or by hunting game. If the homestead was along a major road, women sold handicrafts. Raising livestock often was a subsidiary source of income.

The numerous small towns dotting the eastern half of the country every ten to twenty kilometers were the loci of commercial relations and all effective political and religious authority. A town's inhabitants normally included a few large commercial ranchers, wholesalers and retailers of all kinds and degrees of prosperity, small manufacturers, government officials, and a few professionals such as teachers and pharmacists. There were numerous poor people who eked out a living as servants or laborers. The occupational specialists common to rural Paraguay—barbers, curers, and craftsmen—were typically town dwellers. Most households headed by females were urban; the women earned their livelihood as storekeepers, servants, seamstresses, laundresses, curers, midwives, or cigarmakers.

Peasants attended town functions primarily as observers. Rural families might visit a nearby town during its saint's fiesta, but church would be too far away for regular attendance. The lay functionaries who attended to many church affairs in the community were urban and prosperous. Civic events and fiestas themselves reflected enduring social distinctions based on wealth and breeding: that between *la gente* (the common people) and *la sociedad* (society, those with wealth and the required social graces). Fiestas traditionally included separate dances for the two groups that might be held on different nights or in different locations. There was little doubt about who should attend which function. The only role for *la gente* at the formal dance for the upper crust was as observers.

Migration and Urbanization

Historically, Paraguay had been an overwhelmingly rural country. The 1950 census found only about one-third of the population to be city dwellers. The human landscape for most of the country east of the Río Paraguay—where nearly all Paraguayans lived— was one of scattered homesteads interspersed with small towns of fewer than 1,000 inhabitants.

Most Paraguayan communities existed in varying degrees of isolation. In the late 1980s, only 20 percent of the country's roads were paved (see Transportation, ch. 3). For most people, travel was on foot or on horseback. The two-wheeled ox cart was the most common means of transport for agricultural produce.

The isolation of the countryside masked extensive migration, however. Despite rudimentary transportation facilities, the rural populace was mobile. Slash-and-burn agriculture required a lengthy fallow period, and farmers typically moved as yields declined on their plots. Rural-rural migration was the typical pattern, but the typical move was not over a long distance. According to the 1950 census, in most departments at least 70 percent of all Paraguayans were living in the department of their birth. In the densely settled departments of the central region, the proportion was 90 percent.

There were, however, several migration paths of longer distance and duration. In the first half of the twentieth century, for example, many peasants contracted to work on the yerba maté plantations along the eastern border. Working conditions were so wretched that few workers would willingly stay on past their contracted time. Others worked on the riverboats or in timber or logging operations.

There also was a long history of Paraguayan emigration to Argentina; the 1869 Argentine census enumerated several thousand Paraguayan emigrés. The numbers recorded rose steadily throughout the twentieth century. Estimates of Paraguayans resident in Argentina in the early 1970s ranged from 470,000 to 600,000, or 20 to 25 percent of Paraguay's total population at that time. Between 1950 and 1970, anywhere from 160,000 to 400,000 Paraguayans left their homeland for Argentina. Males predominated slightly, and male migrants tended to be younger than their female counterparts—there were few male Paraguayans over age thirty leaving for Argentina. Even low estimates suggested that approximately 55,000 women between 20 and 29 years of age emigrated between 1950 and 1972. The emigration was sufficient to have a significant impact on Paraguay's natural rate of population increase.

The majority of emigrants came from the central region—an indication of widespread underemployment in agriculture and artisanal industry in that area. Most men went to northeastern Argentina to seek better opportunities on that region's plantations as well as in the textile, tobacco, and lumber industries. The migrants generally were successful—at least they tended to find salaried employment rather than eke out an existence in self-employment. Women, following a pattern typical of Latin American rural-urban migration for females, migrated to Buenos Aires more frequently and found employment in domestic service. Men who migrated to Buenos Aires gravitated to the construction trades.

The path to Argentina was sufficiently travelled to make the way easier for later migrants. Some Argentine companies recruited in Paraguay. Experienced emigrant workers brought friends and relatives with them when returning from visits home, thus sparing the new migrants a lengthy search for housing and employment.

From the early 1960s through the early 1980s, the departments along the country's eastern border also were a favored destination for longer-distance rural-rural migrants. Most came from the central region—an area that, as a result of out-migrations, grew in population at only half the rate for the nation as a whole during the 1972–82 intercensal period. In 1950 the central region accounted for half of Paraguay's total population, but by 1982 the proportion had declined to about 38 percent. Between 1967 and 1972, an estimated 40,000 peasants left the departments of Cordillera, Paraguarí, and Caazapá in search of better living and working conditions. These departments' share of total population declined from more than 21 percent in 1972 to less than 17 percent in 1982. During the same intercensal period, the population of the three departments grew at a scant 0.1 percent in contrast to the 2.7 percent growth rate for Paraguay as a whole.

By contrast, the eastern departments gained population dramatically during the 1972–82 period. The population of the eastern region as a whole grew at a rate more than 2.5 times the national average. The populations of both Alto Paraná and Caaguazú grew at a rate of roughly 10 percent annually. Between 1960 and 1973, the IBR resettled an estimated 250,000 rural Paraguayans in agricultural colonies in underpopulated regions with some potential for increased agricultural production.

Despite Paraguay's essentially rural character, Asunción already had a well-defined role by the end of the colonial era as the hub of government, commerce, and industry. Goods flowed from the capital to the individual towns of the countryside—the towns themselves exchanged little with each other. Agricultural products were routed to Asunción; in return, manufactured goods went out to rural areas. Asunción's preeminence over other cities was made sharply evident by the 1950 census. That census enumerated 7 cities with more than 5,000 inhabitants, but only 1, Asunción (which had a population slightly more than 200,000), with more than 20,000 residents.

Asunción skyline looking toward
the main business and financial district
Courtesy Inter-American Development Bank

Yet even Asunción, political scientist Paul Lewis observed, had the air of a ''sleepy tropical outpost.'' Until the 1960s, automobiles and telephones were rare; perhaps half of the capital's homes had electricity. The city was without a piped water supply and sewage disposal system. Most families bought drinking water from peddlers who sold it door-to-door by mule.

From the 1960s through the early 1980s, however, migrants flocked to the region surrounding and including Asunción. The capital experienced its fastest growth in the 1960s, when its population grew roughly 3 percent annually (see table 3, Appendix). Although Asunción itself lagged during the 1970s, growing at a mere 1.6 percent per year, the metropolitan region grew at rates well above the national average.

Most migrants to Asunción found employment in the service sector or in small artisanal enterprises calling primarily for unskilled laborers. Despite the low wages they offered, these jobs exerted a pull for potential migrants because they were marginally better than what was available in the countryside. The Asunción area had long attracted rural-urban migrants, which meant that many rural dwellers considering a move could find assistance from kin who had made the move earlier. The construction boom in the 1970s also drew substantially greater numbers from rural Paraguay to Asunción.

Urbanization in the 1970s and early 1980s also was fueled by economic expansion along the eastern border. Spurred by the Itaipú hydroelectric project, the urban population of Alto Paraná grew 20 percent annually during the intercensal period from 1972 to 1982. The population of Puerto Presidente Stroessner, the city nearest the project, expanded nearly sixfold during the 1970s, as did the population of nearby Hernandarias. Cities in Amambay also grew during the 1970s, although at a more modest annual rate of 6 percent.

As a result of growth along the eastern border, by 1982 Paraguay had more than 30 cities with at least 5,000 inhabitants. This eastern expansion helped balance the dramatic growth occurring in Asunción and spared Paraguay the "hyper-urbanization" characteristic of many Latin American capitals. In 1950 the metropolitan area had accounted for about 20 percent of total population; by the early 1980s, this proportion had increased modestly to 25 percent.

Religion in Society

In the 1980s an estimated 92 to 97 percent of all Paraguayans were Roman Catholics. The remainder were Mennonites or members of various Protestant groups. The 1967 Constitution guarantees freedom of religion, but recognizes the unique role that Catholicism plays in national life. The president must be a Roman Catholic, but clergy are enjoined from serving as deputies or senators and discouraged from partisan political activity. Relations between church and state traditionally were close, if not always cordial.

A papal decree created the Bishopric of Asunción in 1547, and the first bishop arrived in the diocese in 1556. In 1588 three Jesuits came with the intent of pacifying and converting the Indians. After the arrival of additional Jesuits and Franciscans, the priests began working in the southeastern area of modern Paraguay and on the shores of the Río Paraná in parts of what is now Argentina and Brazil.

The Jesuits soon realized that they had to protect the Indians from enslavement by the growing numbers of Spanish and Portuguese if they were going to convert them. They accomplished this by settling the Indians in *reducciones* (townships) under Jesuit direction. At one point about 100,000 Indians lived in the *reducciones;* the system lasted a century and a half until the Jesuits' expulsion (1767). Following the end of the Jesuit regime, the *reducción* Indians were gradually absorbed into mestizo society or returned to their indigenous way of life (see The Sword of the Word, ch. 1).

For much of the nineteenth century, church-state relations ranged from indifferent to hostile. The new state assumed the prerogatives of royal patronage that the Vatican had accorded to the Spanish crown and sought to control bishops and the clergy. José Gaspar Rodríguez de Francia (1814–40) was committed to a secular state. He suppressed monastic orders, eliminated the tithe, instituted civil marriage, and cut off communication with the Vatican. Francisco Solano López (1862–70) used the church as a branch of government, enlisting priests as agents to report on the population's disaffection and signs of subversion.

Church-state relations reached their nadir with the execution of the bishop of Asunción, Manuel Antonio Palacio, during the War of the Triple Alliance (1865–70). By the war's end, there were only fifty-five priests left in the country, and the church was left leaderless for eleven years.

The modern Paraguayan church was established largely under the direction of Juan Sinforiano Bogarón (archbishop of Asunción, 1930–49) and Aníbal Mena Porta (archbishop of Asunción, 1949–69). Both envisioned a church whose role in the country's endemic political struggles was that of a strictly neutral mediator among the rival factions.

Starting in the late 1950s, the clergy and bishops were frequently at odds with the government. Confrontations began with individual priests giving sermons calling for political freedom and social justice. The activities of the clergy and various lay groups like Catholic Action (Acción Católica) pushed the church hierarchy to make increasingly critical statements about the regime of Alfredo Stroessner Mattiauda (president since 1954).

In the 1960s the Catholic University of Our Lady of Asunción became a center of antiregime sentiment. Students and faculty began cooperation with workers and peasants, forming workers' organizations as an alternative to the government-sponsored union. They organized Christian Agrarian Leagues (also known as peasant leagues) among small farmers. The organizations sponsored literacy programs, welfare activities, and various types of cooperatives. In addition, Catholics operated a news magazine and radio station—both critical of the government.

Throughout the 1970s and 1980s, there were sporadic student demonstrations and government crackdowns. The church criticized the lack of political freedom and the government's human rights record. The government's principal countermeasures included expelling foreign-born clergy and periodically closing the university, news magazine, and radio station. In response, the archbishop of Asunción excommunicated various prominent government officials and suspended Catholic participation at major civic and religious celebrations (see Interest Groups, ch. 4).

On a popular level, Catholicism was an essential component of social life. Even the poorest of homes contained pictures of the saints and a family shrine. Catholic ritual marked the important transitions in life: baptism, confirmation, marriage, and burial. Participation in the rites of the church reflected class and gender expectations. The poor curtailed or delayed rituals because of the costs involved.

Sex roles also affected religious participation. Devotion fell into the female sphere of activities. Men were not expected to show much concern about religion. If they attended mass, it was infrequently, and normally men stood in the rear of the church ready to make a quick exit. Women were supposed to be more devout. Regular participation in church services was seen as a virtue on their part. They were more likely to seek the church's blessing at critical points in the family's existence.

Religion served as perhaps the only institution in society that transcended kinship relations. Both politics and economic activities were enmeshed in the relations of kin; they reflected the family feuds and the accumulated loyalties of generations past. It was in popular religion, however, especially in the communal religious fiestas, that Paraguayans of every social stratum participated and the concerns of family and kin were, to a degree, muted. Fiestas were community and national celebrations; they served as exercises in civic pride and Paraguayan identity. Church holidays were public holidays as much as religious occasions.

The populace enjoyed the celebrations associated with fiestas, but actual belief and practice were typically uninformed by orthodox Catholic dogma. Especially in rural Paraguay, the saints associated with popular devotion were often no more than revered local figures.

Religious societies played an important role, planning and organizing local fiestas and undertaking welfare activities. Various lay brotherhoods assumed responsibility for assisting widows and children, among other duties associated with the care of the poor.

Minority Groups

Although the vast majority of Paraguayans were mestizos and the population was largely homogeneous, minorities became an increasingly significant force during the 1970s and 1980s. Paraguay's population historically had included small numbers of immigrants from Europe, the Middle East, Asia, and Latin

America. During the 1970s, however, thousands of Brazilian settlers crossed the border into Paraguay's eastern departments, dramatically affecting life there. During the same period, thousands of Koreans and ethnic Chinese settled in urban Paraguay. Finally, there were the remnants of the country's original Indian population who continued to follow an indigenous way of life.

Immigrants

A trickle of European and Middle Eastern immigrants began making their way to Paraguay in the decades following the War of the Triple Alliance. The government pursued a pro-immigration policy in an effort to increase population. Government records indicated that approximately 12,000 immigrants entered the port of Asunción between 1882 and 1907; of that total, almost 9,000 came from Italy, Germany, France, and Spain. Migrants also arrived from neighboring Latin American countries, especially Argentina.

Most migrants—even many who began their lives in Paraguay's agricultural settlements—typically found their way into urban trades and commerce and became the backbone of the country's small middle class. Middle Easterners tended to remain culturally and socially distinct even after several generations. European and Latin American immigrants were more readily assimilated. Nonetheless, in small towns non-Paraguayan family origins were noted for generations after the original migrant's arrival.

Although most minority groups tended to prefer urban life, Japanese immigrants founded and remained in agricultural colonies. Until the twentieth century, Japanese immigration was limited by Paraguay's unwillingness to accept Asian colonists; Japanese themselves preferred the more lucrative opportunities offered by the expanding Brazilian economy. When Brazil set quotas on Asian immigration in the 1930s, however, a Japanese land company set up an agricultural settlement southeast of Asunción. Two more colonies near Encarnación followed in the 1950s. A 1959 bilateral agreement between the Japanese and Paraguayan governments encouraged further immigration. By the 1980s there were about 8,000 Japanese settlers in agricultural colonies. The colonists made a concerted effort to preserve Japanese language and culture with varying degrees of success. Until the end of World War II, the earliest settlement supported a parallel educational system with subjects taught entirely in Japanese; the colonists eventually limited this to supplemental Japanese language classes. By the late 1960s, many Japanese children could speak in Japanese, Guaraní, and

Spanish. But there was strong bias against Japanese-Paraguayan intermarriage.

Like the Japanese, most German-speaking Mennonite immigrants remained in agricultural colonies. The bulk of the Mennonite population came between the 1920s and the 1940s and established three colonies in the central Chaco. In 1926 approximately 2,000 persons left Canada after the passage of legislation requiring English to be the language of instruction in Mennonite schools. The Paraguayan government, eager to develop the Chaco, readily allowed Mennonites to conduct their own schools in German and exempted the immigrants from military service.

The original Menno Colony was followed by the establishment of the Fernheim Colony in 1930 and the Neuland Colony in 1947. These latter two groups of colonists, also German-speaking, fled religious persecution in the Soviet Union. The Fernheimers, who had higher levels of education and more exposure to urban life than did the Mennos, also founded the town of Filadelfia, which eventually became an important agricultural supply center for the central Chaco. Some Fernheimers and Neulanders left the Chaco to establish small colonies in Eastern Paraguay. In the early 1980s, there were approximately 15,000 Mennonites in Paraguay; two-thirds lived in the Chaco, with the remainder in Caaguazú, San Pedro, and Itapúa departments and in Asunción (see Agriculture, ch. 3).

Until the 1970s, the Brazilian presence in Paraguay was relatively minor and was confined primarily to privately organized agricultural colonies along the easter border. In 1943 there were fewer than 500 Brazilian farmers in all of Paraguay; throughout the 1950s and 1960s, the proportion of Brazilians in the eastern border region held constant at between 3 and 4 percent of the total population of the area.

In the early 1970s, however, Brazilian immigrants, persuaded by a variety of factors, began streaming into the region from the neighboring Brazilian state of Paraná. In 1967 the Paraguayan government repealed a statute that had prohibited foreigners from purchasing land within 150 kilometers of the country's borders. During the same era, increased mechanization of soybean production in Paraná generated a growing concentration of landholdings in that area. Brazilian farmers whose holdings were too small to support increased production costs sold their land in Brazil and bought cheap land in Paraguay. In the late 1970s, land along Paraguay's eastern frontier was seven to eight times cheaper than comparable land in Brazil. The disparity in prices

Mennonite farmers from San Pedro Department
Courtesy Richard S. Sacks

drew large investors who cleared the land of saleable timber, then subdivided it and sold it to Brazilian immigrants.

Official records gave only an imprecise sense of the number of Brazilians who had come to the country. According to the 1982 census, there were 99,000 Brazilians residing in Paraguay. Most analysts discounted this figure, however, and contended that between 300,000 and 350,000 Brazilians lived in the eastern border region. Along the border, the Brazilian cruzeiro was more commonly used than the guaraní (for value of the guaraní—see Glossary), and Portuguese was heard more often than Spanish or Guaraní. Many Paraguayan peasants and Indians were evicted from lands purchased by immigrants. The pace of land sales increased to such a point that undercapitalized Paraguayan farmers who had settled in the region as part of IBR's colonization programs were selling their lands to Brazilian farmers and financial groups.

Analysts also rejected government figures on the number of immigrants from the Republic of Korea (South Korea), Hong Kong, and Taiwan. The 1982 census reported that there were 2,700 Koreans in Paraguay, along with another 1,100 non-Korean or non-Japanese Asian immigrants. The actual number of Koreans and ethnic Chinese, however, was believed to be between 30,000 and 50,000. Virtually all Koreans and ethnic Chinese lived in

Puerto Presidente Stroessner or Asunción and played a major role in the importation and sale of electronic goods manufactured in Asia.

Indians

Sixteenth-century Iberian explorers in South America found the Atlantic Coast of modern-day Brazil in the control of Guaraní Indians; the groups on the southern Brazilian coast, known as the Tupinambá, had extended their territory inland to the Río Paraguay, Río Paraná, and Río Uruguay. Various migrations eventually brought these and other closely related groups to the eastern flanks of the Andes.

The Spanish rapidly subjugated and assimilated the Guaraní they encountered in what later became Eastern Paraguay (see The Young Colony, ch. 1). High rates of intermarriage or concubinage between Spanish settlers and Guaraní women created a society that was overwhelmingly mestizo. In the resulting synthesis, the dominant social institutions and culture were Hispanic; the commonly spoken language, however, was Indian in origin.

As many as 100,000 Indians lived in Jesuit-run *reducciones* during the seventeenth and eighteenth centuries. After the expulsion of the Jesuits from Paraguay in 1767, the *reducciones* were taken over by civil authorities; subsequent mismanagement caused their population to decline. The survivors either were assimilated into the rural mestizo population or fled to the hinterland (see Religion in Society, this ch.).

Over the next two centuries, relations between vestigial groups of Indians and the dominant rural Paraguayans were infrequent. When interaction occurred at all, it was often violent. Nevertheless, the War of the Triple Alliance reduced the Paraguayan population sufficiently to reduce pressure on forest lands and thus buffered the remaining tribes.

The Indians' situation remained relatively stable until the mid-twentieth century. Although much land along the eastern border was held by foreign investors, these vast estates were not worked intensively. Hunters and gatherers therefore had sufficient reserves of land, as did the more sedentary populations. Although Indians might occasionally serve as laborers, they were not pressured by other rural settlers or missionaries. In the Chaco most tribes adopted sheep and goat herding; the inhospitable nature of the region provided a natural barrier to mestizo settlement and protected many groups from outside interference until the Chaco War of 1932–35.

In the early 1980s, the Paraguayan Indian Institute (Instituto Paraguayo del Indígena—Indi) estimated the country's Indian population at nearly 40,000. Indi's efforts to count the Indians met with significant resistance from some indigenous leaders. Various anthropologists placed the count higher, at 50,000 to 100,000, or 1.5 to 3 percent of the total population. But all the numbers represented only the roughest of approximations.

Paraguay's indigenous peoples were divided into seventeen tribal groups representing six language families. Even in the ethnographic literature, there was confusion about the precise distinctions among tribes and the linguistic relationships involved.

In general, observers relied upon a person's self-identification and that of those in contact with him or her in categorizing the individual as an Indian. Those who viewed themselves as tribal members—separate and distinct from the national culture—and who were seen by others as *indios* or *indígenas,* were classified as Indians. Language was a less certain cultural marker, but in general Indians spoke as their primary language neither Spanish nor the variety of Guaraní used by most Paraguayans.

Despite pride in their Guaraní heritage and language, many Paraguayans had negative feelings toward the country's remaining Indians and viewed nomadic tribes as subhuman. A survey of attitudes toward Indians in the 1970s found that 77 percent of respondents thought: "They are like animals because they are unbaptized." Indianness was a stigma; even Indians who became sedentary and Christian faced continued discrimination in employment and wages. According to estimates in the 1980s, the 3 percent of the population considered Indians accounted for roughly 10 percent of the poorest segment of Paraguayan society.

The Río Paraguay split the country's Indians: the four groups in Eastern Paraguay all spoke varieties of Guaraní, whereas the approximately thirteen tribes of the Chaco represented five language families. In the 1970s and 1980s, the situation of specific tribes varied according to a number of circumstances. The principal factor affecting a tribe's well-being was the extent and kind of pressure brought to bear on Indians and their traditional territories by outsiders.

The Guaraní speakers of Eastern Paraguay were scattered throughout the (formerly) remote regions to the northeast, along the country's border with Brazil. Although much land occupied by Indians had been legally owned by large estates, the tribes traditionally had been able to practice slash-and-burn agriculture and hunting and gathering largely undisturbed. Members of some tribes occasionally worked as wage laborers on the immense yerba maté plantations, whereas others had no peaceful relations with the larger society. Beginning in the 1960s, however, the tribes' customary ways of life were eroded by the IBR-sponsored settlements, the influx of Brazilian migrants, the purchase and more efficient operation of many estates by multinational firms, and the initiation of large-scale hydroelectric projects. As a result of increasing intrusions into traditional Indian lands, almost all Indians in Eastern Paraguay were involved in wage labor to some degree by the late 1970s.

For the past century, the largest tribe in Eastern Paraguay, the Paiú-Tavyteraú, subsisted through a combination of slash-and-burn farming, fishing and hunting, and periodic wage labor. For them the far-reaching changes of the 1960s and 1970s meant loss of land, the depletion of hunting and fishing resources, and increased dependence on wage labor. By the early 1970s, anthropologists found malnutrition widespread and tuberculosis endemic among tribal members. Estimates of mortality during the first two years of life were as high as 50 percent. The Avá-Chiripá, to the south of the Paiú territory, had been subject to even more outside pressure: they were well on the way to being dispossessed of their traditional lands and becoming dependent on wage labor.

Contact between the Aché tribe and the larger society had never been peaceful. During the 1960s and 1970s, a variety of rural Paraguayans raided and enslaved some of the Aché, who continued to follow a seminomadic existence in Eastern Paraguay's forests. By the late 1970s, the Aché survived only in a few communities run by missionaries and on a few ranches in Eastern Paraguay. Because of the Aché's more secure position on missions and ranches, organized raiding was largely eliminated by the early 1980s. Nonetheless, small groups of Aché on return trips to the forest to forage and hunt were often the targets of rural Paraguayans, and reports persisted in the mid-1980s of Indians being held involuntarily by Paraguayan families.

The Chaco Indians had a more varied history of contact with outsiders. They tenaciously resisted colonial efforts at pacification and conversion. Indeed, the warlike Indians, in combination with the inhospitable Chaco terrain and climate, presented an effective barrier to Spanish expansion west of the Río Paraguay. The Chaco Indians subsisted in a traditional manner by hunting and gathering and raising livestock. The sale of animal skins and periodic wage labor in tanning factories along the Río Paraguay or on sugar plantations in Argentina provided a source of cash income.

The tribes lived without undue interference until the Chaco War (and the subsequent expansion of ranching in the region) and

86

A vocational arts secondary school in Limpio, Central Department
Courtesy Inter-American Development Bank

Mennonite colonization in the central Chaco. Almost all Chaco tribes became more sedentary after the war. The Mascoi-Toba speakers of the central and southeastern Chaco were especially affected, and by the 1980s many spoke only or primarily Guaraní. Some tribes that provided scouts for the army during the war later found occasional employment with military garrisons. The increase in ranching meant less land and game available to hunters and gatherers and a concomitant rise in the need for wage labor. After the government banned the sale of skins in an effort to preserve the declining animal population, the Indians became increasingly dependent on the region's cattle ranches for wage labor. Dependence also increased following the closing of most of the tanning factories. Demand for labor in ranching, however, declined precipitously as lands were cleared and fenced. In addition, the opening of the Trans-Chaco Highway meant that Indians had to compete with migrants, usually single males, from elsewhere in the country. Ranchers often preferred employing these transients to assuming responsibility for allowing Indians with families to settle and work on their ranches.

Language use among the Chaco tribes reflected the various ways that groups adapted to the presence of outsiders and the changing economy. Migration and wage labor brought with them a significant amount of intertribal marriage. Guaraní or (less frequently)

87

Spanish came to serve as a lingua franca. In groups that had a history of several generations of labor in the tanning factories, husbands and wives from different tribes often spoke Guaraní in their home. Their children were monolingual in that tongue until they learned Spanish at school. By the 1980s, it appeared that a number of languages—Angaité, Guaná, and Mascoi-Toba among them—might die out within the next generation. By contrast, a group of Mac'á who settled on the west bank of the Río Paraguay under the patronage of General Juan Belaieff, whom they had assisted in the Chaco War, remained almost entirely monolingual in Mac'á except when engaged in commerce.

In the late 1970s, researchers estimated that more than half of all Indians lived on settlements under the auspices of various mis sionary organizations. This was particularly true of those groups whose first intensive contacts with Paraguayan society dated from the 1960s and 1970s. In the Chaco almost all Indians who were not scattered on individual ranches lived under the patronage of the missions.

Historically, official government policy had often left Indians to the care of religious groups. Until the 1960s, the government's only defined Indian policy was in the form of a 1909 law that enjoined Paraguay ''to take measures leading to the conversion of the Indians to Christianity and civilization . . . .'' Because the legislation permitted missionaries to acquire land for Indian settlements, some tribes were able to obtain land. At the same time, however, the law increased the tribes' dependence on missionaries as advocates in dealing with the larger society.

The missionaries offered the Indians under their care a measure of protection from the worst predations of rural Paraguayans. In some cases, mission educational programs taught in Indian languages offered the only hope that these tongues would be preserved at all. The impact of Christian proselytizing on indigenous belief and social institutions was less positive, however. Fundamentalist groups were particularly unrelenting in their efforts to eliminate indigenous beliefs. Anthropologists David Maybury-Lewis and James Howe noted that efforts to ''crush witch doctors'' drove a wedge between Christian and traditional believers within the same tribe. Critics charged that fundamentalist groups' aggressive proselytization destroyed Indian culture in the process of conversion.

Roman Catholics had the longest history of missionary activity. Their efforts were focused on protecting Indians from the worst effects of outside incursions, in particular forced removals from tribal lands. The philosophy of the Second Vatican Council

(1962–65) called for a process of gradual conversion that included respect for indigenous beliefs.

Anglicans had been active in the southeast Chaco since the turn of the century. By the late 1970s, the Lengua converts at the Anglican mission were generally in charge of running the settlement. The most serious problems came from overcrowding as more and more Indians displaced from elsewhere in the Chaco sought refuge at the mission.

Mennonites used Indians as a ready source of labor when they first settled in the central Chaco. As Mennonite-Indian relations became more complex, the Mennonites formed the Association of Indian-Mennonite Cooperative Services (Asociación de los Servicios de Cooperación Indígena-Menonita—ASCIM) to proselytize and assist the Indians. As was the case with other mission settlements, the problems ASCIM faced grew as Indians forced off their lands elsewhere in the Chaco flocked to the Mennonite settlements. Although ASCIM had resettled about 5,000 Indians on their own land by the late 1970s, large numbers of landless people remained around Filadelfia, hoping for employment on Mennonite farms.

A number of secular and official organizations attempted to assist Indians over the years. Inspired by the indigenist movement that flourished in Latin America in the early twentieth century, middle- and upper-class Paraguayans founded the Indigenist Association of Paraguay (Asociación Indigenista del Paraguay—AIP) in the early 1940s. Over the years AIP campaigned for Indian rights and publicized the problems Indians faced. In the late 1970s and early 1980s, the association was active in sponsoring legal defense and regional development projects for the tribes of Eastern Paraguay and in drafting legislation that established Indi. Indi's mandate was to help Indians improve their legal status, especially in matters pertaining to employment and landholding. The efforts of Indi and other advocates for Indian rights resulted in enactment of legislation in 1981 that formally recognized the Indians' right to pursue their culture and way of life, stated that landholding was integral to the continued survival of Paraguay's Indians, and expanded the means through which communities could obtain formal legal status and title to their lands.

Education

Education in the colonial era was largely limited to the upper class. The wealthy either hired tutors or sent their children abroad. Although there were a few private schools in operation following the declaration of independence in 1811, they languished throughout most of the nineteenth century. The only secondary school closed in 1822. By the end of the War of the Triple Alliance, perhaps as little as 14 percent of the populace was literate.

Starting with the inauguration of the public secondary school system in 1877, public education grew steadily in the decades following the war. In 1889 the National University of Asunción was founded, and in 1896 the first teacher-training school began operation. By the eve of the Chaco War, there were several teachers' colleges, a number of secondary schools, and a few technical schools. The decades following the Chaco War were marked by widespread expansion of the educational system. Between the end of that war and the beginning of World War II, enrollments nearly doubled. They continued to expand in subsequent decades. Enrollments grew even faster at universities and secondary schools than at the elementary level.

Paraguay had two universities: the National University and the Catholic University. Both had branches in several interior cities. In the mid-1980s, about 20,000 students were enrolled in the National University and some 8,000 in the Catholic University. The number of applicants for university admission grew because of the growing numbers of students completing secondary school. In the mid-1970s, both universities began offering a variety of short-term degree programs in an effort to meet the increased demand for admission. The programs were designed to reduce pressure on traditional professional courses of study such as engineering, law, and medicine.

Formal education was under the direction of the Ministry of Education and Worship. The six-year cycle of primary school was free and compulsory for children from ages seven to fourteen. Secondary education consisted of two three-year programs, each leading to a baccalaureate degree. The diversified program emphasized training in the humanities and was preparatory to study at a university or teacher-training institute. The technical program was designed for students entering any of a number of postsecondary schools offering training in commerce, industry, or agriculture.

Schools were financed by the government and a variety of user sources. The Ministry of Education and Worship's budget represented slightly less than 15 percent of the government budget in the early 1980s. Virtually all of the costs of rural primary schools and nearly 90 percent of the costs of urban primary schools were covered by government funds. Public secondary schools received from half to three-quarters of their budget for current expenditures from the national government.

There was a perennial shortage of adequately trained teachers; this was especially true of rural teachers, who were often uncertified. Primary school teachers were required to complete a two-year

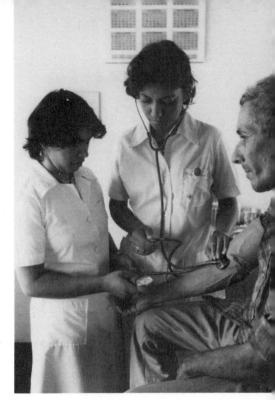

*A rural health clinic
near Villarrica
Courtesy
Inter-American
Development Bank*

postsecondary school training program. Secondary teachers were supposed to have an additional two years of specialized training. Curricula changes demanded extensive upgrading of teachers' skills. There were retraining programs available through the Higher Institute of Education and several regional centers.

Reforms in the 1980s attempted to make the educational system more responsive to the needs of the population. Rural Paraguayans had long faced a lack of educational facilities, materials, and teachers. The reforms attempted to meet some of these needs through multigrade programs designed to achieve a more efficient allocation of scarce resources. By the early 1980s, there were about 2,000 multigrade programs reaching more than 55,000 students.

Student enrollments increased at all levels during the 1970s and early 1980s. Overall enrollment grew nearly 6 percent per year in the late 1970s. The number of students enrolled in the basic cycle of secondary school grew from 49,000 in 1975 to 76,000 in 1980. The number of students attending primary school increased by roughly one-quarter during this period; rural school children, who historically had had very limited access to education, represented most of the increase. The number of rural children attending primary school increased by more than one-third between 1972 and 1981.

Despite the growth of school enrollments, the proportion of

school-age children enrolled in classes actually remained constant or declined between 1965 and 1985. Only in higher education did enrollments grow faster than the school-age population (see table 4, Appendix).

In the mid-1980s, the official literacy rate was above 80 percent. More males than females were able to read and write, although literacy was increasing faster among females. About 90 percent of city dwellers could read; rural Paraguayans lagged behind their urban counterparts by about 10 percent.

Critics charged that the official literacy figures greatly overestimated the numbers who could actually read and write. They argued that the government counted as literate anyone who attended primary school—a dubious assumption given the large number of monolingual Guaraní speakers who entered but failed to complete elementary school. Such speakers represented an estimated 90 percent of the children entering rural primary schools. Many men who entered the armed forces as conscripts first learned to read during their military service.

In the early 1970s, less than 5 percent of those entering rural elementary schools finished this course of study, as compared to 30 percent of urban youngsters. Only 1 percent of rural children finished secondary school; the figure for city children was 10 percent. Rural schools also were plagued with high rates of student absenteeism and grade repetition. A 1980 survey showed a substantial improvement in the percentage of children completing the elementary school cycle. The figure for who completed their course of primary school studies had risen to 38 percent. Although the completion rate for rural students climbed to 25 percent, this figure was substantially below that for urban youngsters.

In the late 1970s, the Ministry of Education and Worship attempted to deal with the crisis in rural education by developing a bilingual program for monolingual Guaraní speakers. The program was designed to develop basic oral skills in Guaraní and oral and written skills in Spanish. Guaraní literature also was available at the secondary and university levels.

Health and Welfare

The Ministry of Public Health and Social Welfare was responsible for approving and coordinating all public and private activities and programs dealing with health. Other agencies involved in the health sector included the Social Insurance Institute, the Military Health Service, and the Clinical Hospital of the National University. Health services were organized through a system of four hierarchical levels, each of increasing complexity and sophistication. Health services at the first level aimed at providing basic care for the community. Intermediate levels offered services of greater complexity to towns and cities, whereas the fourth level provided specialized services to the entire nation.

Paraguay recorded impressive gains in health-care delivery in the 1970s and early 1980s. Following the government's launching of a massive immunization campaign in the late 1970s, the percentage of infants vaccinated against diphtheria, pertussis, tetanus, and measles went from 5 percent in 1977 to over 60 percent in 1984 (see table 5, Appendix). From 1973 to 1983, the proportion of infants receiving medical care rose from 51 percent to nearly 75 percent, and prenatal care from 53 percent to nearly 70 percent. The supply of nurses relative to the population more than doubled between 1965 and 1981. By the early 1980s, surveys indicated that 60 to 70 percent of the populace had easy access to health care.

Despite these achievements, the health-care system was beset by a number of problems. First of all, the proportion of the national budget allocated to health decreased as a result of the economic downturn of the early 1980s. In addition, international health agencies noted a lack of coordination among the agencies and institutes whose work affected health. Mechanisms for gathering information about the delivery of health services were inadequate; even the reporting of vital events and infectious diseases was limited. Government health services also lacked many necessary supplies. Finally, the heavy concentration of doctors and other health providers in urban areas resulted in a shortage of personnel for rural residents.

In response to these problems, the government designed a broadly based program to augment community health organization and increase community participation. The program's objectives included upgrading the training of lay midwives, expanding health education, training traditional health practitioners and other volunteers, increasing the number of health centers in rural areas, and integrating health-care services with existing community organizations. Other priorities included lowering the morbidity and mortality rates among mothers and young children, controlling infectious diseases and diseases that could be checked through vaccination, and improving child nutrition.

The Sanitary Works Corporation (Corporación de Obras Sanitarias—Corposana) provided drinking water and sewage disposal services for towns of more than 4,000 inhabitants. The National Service for Environmental Sanitation (Servicio Nacional de Sanitaria Ambiental—Senasa) provided the same services for

93

smaller communities and also dealt with issues relating to national environmental health. By the mid-1980s, however, only 25 percent of the population had easy access to potable water. Like other health-related services, potable water was far more available in urban areas. About half the urban population had drinking water, whereas only 10 percent of rural residents did. Approximately half the population had access to sewage disposal services.

Sanitary conditions were not adequate to ensure proper food storage and processing. The main sources of contamination were unpasteurized milk and meat products processed in poorly refrigerated slaughterhouses.

Housing was rudimentary in much of the country; some 80 percent of Paraguayan homes were owner-built. Flooding along the country's major rivers (Río Paraguay, Río Paraná, and Río Pilcomayo) and their tributaries in 1982 and 1983 destroyed much housing around Asunción and other river cities. Many residents continued to live in ramshackle huts years after the floods. Provision of services in such settlements was typically inadequate. The presence of rodents and insects represented a significant health risk.

In the late 1980s, life expectancy at birth was sixty-nine years for females and sixty-five for males—an increase of two years for each sex from 1965 to 1986. General mortality was 6.6 per 1,000 inhabitants in the mid-1980s (see table 6, Appendix). Experts projected the death rate to continue its decline to a low of approximately 5.2 per 1,000 inhabitants by the turn of the century. Heart and cerebrovascular diseases, diarrhea, cancer, and acute respiratory infections were the main causes of mortality among the population. The main infectious and parasitic diseases were malaria, Chagas' disease, diarrhea, and acute respiratory infections. Rabies was the most damaging of diseases transmitted by animals. In late 1987 Paraguay reported a total of seven known cases of acquired immune deficiency syndrome (AIDS), which had resulted in four deaths.

Although Paraguay recorded notable declines in its infant mortality rate (IMR) and postneonatal mortality rate in the early 1980s, significant regional disparities occurred. From 1981 to 1984, the IMR in Asunción declined by more than 25 percent; in contrast, the drop was less than 15 percent in the rest of the country. The picture for postneonatal mortality was similar: the rate in the capital declined by nearly 30 percent, whereas the rate for the rest of Paraguay fell only about 10 percent.

Through the mid-1980s, diarrhea, pneumonia, and malnutrition remained the principal threats to the health of infants and children. Among infants the death rate from malnutrition was 1.6 per

*Construction of a
water treatment plant
at Coronel Oviedo
Courtesy
Inter-American
Development Bank*

1,000; nearly 10 percent of early childhood deaths were caused by nutritional deficiencies.

In the late 1980s, Paraguay had a social security system that had been established and modified by laws in 1943, 1950, 1965, and 1973. The system, administered by the Social Insurance Institute, offered old-age pensions, invalidity pensions, survivor settlements, sickness and maternity benefits, and work-injury benefits for temporary or permanent disabilities to employed persons and to self-employed workers who elected voluntary coverage. Railroad, banking, and public employees had special systems. Both employers and employees contributed a percentage of salaries to fund the program. Employees generally contributed 9.5 percent of earnings (except, for example, pensioners who contributed only 5 percent, and teachers and professors, who contributed only 5.5 percent), employers 16.5 percent, and the government, 1.5 percent. The Social Insurance Institute operated its own clinics and hospitals to provide medical and maternal care.

* * *

In the late 1980s, there was a dearth of current, English-language studies on Paraguayan society. Elman R. and Helen S. Service's *Tobatí: Paraguayan Town,* although dated (1954), contains valuable information on rural Paraguay. Paul H. Lewis provides useful data

95

on contemporary social relations in *Paraguay Under Stroessner*. Guillermina Engelbrecht and Leroy Ortiz's "Guaraní Literacy in Paraguay" and Joan Rubin's *National Bilingualism in Paraguay* examine the role of the Guaraní language in national life. Fran Gillespie and Harley Browning's "The Effect of Emigration upon Socioeconomic Structure: The Case of Paraguay" deals with migration and urbanization in Paraguay. David Maybury-Lewis and James Howe's *The Indian Peoples of Paraguay: Their Plight and Their Prospects* and Harriet Manelis Klein and Louisa R. Stark's "Indian Languages of the Paraguayan Chaco" provide an excellent overview of the status of Indians. R. Andrew Nickson's "Brazilian Colonization of the Eastern Border Region of Paraguay," Calvin Redekop's *Strangers Become Neighbors: Mennonite and Indigenous Relations in the Paraguayan Chaco*, and Norman R. Stewart's *Japanese Colonization in Eastern Paraguay* all describe the experience of some of Paraguay's immigrants. (For further information and complete citations, see Bibliography.)

Chapter 3. The Economy

A farmer sacks cotton for transport to market.

PARAGUAY IS A MIDDLE-INCOME COUNTRY that changed rapidly in the 1970s and 1980s as a result of hydroelectric development, agricultural colonization, construction, and cash crop exports. Nevertheless, the country's gross domestic product (GDP—see Glossary) in 1986 was approximately US$3.4 billion, or roughly US$1,000 per capita, ranking Paraguay only ahead of Bolivia among the Spanish-speaking countries of South America. Paraguay was the most agricultural economy of South America, and that sector influenced the performance of virtually every other sector of the economy.

Traditionally isolated and underpopulated, Paraguay was one of the last countries in Latin America to enjoy the region's rapid growth in the post-World War II period. Paraguay entered a phase of sustained economic growth in the late 1950s. Its economy grew at the fastest pace of all the Latin American countries during most of the 1970s as the Paraguayan-Brazilian project, Itaipú, the world's largest hydroelectric plant, was constructed. During that decade, cotton and soybeans came to dominate agriculture, mostly as a result of high export prices and agricultural colonization. Paraguay's economy also was characterized by a large underground sector, in which smuggling and contraband had become normal features by the 1970s.

The Paraguayan economic miracle of the 1970s came to a halt in 1982 because of the completion of construction at Itaipú, lower commodity prices for cotton and soybeans, and world recession. The economy recovered in 1984 and 1985, stagnated in 1986, and continued to expand in 1987 and 1988. Despite its rapid growth, the Paraguayan economy became increasingly dependent on soybeans and cotton for exports and overall economic dynamism. These two crops, however, remained subject to external price fluctuations and local weather conditions, both of which varied considerably.

Economic growth in the post-World War II period occurred in the context of political stability characterized by authoritarian rule and patronage politics. Government economic policies deviated little from 1954 to the late 1970s, consistently favoring a strong private-enterprise economy with a large role for foreign investment. Unlike most Latin American economies, in Paraguay import tariffs were generally low, fiscal deficits manageable, and exchange rates not overvalued. These trends faltered in the 1980s as the government took a more active part in industry, deficits rose, and the national currency was generally overvalued and devalued numerous times. Throughout the post-World War II era, Paraguay had no personal income tax, and government revenues as a percentage of GDP were among the lowest in the world.

Despite the sustained economic growth that marked the post-war period, the distribution of economic benefits was highly inequitable. Although GDP expanded rapidly in the 1970s, most economists estimated that income distribution worsened during the decade. Government spending on social services was particularly lacking. Paraguay's poverty was mostly a rural phenomenon, which increasingly involved competition for land in the eastern region near the Brazilian border, especially in the departments (administrative divisions) of Alto Paraná, Canendiyú, and Caaguazú (see fig. 1). Nonetheless, land tenure was not generally the acute social problem it was in many developing countries.

Although Paraguay faced significant obstacles to future economic development, it displayed extraordinary potential. Paraguay contained little oil and no precious metals or sea coasts, but the country was self-sufficient in many areas and was endowed with fertile land, dense forests, and swift rivers. The process of opening up the eastern border region to economic activity and continued agricultural expansion was expected to effect rapid changes in once-isolated Paraguay. Likewise, the development of a series of hydroelectric plants along the Río Paraná linked Paraguay to its neighbors and provided it access to cherished energy resources and badly needed export revenues. Finally, road construction united different departments of Paraguay and provided the country its first access to the Atlantic Ocean via Brazil. These processes of infrastructure development, hydroelectric expansion, agricultural colonization, and a cash crop explosion allowed Paraguay by the late 1980s to begin to tap its potential.

Growth and Structure of the Economy

Until the Spanish established Asunción in 1537, economic activity in Paraguay was limited to the subsistence agriculture of the Guaraní Indians. The Spanish, however, found little of economic interest in their colony, which had no precious metals and no sea coasts. The typical feudal Spanish economic system did not dominate colonial Paraguay, although the *encomienda* system was established (see The Young Colony, ch. 1). Economic relations were distinguished by the *reducciones* (reductions or townships) that were established by Jesuit missionaries from the early seventeenth century until the 1760s (see The Sword of the Word, ch. 1). The incorporation of Indians into these Jesuit agricultural communes laid the foundation for an agriculture-based economy that survived in the late twentieth century.

Three years after Paraguay overthrew Spanish authority and gained its independence, the country's economy was controlled by the autarchic policies of José Gaspar Rodríguez de Francia (1814–40), who closed the young nation's borders to virtually all international trade (see El Supremo Dictador, ch. 1). Landlocked, isolated, and underpopulated, Paraguay structured its economy around a centrally administered agricultural sector, extensive cattle grazing, and efficient shipbuilding and textile industries. After the demise of Francia, government policies focused on expanding international trade and stimulating economic development. The government built several roads and authorized British construction of a railroad.

The War of the Triple Alliance (1865–70) fundamentally changed the Paraguayan economy (see The War of the Triple Alliance, ch. 1). Economic resources were employed in and destroyed by the war effort. Paraguay was occupied by its enemies in 1870; the countryside was in virtual ruin, the labor force was decimated, peasants were pushed into the environs of Asunción from the east and south, and the modernization of the preceding three decades was undone. Sleepy, self-sufficient Paraguay, whose advances in agriculture and quality of life had been the envy of many in the Southern Cone (see Glossary), became the most backward nation in that subregion.

To pay its substantial war debt, Paraguay sold large tracts of land to foreigners, mostly Argentines. These large land sales established the base of the present-day land tenure system, which is characterized by a skewed distribution of land. Unlike most of its neighbors, however, Paraguay's economy was controlled not by a traditional, landed elite, but by foreign companies. Many Paraguayans grew crops and worked as wage laborers on *latifundios* (large landholdings) typically owned by foreigners.

The late 1800s and the early 1900s saw a slow rebuilding of ports, roads, the railroad, farms, cattle stock, and the labor force. The country was slowly being repopulated by former Brazilian soldiers who had fought in the War of the Triple Alliance, and Paraguay's government encouraged European immigration. Although few in number, British, German, Italian, and Spanish investors and farmers helped modernize the country. Argentine, Brazilian, and British companies in the late 1800s purchased some of Paraguay's best land and started the first large-scale production of agricultural goods for export. One Argentine company, whose owner had purchased 15 percent of the immense Chaco region, processed massive quantities of tannin, which were extracted from the bark of the Chaco's ubiquitous quebracho (break-axe) hardwood (see fig. 3). Large quantities of the extract were used by the region's thriving hide industry. Another focus of large-scale agro-processing was the yerba maté bush, whose leaves produced the potent tea that is the national beverage. Tobacco farming also flourished. Beginning in 1904, foreign investment increased as a succession of Liberal Party (Partido Liberal) administrations in Paraguay maintained a staunch laissez-faire policy.

The period of steady economic recovery came to an abrupt halt in 1932 as the country entered another devastating war. This time Paraguay fought Bolivia over possession of the Chaco and rumors of oil deposits. The war ended in 1935 after extensive human losses on both sides, and war veterans led the push for general social reform (see The Chaco War and the February Revolution, ch. 1). During the 1930s and 1940s, the state passed labor laws, implemented agrarian reform, and assumed a role in modernization, influenced in part by the leadership of Juan Domingo Perón in Argentina and Getúlio Dornelles Vargas in Brazil. The 1940 constitution, for example, rejected the laissez-faire approach of previous Liberal governments. Reformist policies, however, did not enjoy a consensus, and by 1947 the country had entered into a civil war, which in turn initiated a period of economic chaos that lasted until the mid-1950s. During this period, Paraguay experienced the worst inflation in all of Latin America, averaging over 100 percent annually in the 1950s.

After centuries of isolation, two devastating regional wars, and a civil war, in 1954 Paraguay entered a period of prolonged political and economic stability under the authoritarian rule of Alfredo Stroessner Mattiauda. Stroessner's economic policies took a middle course between social reform, *desarrollismo* (see Glossary), and laissez-faire, all in the context of patronage politics. Relative to previous governments, Stroessner took a fairly active role in the economy but reserved productive activities for the local and foreign private sectors. The new government's primary economic task was to arrest the country's rampant and spiraling price instability. In 1955 Stroessner fired the country's finance minister, who was unwilling to implement reforms, and in 1956 accepted an International Monetary Fund (IMF—see Glossary) stabilization plan that abolished export duties, lowered import tariffs, restricted credit, devalued the currency, and implemented strict austerity measures. Although the sacrifice was high, the plan helped bring economic stability to Paraguay. Labor unions retaliated with a major strike in 1958, but the new government, now firmly established, quelled the uprising and forced many labor leaders into exile; most of them remained there in the late 1980s.

By the 1960s, the economy was on a path of modest but steady economic growth. Real GDP growth during the 1960s averaged 4.2 percent a year, under the Latin American average of 5.7 percent but well ahead of the chaotic economy of the two previous decades. As part of the United States-sponsored Alliance for Progress, the government was encouraged to expand its planning apparatus for economic development. With assistance from the Organization of American States (OAS), the Inter-American Development Bank (IDB), and the United Nations Economic Commission for Latin America (ECLA), in 1962 Paraguay established the Technical Planning Secretariat (Secretaría Técnica de Planificación—STP), the major economic planning arm of the government. By 1965 the country had its first National Economic Plan, a two-year plan for 1965–66. This was followed by another two-year plan (1967–68) and then a series of five-year plans. Five-year plans—only general policy statements—were not typically adhered to or achieved and played a minimal role in Paraguay's economic growth and development. Compared with most Latin American countries, Paraguay had a small public sector. Free enterprise dominated the economy, export promotion was favored over import substitution, agriculture continued to dominate industry, and the economy remained generally open to international trade and market mechanisms.

In an economic sense, the 1970s constituted Paraguay's miracle decade. Real GDP grew at over 8 percent a year and exceeded 10 percent from 1976 to 1981—a faster growth rate than in any other economy in Latin America. Four coinciding developments accounted for Paraguay's rapid growth in the 1970s. The first was the completion of the road from Asunción to Puerto Presidente Stroessner and to Brazilian seaports on the Atlantic, ending traditional dependence on access through Argentina and opening the east to many for the first time. The second was the signing of the Treaty of Itaipú with Brazil in 1973. Beyond the obvious economic benefits of such a massive project, Itaipú helped to create a new mood of optimism in Paraguay about what a small, isolated country could attain. The third event was land colonization, which resulted from the availability of land, the existence of economic opportunity, the increased price of crops, and the newly gained accessibility of the eastern border region. Finally, the skyrocketing price of soybeans and cotton led farmers to quadruple the number of hectares planted with these two crops. As the 1970s progressed, soybeans and cotton came to dominate the country's employment, production, and exports.

These developments shared responsibility for establishing thriving economic relations between Paraguay and the world's sixth largest economy, Brazil. Contraband trade became the dominant economic force on the border between the two countries, with Puerto Presidente Stroessner serving as the hub of such smuggling activities. Observers contended that contraband was accepted by many Paraguayan government officials, some of whom were reputed to have benefited handsomely. Many urban dwellers' shelves were stocked with contraband luxury items.

The Paraguayan government's emphasis on industrial activity increased noticeably in the 1970s. One of the most important components of the new industrial push was Law 550, also referred to as Law 550/75 or the Investment Promotion Law for Social and Economic Development. Law 550 opened Paraguay's doors even further to foreign investors by providing income-tax breaks, duty-free capital imports, and additional incentives for companies that invested in priority areas, especially the Chaco. Law 550 was successful. Investments by companies in the United States, Europe, and Japan comprised, according to some estimates, roughly a quarter of new investment. Industrial policies also encouraged the planning of more state-owned enterprises, including ones involved in producing ethanol, cement, and steel.

Much of Paraguay's rural population, however, missed out on the economic development. Back roads remained inadequate, preventing peasants from bringing produce to markets. Social services, such as schools and clinics, were severely lacking. Few people in the countryside had access to potable water, electricity, bank credit, or public transportation. As in other economies that underwent rapid growth, income distribution was believed to have worsened in Paraguay during the 1970s in both relative and absolute terms. By far the greatest problem that the rural population faced, however, was competition for land. Multinational agribusinesses, Brazilian settlers, and waves of Paraguayan colonists rapidly increased the competition for land in the eastern border region. Those peasants who lacked proper titles to the lands they occupied were pushed to more marginal areas; as a result, an increasing number of rural clashes occurred, including some with the government.

In the beginning of the 1980s, the completion of the most important parts of the Itaipú project and the drop in commodity prices ended Paraguay's rapid economic growth. Real GDP declined by 2 percent in 1982 and by 3 percent in 1983. Paraguay's economic performance was also set back by world recession, poor

*Selling perfume on the
streets of Puerto
Presidente Stroessner
Courtesy Richard S. Sacks*

weather conditions, and growing political and economic instability in Brazil and Argentina. Inflation and unemployment increased. Weather conditions improved in 1984, and the economy enjoyed a modest recovery, growing by 3 percent in 1984 and by 4 percent in 1985. But in 1986 one of the century's worst droughts stagnated the economy, permitting no real growth. The economy recovered once again in 1987 and 1988, growing between 3 and 4 percent annually. Despite the economy's general expansion after 1983, however, inflation threatened its modest gains, as did serious fiscal and balance-of-payments deficits and the growing debt (see Balance of Payments and Debt, this ch.).

Economic Policy

Fiscal Policy

In the 1970s, the government pursued cautious fiscal policies and achieved large surpluses on the national accounts, mainly as a result of the vibrant growth in the second half of the decade. By the early 1980s, there were growing demands for increased government expenditure for social programs. By 1983, the first fiscal year (see Glossary) of increased government spending and the first full year of a recession, the government had entered into a significant fiscal crisis as the budget deficit reached nearly 5 percent of GDP (the deficit had been only 1 percent of GDP in 1980). In 1984 the government imposed austere measures to remedy national accounts. Cuts in current expenditures curtailed already meager social and economic programs. In addition, from 1983 to 1986, real wages of government employees were allowed to drop by 37 percent. Capital expenditures were cut back more seriously. Capital expenditures as a percentage of total expenditure dropped from 31 percent in 1984 to 10 percent by 1986. Austerity measures were successful in economic terms, and by 1986 budget deficits were under 1 percent of GDP. In 1986 the government announced a high-profile Adjustment Plan, which continued previous policies of expenditure cutbacks but also proposed more structural changes in fiscal and monetary policies. The most prominent of these was a proposal for the country's first personal income tax. Many observers characterized the plan as mainly rhetorical, however, citing the government's lack of political will to implement many of its proposals.

Despite the government's ability to control budgetary matters, fiscal policy faced two new and growing problems in the 1980s. The first was the poor financial performance of state-owned enterprises. The overall public-sector deficit, which reached 7 percent of GDP in 1986, had swelled in part because of the high operating costs of parastatals (state-owned enterprises), which accounted for 44 percent of the overall deficit in 1986. Rather than continually increasing the price of utilities and the services of parastatals, the government accepted the loss to avoid the inflationary pressures of increasing costs to consumers. This policy, however, was seen by critics as only a stopgap measure, short of more painful structural solutions, such as examining the financial viability of certain parastatals. The second growing fiscal problem in the 1980s directly involved the country's complex exchange-rate system. Created in July 1982, the multitiered system allowed a preferential exchange rate for the imports of certain government-owned companies. It was the Central Bank, however, that forfeited the losses involved in these exchange transactions, which were recorded as part of the overall public-sector deficit. In 1986 Central Bank losses of this kind accounted for nearly half of all the public sector's deficit. Again to avoid inflation, the government chose to maintain the multitiered system, at least in the short run.

Expenditures

Government expenditures in 1986 reached only 8 percent of GDP, a very low figure compared with those for many developing countries where state expenditures accounted for a third of GDP or more. Expenditures were separated into current and capital accounts. As a result of large fiscal deficits, mostly caused by parastatals, fiscal policy in the 1980s sought to cut public expenditures, primarily capital expenditures. The extremely sharp decline in capital expenditures in 1986 brought capital investment to less than 1 percent of GDP, a dangerously low level according to many economists. This decline signified that Paraguay was sacrificing long-term development for short-term corrections.

The two major segments of the current account were government salaries (39 percent) and subsidies and transfers (24 percent). Defense spending represented an additional 10 percent of total government expenditures (see Defense Spending, ch. 5). Unilateral transfers to individuals for social services were minimal, and the country's social security program, which served only one-fifth of the population, was essentially self-financed by workers and employers. Interest payments on the country's mounting debt, 4 percent of current expenditures in 1980, doubled to 8 percent by 1986. Most capital expenditures in the 1980s went toward state-owned enterprises. Other major infrastructural projects and development finance institutions absorbed the balance in widely varying percentages depending on the given year.

Revenues

The most striking feature of fiscal policy in Paraguay, and the best empirical evidence of the limited role of the government in the economy, was the level of government revenues as a percentage of GDP. Revenues in 1986 equalled slightly less than 8 percent of GDP, the lowest rate in Latin America and one of the lowest in the world. Tax revenues represented 87 percent of total revenues in 1986 and came from taxes on goods and services (32 percent), net income and profits of managers and corporations (15 percent), international trade, mainly imports (14 percent), and real estate (11 percent). The remaining 28 percent came from a variety of other sources, including stamp taxes. Paraguay had no personal income tax, state tax, or local taxes. Nontax revenues, which included profits from parastatals, represented the remaining 13 percent of total revenues. Although revenues were greater than expenditures in 1986, there was a small budget deficit as a consequence of certain exchange-rate adjustments.

The tax system was a focus of great concern. Generally outdated, it had become increasingly inefficient through numerous ad hoc additions to the tax code over the years. The tax system, headed by the Income Tax Bureau, also was difficult to administer, suffered from low collection rates, and was organizationally complex. For example, the system comprised four autonomous collection agencies whose boundaries were not always clear. Another of the system's fundamental drawbacks was its lack of practical taxes, such as a personal income tax, through which the government could systematically capture tax revenues. More important, the lack of tax revenues limited the government's ability to undertake public works and provide social services. Paraguay was perhaps the only country in Latin America whose government received encouragement from the major multilateral lenders—the IMF, the World Bank (see Glossary), and the IDB—to increase its taxes. As part of the 1986 Adjustment Plan, the government proposed a progressive personal income tax, a value-added tax, and some administrative reshuffling of the tax administration. In 1988, however, it was still unclear whether these policies would be enacted or had been proposed merely for political effect.

Monetary Policy

In 1943 the guaraní (see Glossary) replaced the gold peso (which had been pegged to the Argentine peso) as the national currency, laying the foundation for the country's contemporary monetary system. Guaraníes are issued exclusively by the Central Bank (Banco Central) in notes of 1, 10, 100, 500, 1,000, 5,000 and 10,000 and as coins of 1, 5, 10, and 50 guaraníes. One guaraní is worth 100 céntimos.

Changes in banking laws in the 1940s set the stage for the creation of the country's new Central Bank, which was established in 1952, replacing the Bank of Paraguay and the earlier Bank of the Republic. As the center of the financial system, the Central Bank was charged with regulating credit, promoting economic activity, controlling inflation, and issuing currency. As a result of the growth in the financial system, a new general banking law was introduced in 1973, authorizing greater Central Bank regulation of commercial banks, mortgage banks, investment banks, savings and loans, finance companies, and development finance institutions, among others. In 1979 the Central Bank also began to regulate the nation's growing capital markets.

The Central Bank also controlled monetary policy. One of the major aims of monetary policy in the 1980s was price stability. After experiencing extreme price instability—a familiar threat to the economies of the Southern Cone—in the 1940s and 1950s, Paraguay entered into two decades of price stability, credit expansion, economic growth, and a stable exchange rate. Inflation was only 38 percent in the 1960s, a dramatic turnaround from the 1,387-percent figure recorded during the previous decade. Although the rate climbed to 240 percent in the 1970s, it remained far below the postwar level. The pace of inflation accelerated in the 1980s, however,

Street markets in Asunción
Courtesy Tim Merrill

after the economic downtown in 1982. Inflation, as measured by Paraguay's consumer price index, reached an annual rate of 27 percent in 1986 and climbed to well over 30 percent in 1987. Government authorities wrestled with how to control inflation without implementing policies that could unleash even greater inflation and popular discontent. Although influenced by many factors, inflation in the 1980s was exacerbated by fiscal deficits, exchange-rate losses of the Central Bank, the exchange-rate system in general, the country's declining terms of trade, and the inflation of neighboring trading partners, Brazil and Argentina.

The Central Bank regulated the allocation of credit, the supply of credit, and the country's interest rate in an attempt to promote economic growth and restrain inflation. The Central Bank held considerable control over the national banking system, but many regulations were loosely enforced.

Exchange-Rate Policy

From 1960 to 1982, Paraguay enjoyed extraordinary exchange-rate stability as the guaraní remained pegged to the United States dollar at ₲126=US$1. After the virtual financial chaos of 1947–54, this stability was especially welcome in Paraguay. Although the country's exchange rate was overvalued in the 1970s, it was not until the 1982 recession that the government devalued the guaraní.

Exchange-rate policy in the 1980s came to be characterized by numerous devaluations and almost annual changes in the number of exchange rates employed. In early 1988 five exchange rates were in use, making exchange-rate policy very complicated. The first rate of ₲240=US$1 was used for the imports of certain state-owned enterprises and for external debt service payments. The second rate of ₲320=US$1 was applied to petroleum imports and petroleum derivatives. The third rate of ₲400=US$1 was reserved for disbursements of loans to the public sector. The fourth rate of ₲550=US$1 was used for agricultural inputs and most exports. The fifth rate, the only one not set by the Central Bank, was a free-market rate set by the commercial banks. The free-market rate, which was applied to most of the private sector's nonoil imports, exceeded ₲900=US$1 by 1988. Exchange-rate adjustments were expected to continue in the late 1980s.

One of the most distinctive and complex features of the nation's exchange-rate policy was a system of official minimum export prices for selected agricultural commodities. The system, called Aforo, was essentially a way of guaranteeing foreign-exchange earnings to the Central Bank. Aforo values, assessed by the government immediately before a harvest or slaughter, designated the minimum prices exporters should receive for the goods and determined what percentage of foreign-exchange earnings must be turned over to the Central Bank. The difference between the Aforo price and the actual price was traded in the free-exchange market. In 1987 the official export rate for Aforos was ₲550=US$1, whereas the free-market rate was upwards of ₲900=US$1. Lower Aforos generally made Paraguayan exporters more competitive but guaranteed less revenue to the Central Bank. Aforos were one of several government policies that fueled contraband trading.   cop. 2

As the manipulation of Aforos demonstrated, exchange-rate policy was an important economic policy tool of the Paraguayan government and directly affected most sectors of the economy. Although the government ostensibly intended to reduce the gaps among the various tiers of the exchange rate, it was reluctant to reunify the rates in fear of greatly speeding inflation. Paradoxically, however, the multitiered exchange-rate system increased inflationary pressures in numerous indirect ways. One of its most important effects was the fall in Central Bank reserves associated with the exchange-rate subsidies for parastatals, a policy that created a growing public-sector deficit. Likewise, Central Bank losses encouraged a more expansionary monetary policy, most notably through rediscounting rates. An overvalued exchange rate also hampered export growth in general, which in turn aggravated Paraguay's balance-of-payments deficits and potentially its external debt.

Labor

Paraguay's labor force surpassed 1.4 million in 1986, or approximately 37 percent of the country's estimated population. Government statistics recorded an unemployment rate of 14 percent in 1986, but that figure dropped to 8 percent in 1987. Estimates of unemployment varied widely outside Paraguayan government circles. For example, the United Nations Economic Commission for Latin America and the Caribbean (ECLAC) estimated unemployment as high as 18 percent in 1986 with as much as 50 percent underemployment in urban areas. Males dominated the official labor force, accounting for 79 percent of registered workers. Women were visibly a much higher percentage of the work force than official statistics reflected. But, unlike in most Latin American countries, Paraguay's female labor force was not growing faster than the male labor force; males were expected to continue to constitute a disproportionate share of the labor force for some time to come.

Statistics on the distribution of labor by economic sector in 1987 showed 48 percent of workers in agriculture, 31 percent in services, and 21 percent in industry. Males dominated agricultural labor, whereas women were most prominent in the services sector. The country maintained the highest percentage of labor in agriculture in all of South America and one of the lowest services percentages on the continent. Nevertheless, according to data from the IDB, a large portion of the labor force in Asunción was in the informal sector (see Glossary), generally in services. In fact, Asunción ranked second among Latin American cities in the percentage of labor force in the informal sector.

Unlike most Latin American countries, the distribution of Paraguay's labor force had changed little in thirty-five years. In 1950 agriculture comprised 55 percent of the labor force, services 25 percent, and industry 20 percent. The greatest fluctuations within economic sectors during the 1980s occurred in the construction industry, which was directly affected by hydroelectric development. After the end of Itaipú's construction phase in the early 1980s, observers estimated that the number of construction workers dropped from 100,000 to 25,000, but they expected that the start-up of construction at the Yacyretá hydroelectric project would restore many of those jobs.

Comprehensive labor laws had been passed since 1961, but they were not universally enforced. Laws theoretically regulated maximum hours to be worked per week, child labor, union activities, female labor, maternity leave, holidays, and social security and established a minimum wage. Minimum wages, in effect since 1974, were set by the Labor Authority according to geographic location and task performed. Minimum wages in the 1970s and 1980s did not keep pace with inflation, and the real minimum wage was eroding. The real wages of the work force at large, however, eroded even more quickly than minimum wages over the same period. Employees typically worked from 6:00 A.M. to 8:00 P.M. with an almost universal midday siesta.

Organized labor provided the best example of the loose enforcement of labor laws. Although the country's labor laws permitted free association by labor unions, most labor movements had been thwarted by the government since 1958, the year of a major strike by the Paraguayan Confederation of Workers (Confederación Paraguaya de Trabajadores—CPT). There was a growing independent workers' movement developing in the 1980s, which was fueled mostly by dissatisfaction with the declining real wage of the Paraguayan worker. Nonetheless, unionized labor remained dominated by the CPT, which was generally more progovernment than prolabor and rarely challenged government policy (see Interest Groups, ch. 4).

Agriculture

Throughout Paraguay's history, agriculture has been the mainstay of the economy. This trend continued unabated in the late 1980s as the agricultural sector generally accounted for 48 percent of the nation's employment, 23 percent of GDP, and 98 percent of export earnings (see fig. 6). The sector comprised a strong food and cash crop base, a large livestock subsector, and a vibrant timber industry.

Growth in agriculture was very rapid from the early 1970s to the early 1980s, a period when cotton and soybean prices soared and cropland under cultivation expanded as a result of agricultural colonization. Growth in agriculture slowed from an average of 7.5 percent annual growth in the 1970s to approximately 3.5 percent in the mid- to late 1980s. Agricultural output was routinely affected by weather conditions. Flooding in 1982 and 1983 and severe droughts in 1986 hurt not only agriculture, but, because of the key role of the sector, virtually every other sector of the economy as well.

In the aggregate, however, the advances experienced by the sector during the 1970s and 1980s did not reach many of the small farmers, who continued to use traditional farming methods and lived at a subsistence level. Despite the abundance of land, the distribution of the country's farmlands remained highly skewed, favoring large farms. Epitomizing the country's economic activity in general, the agricultural sector was consolidating its quick expansion over the two previous decades and only beginning to tap its potential in the late 1980s.

Land Tenure

The history of land tenure in Paraguay is distinct from that in most Latin American countries. Although there had been a system of land grants to conquistadors, Paraguay was distinguished by Jesuit *reducciones* that dominated rural life for over a century. After the expulsion of the Jesuits in 1767 and later the Spanish, the state had become the owner of 60 percent of the country's land by the mid-1800s. Large tracts of land were sold, mostly to Argentines to pay the country's war debt from the War of the Triple Alliance. This was the beginning of the concentration of land in Paraguay not in the hands of the Spanish or of a local elite but rather of foreign investors. Land policy remained controversial until the 1930s, when there was a broader consensus for the titling of land to users of the land and mediating between *latifundio* and *minifundio* (small landholding). After 1954 multinational agribusinesses, mostly Brazilian and American, played an increasing role

113

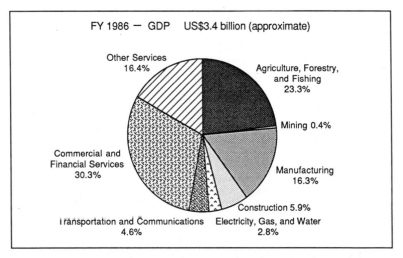

FY 1986 — GDP   US$3.4 billion (approximate)

Other Services
16.4%

Agriculture, Forestry,
and Fishing
23.3%

Mining 0.4%

Commercial and
Financial Services
30.3%

Manufacturing
16.3%

Construction 5.9%

Transportation and Communications
4.6%

Electricity, Gas, and Water
2.8%

Source: Based on information from Economist Intelligence Unit, *Country Report: Uruguay, Paraguay,* No. 3, London, 1988, 3.

Figure 6. Gross Domestic Product (GDP) by Sector, 1986

in the economy, often purchasing enormous tracts of land devoted to raising cattle, cotton, soybeans, and timber.

The most recent data on land tenure was the agricultural census of 1981, which followed earlier major agricultural censuses of 1956 and 1961. The most striking change from 1956 to 1981 was the kind of ownership of the farms. In the 1956 census, 49 percent of all farmers squatted on their land compared with only 30 percent in the 1981 census. This data suggested an increasing interest on the part of small farmers in obtaining title to their land in the face of growing land pressures. The 1981 census also indicated that 58 percent of all farms were owned outright and 15 percent were sharecropper farms; the 1956 census showed that 39 percent of farms belonged to farmers and 12 percent were worked by sharecroppers.

Another striking element of the 1981 agricultural census was the great disparity between small and large landholdings. According to the census, 1 percent of the nation's more than 273,000 farms covered 79 percent of the nation's farmland in use. These large farms had an average landholding of almost 7,300 hectares. Many of the largest holdings were cattle farms in the Chaco region. By contrast, the smallest farms, which made up 35 percent of all farms, covered only 1 percent of the land, making the average size of a *minifundio* 1.7 hectares, or less than was necessary for one family's subsistence. Still, the 1981 census figures were somewhat more encouraging than those in the 1956 census, which showed that 1 percent of farms covered 87 percent of the land, and 46 percent of farms covered only 1 percent of the farmland. Another encouraging trend that the census quantified was the declining number of farms under 5 hectares in size and the growth of small to medium-size farms (5 to 99.9 hectares).

Despite these positive trends, the 1981 census pointed to an increasing problem of landlessness. Census figures indicated that roughly 14 percent of all peasants were landless. Landlessness historically had been mitigated by the undeveloped nature of the eastern border region. Because the owners of estates in the region used only a portion of their holdings, peasants could squat on the properties without retribution. Land pressures also were alleviated by the vast tracts of untitled land in the east. Beginning in the 1960s, however, competition for land in the area increased dramatically. Many estate owners sold their lands to agribusinesses; the new proprietors, who were committed to an efficient and extensive use of their holdings, sometimes called upon the government to remove squatters from the lands.

Squatters also came into competition with Paraguayan colonists and Brazilian immigrants. Thousands of colonists were resettled in the eastern region under the government's agrarian reform program (see Land Reform and Land Policy, this ch.). The Brazilian immigration occurred as a result of a dramatic increase in land prices in the 1970s in the neighboring Brazilian state of Paraná. Many farmers sold their properties and crossed into Paraguay, where land was much cheaper. By the late 1980s, at least half of the population in the departments of Canendiyú and Alto Paraná was Brazilian.

Land Reform and Land Policy

After decades of public controversy over government land policy, two important agrarian laws were enacted in 1963 that guided land policy through the late 1980s. The Agrarian Statute, as the laws were called, limited the maximum size of a single landholding to 10,000 hectares in Eastern Paraguay and 20,000 hectares in the Chaco, with landholdings in excess of this size subject to taxes or possible purchase. This law, however, like many of the laws involved in economic policy, was enforced only loosely or not at all. A more fundamental component of the Agrarian Statute was the creation of the Rural Welfare Institute (Instituto de Bienestar Rural—IBR). The IBR, which superceded the Agrarian Reform Institute, became the central government agency mandated to plan colonization programs, issue land titles to farmers, and provide new colonies with support services such as credit, markets, roads, technical assistance, and other social services as available. From 1963 to the late 1980s, the IBR titled millions of hectares of land and created hundreds of colonies, directly affecting the circumstances of roughly one-quarter of the population. In the late 1980s, the IBR remained the key government agency, along with the Ministry of Agriculture and Livestock, in serving the land needs of small farmers.

Although the IBR played an important role in stimulating the celebrated ''March to the East,'' the exodus from Paraguay's central zone to the eastern border region that began in the 1960s was a spontaneous process. The task of the IBR was so enormous and its resources so limited that many of the country's farmers bypassed the institute in order to participate in the eastward land grab. Thousands of Paraguayans took it upon themselves to trek eastward to the abundant, fertile, but forested land of Alto Paraná, Itapúa, and other eastern departments. Many of the colonists were pioneers in the truest sense, clearing densely forested areas for farming mostly by axe. Few farmers had access to institutional credit, and these newly colonized areas generally lacked schools, roads, and other amenities.

Land Use

Paraguay comprises a total of 40.6 million hectares of land. But based on soil surveys, analysts have estimated that only one-fifth of that area is appropriate for normal crop production. According to the 1981 agricultural census, 7 percent of the land was dedicated to crop production, 20 percent to forestry, 26 percent to livestock, and 47 percent to other purposes. These figures indicated the great agricultural potential that remained in Paraguay in the late 1980s. One of the most important trends in Paraguayan agriculture was the increase in the percentage of land under cultivation, which had been only 2 percent in 1956. Livestock activity fluctuated greatly during the 1970s and 1980s but generally had increased, rising above the 22-percent land use reported in 1956. The improved utilization of agricultural resources resulted from increased colonization, favorable price movements for cash crops, further mechanization, and infrastructure improvements connecting produce with markets.

For agricultural purposes, the country can be divided into three regions: the Chaco, the central region, and the eastern region. The semiarid Chaco contained extensive grazing land that supported 40 percent of the country's livestock. Although the Chaco region covered 60 percent of the country's land mass, it contained only 3 percent of the population and accounted for less than 2

A farmer in Paraguarí holding a sample of his watermelon crop
Courtesy Inter-American Development Bank

percent of crop production. With the exception of the Mennonite colonies in the central Chaco, there was little crop activity (see Minority Groups, ch. 2). A more suitable location for crops was the central region in the vicinity of Asunción, where traditional crop production had dominated since peasants were pushed toward the capital at the end of the War of the Triple Alliance. But government policies since the 1960s had favored breaking up *minifundios* in the central region and establishing larger, more efficient farms in the fertile eastern border region, which is endowed with rich, varied soils, well distributed annual rainfalls, and millions of hectares of hardwood forests. Together these regions cover some 16 million hectares, 40 percent of the country's land and approximately 98 percent of the country's crop land. Agricultural surveys in the east, the new focus of agricultural activity, have determined that 30 percent of the region is suitable for intensive agriculture, 40 percent for livestock, 20 percent for moderate agriculture or livestock use, and 10 percent for forestry.

The country's land use changed rapidly in the 1970s and 1980s as foreign investment, Paraguayan and Brazilian colonists, the construction of Itaipú, favorable commodity prices, and new infrastructure all contributed to the penetration of the dense eastern region. Increased prices for soybeans and cotton beginning in the early 1970s changed the Paraguayan landscape more drastically

117

than any other factor. By the late 1980s, cotton and soybeans accounted for over 1.1 million hectares, or over 40 percent of all land in crops and contributed over 60 percent of exports. Although government policies favored export crops, the rapid expansion of cash crops was largely a direct response that Paraguay's free-market economy made to the rise in the international demand for these products.

Crops

Export Crops

Soybeans had replaced cotton as the country's most important crop by the 1980s. A relatively new crop for Paraguay, soybeans were not produced in any quantity until 1967, when they were introduced as the summer rotation crop in a national plan for self-sufficiency in wheat. After soybean prices nearly tripled in 1973, however, much of the land slated for wheat was sown with soybeans instead. As the lucrative nature of soybean cultivation and processing became apparent, several large agribusinesses from Brazil, the United States, and Italy engaged in large-scale, commercial production of soybeans and soybean oil. It is difficult to exaggerate the drastic growth soybeans enjoyed in Paraguay. In 1970 soybeans covered only 54,600 hectares and had an annual production of over 75,000 tons. By 1987 soybeans covered some 718,800 hectares, more than any other crop, with an annual output of 1 million tons and export revenues of approximately US$150 million. The soybean crop grew primarily in the newly colonized departments of Itapúa, Alto Paraná, Canendiyú, and Amambay. Soybeans were produced principally for the world market and sold both as a raw bean and as a processed oil, which was also consumed locally. Soybean prices generally rose beginning in the 1970s but experienced significant fluctuations in the early to mid-1980s before recovering in the late 1980s. The major constraint on growth in soybean output, besides price fluctuations, was the lack of storage, drying facilities, and local processing capacity.

Cotton was one of Paraguay's oldest crops, grown since the time of the Jesuit missions. The government encouraged cotton production after the crop was nearly wiped out by the War of the Triple Alliance. Cotton was especially suited to the Paraguayan climate and soils and was grown primarily by small farmers in the central region. Cotton farming also experienced extremely rapid growth in the 1970s and 1980s. In 1970 only 46,900 hectares were sown with cotton, producing a volume of over 37,000 tons. By 1985, however, 385,900 hectares were covered with cotton, yielding almost 159,000 tons. Those figures had dropped to 275,000 hectares and 84,000 tons during the drought of 1986. Foreign-owned, large-scale, commercial production in the eastern border region was surpassing central region production in the late 1980s. Despite the advances in cotton production, cotton cultivation in the 1980s was still characterized by low yields and a low technological level. Even more so than soybeans, cotton suffered wide price fluctuations, and many small farmers who came to rely on cotton revenues in the 1970s became vulnerable to external price fluctuations in the following decade. Some cotton fiber was used domestically, but about 80 percent of the country's crop was processed into cotton lint at more than ten textile-processing factories. Cotton exports in 1987 earned about US$100 million, with most exports going to Uruguay, Britain, France, the Federal Republic of Germany (West Germany), and Japan.

Another key export crop was tobacco. Used domestically for centuries, cigarettes and cigars also earned foreign exchange. During parts of the early 1900s, tobacco was Paraguay's principal agricultural export to Western Europe. Tobacco production slowed in the 1970s with the advent of massive soybean and cotton production. Another reason for the tobacco crop's decline was the inability of the domestic cigarette factories to improve quality control and compete with smuggled brands. Wide price fluctuations of tobacco also explained dwindling production. Despite these difficulties, tobacco made a slight recovery in the 1980s. The area cultivated rose from 7,600 hectares in 1980 to over 8,000 hectares in 1987. Output increased from 11,500 to 12,000 tons. Tobacco was grown throughout Paraguay, mostly by small farmers. Cigarettes and cigars were exported to Argentina, France, and Spain. Tobacco exports were valued at approximately US$9 million in 1987.

Coffee was another export crop but of much less importance. Cultivated since the times of the Jesuits, coffee was grown in the central and eastern border regions for local and export markets. Most modern coffee production methods derived from the practices of German colonists in the eastern region. Coffee production boomed in the late 1970s but waned in the early 1980s. In the late 1980s, coffee output rose again, following a pattern of fluctuating production based on price movements. In 1987 approximately 9.2 million hectares of coffee yielded 18.4 million tons of exports with an estimated value of US$44.7 million.

Sugarcane remained an important cash crop for small farmers in the late 1980s. Unlike many countries in the Western Hemisphere, Paraguay saw sugarcane as a crop of the future, not because of its use for refined sugar and molasses, but as an input to ethanol, an increasingly popular energy alternative for the country. Sugarcane was planted in Paraguay as early as 1549 with seedlings from Peru, and sugar had been exported since 1556. After the devastation of Paraguay's two major wars, however, local output did not meet domestic demand until the mid-1900s, after which exports were revived. Since then, sugar production has fluctuated with price changes but generally has increased. Paraguay's climate is appropriate for sugarcane cultivation, but traditional methods and inefficient small-scale production limited harvests. Besides low yields, the industry suffered from outdated milling facilities and high production costs. Sugar production, however, was expected to be modernized and increasingly commercialized as a result of its high government priority as an input to an alternative energy source. Some 65,000 hectares of sugarcane produced 3.2 million tons of sugar in 1987, including 7,500 tons of sugar exports valued at US$2.3 million. These figures were highs for the decade.

Numerous crops were grown partially or entirely for their value as exported processed oils. Oilseeds represented one of Paraguay's largest agro-industries. One of Latin America's largest oilseed exporters, Paraguay processed cottonseed, soybean, peanut, coconut, palm, castor bean, flaxseed, and sunflower-seed oils. Industrial countries in particular consumed oilseeds as a lower-priced substitute for more traditional oils, which also were higher in cholesterol. Some oil was used locally as well. Paraguay also produced a number of nonvegetable oils, such as tung oil and petit-grain oil. Tung oil, derived from tung nuts, was used as a drying agent in paints. Petit-grain oil, derived from Paraguay's bitter oranges, was used in cosmetics, soaps, perfumes, and flavorings. In the 1980s Paraguay remained one of the world's leading exporters of petit-grain oil.

Food Crops

Manioc (cassava), corn, beans, and peanuts, the four basic crops of the Guaraní Indians, were still the country's major food crops in the 1980s. Manioc, the staple of the Paraguayan diet, had been cultivated in nearly every area of the country for centuries. Called *mandioca* in Paraguay, the root crop was the main starch of the diet. Manioc did not experience the rapid explosion of cultivation that cotton, soybean, and corn did. Nevertheless, manioc yields ranked as some of the best in Latin America. In 1986 about 220,000 hectares produced 3.4 million tons of manioc. These figures compared favorably with 1976 data, which recorded 106,500 hectares producing 1.6 million tons.

Corn was Paraguay's most rapidly growing food crop. From the early 1960s to the late 1980s, corn output multiplied rapidly, covering more hectares than any crop except soybeans. After the doubling of both hectares cultivated and total output in the 1970s, corn production accelerated even further in the 1980s, mostly because of continued agricultural colonization. In 1980 approximately 376,600 hectares yielded 584,700 tons of corn, compared with an unprecedented 547,000 hectares of corn in 1987, which harvested 917,00 tons. Like manioc, corn was grown throughout the country, but the departments of Itapúa, Paraguarí, Caaguazú, and Alto Paraná were responsible for most of the harvest. White corn was the traditional corn of Paraguay, but yellow, high-yield hybrids were increasingly common, especially on larger farms. Most corn went to domestic human consumption; roughly a third of domestic corn consumption took place in the form of feed grain for the livestock sector. In addition, some surplus corn was exported to Brazil and Argentina, depending on weather conditions and annual output.

Other principal food crops included beans, peanuts, sorghum, sweet potatoes, and rice. Many types of beans were grown in Paraguay, including lima beans, green beans, and peas. Since the 1970s, however, bean production had been declining because of the profitability of other crops. Peanuts, a traditional though marginal crop, expanded in the 1970s and 1980s and often were intercropped with cotton. Peanuts also were processed as an oilseed. Sorghum, a drought-resistant crop, was grown primarily as feed for livestock and was considered a potential crop for the arid Alto Chaco. Sweet potatoes, another main staple crop, like many other food crops, did not expand significantly in the 1970s, and harvests contracted measurably in the 1980s. Rice production, by contrast, expanded after high-yield varieties were introduced in the 1960s. Rice is not a dietary staple in Paraguay as it is in many Latin American countries, but it is popular and consumed in ever-greater quantities. Self-sufficient in rice, Paraguay showed potential as a regional exporter because of its rich soils and irrigation potential along the Río Paraná.

After attempting for twenty years to become self-sufficient in wheat production, Paraguay reached wheat self-sufficiency in 1986. For two decades, the government's national wheat program had encountered numerous obstacles: seeds inappropriate for Paraguay's climate, skyrocketing prices for alternative crops, poor weather, blight infection, and a lack of proper farming practices. From 1976 to 1986, however, the number of hectares covered with wheat multiplied some sixfold, from 24,200 to over 140,000. Wheat output reached 233,000 tons in 1986, 33,000 tons above national consumption. In 1987 approximately 175,000 hectares of wheat fields yielded 270,000 tons, a record high. Over half of all wheat was grown in Itapúa, where most soil testing, tractors, and fertilizers were used. Despite the rapid expansion, wheat production in the 1980s was hurt by floods, droughts, and cheap contraband, all of which caused flour mills to operate at about half of capacity. Smuggled Brazilian flour sometimes was half the price of Paraguayan flour. Future growth in the wheat industry was constrained by a lack of adequate grain-cleaning and storage facilities.

Paraguayans cultivated numerous other fruits, vegetables, and spices for both domestic consumption and export. Most common were citrus fruits, which were ideal for Paraguay's subtropical and tropical climate. Paraguay also produced pineapples, which according to some sources originated in Paraguay, and peaches, which were farmed commercially by fruit companies from the United States. Bananas, plums, strawberries, pears, avocados, guavas, papayas, mangoes, grapes, apples, watermelon, and other melons were cultivated to varying degrees as well. Vegetable production included gourds, squash, tomatoes, and carrots. Onions and garlic were widely grown and commonly used in cooking.

A uniquely Paraguayan crop was the yerba maté plant. Yerba maté was grown throughout the country—especially Eastern Paraguay—for both domestic and regional markets. Large-scale production was traditionally dominated by Argentine and British interests. Despite its popularity, yerba maté output fell significantly in the 1970s and 1980s, as farmers switched to more lucrative crops.

Paraguay was also believed to be an expanding producer of marijuana in the 1980s. One United States Congressional report in the 1980s estimated annual production at 3,000 tons.

Farming Technology

In the 1980s most farmers held small plots of land, used low levels of agricultural inputs, such as equipment, fertilizer, and irrigated water, and produced primarily food crops for domestic consumption and some cash crops for additional income. Large holdings, many foreign-owned, operated with much higher levels of farming technology and produced almost exclusively cash crops for the export market. Although agricultural colonization and greater cultivation of cash crops by small farmers were modifying this pattern, the basic agricultural dichotomy generally continued in the late 1980s. Although farming techniques were steadily improving, Paraguay continued to display some of the lowest yield rates in

Harvesting bananas in Santa Catalina
Courtesy Inter-American Development Bank

all of Latin America, indicating that agricultural modernization was still far away.

The Mennonite colonies in the central Chaco offered a notable exception to the country's low yields. When Mennonites first arrived in 1926, the central Chaco was a virtual desert. Mennonite pioneers suffered great hardship for at least a generation to make the region's semiarid soils fertile. With time, the Mennonites converted the central Chaco into the major supplier of food for the entire Chaco and made it self-sufficient in almost every crop. The success of the Mennonites was generally attributed to their dedication, superior farming techniques, and access to foreign capital.

A "land without people and people without land," a phrase often used to describe Paraguay, helped explain the country's longstanding farming methods. As a traditionally underpopulated nation, Paraguay suffered from labor shortages and negligent soil practices that favored clearing new land rather than preserving cultivated land. Because of the poor distribution of land, many farmers could not obtain sufficient income from working their own land and often engaged in seasonal wage labor in Argentina. Cultivation practices typically were slash and burn with little use of crop rotation. New forestlands were then cleared by axe, and the cuttings were burned; little plowing was done before planting. These practices became increasingly impractical in the 1980s as the market for fertile land tightened, especially in the eastern border region. The need for maintaining and improving soil fertility was greater than ever by the late 1980s.

The use of purchased inputs in agriculture, such as fertilizers, insecticides, farm equipment, and irrigated water, remained low in Paraguay in the 1980s and occurred mostly on large estates. The country's aggregate level of fertilizer use stood at five kilograms per hectare in the mid-1980s, one of the lowest in Latin America. Some fertilizers were produced locally; most were imported from Brazil. Most fertilizer use was targeted at a few specific crops such as wheat, cotton, and soybeans. Although Paraguay's lands were naturally fertile, most agronomists felt there was an increasing need for higher yields rather than more colonization. Insecticide and herbicide use was even less prevalent than fertilizer use. Weed and insect damage was considerable among some crops, another factor contributing to low agricultural productivity. Because most farms were small, the use of mechanized equipment generally was not appropriate for most farmers, and small farmers tended to use simple hand tools, rudimentary vehicles, and animal-pulled plows. By contrast, tractor use was common among large landholders, accounting for nearly all of the 4.4 tractors per 1,000 hectares that were reported in the mid-1980s. Irrigated farmland represented only 3 percent of all land under cultivation; this figure also was low by Latin American standards.

One of the principal reasons for the continued use of traditional farming practices was the limited scope of government extension services. Although the Ministry of Agriculture and Livestock was dedicated to improving extension services and increasing productivity, its greatest obstacle remained a lack of financial commitment on the part of the central government, which allocated only 2 to 4 percent of the national budget to agriculture in the 1980s, despite the sector's fundamental role in the economy. The Ministry's Agriculture and Livestock Extension Service (Servicio de Extensión Agrícola y Ganadera—SEAG) operated only in the eastern border region through 13 extension offices with a staff of under 500. SEAG was able to reach only approximately 15 to 20 percent of the subregion's farmers, offering mostly crop-specific advice rather than more general technical assistance. Livestock extension was generally neglected, and few efforts were made to integrate crop and livestock activity. Only limited technical assistance was available from international development organizations. Other constraints to increased productivity were the lack of necessary support services in rural areas, such as health clinics and schools.

Likewise, a lack of basic infrastructure, including feeder roads and rural markets, hindered output.

The Ministry of Agriculture and Livestock also played the leading role in the country's agricultural research. Most research took place inside the Department of Agriculture and Forestry Research. Research was oriented toward specific crops, mainly cotton, soybeans, wheat, rice, sugarcane, tobacco, and certain fruits and vegetables. The principal goals of agricultural research were greater soil conservation and the introduction of high-yielding seeds. As with government extension services, the prime obstacle to expanded research efforts was financial.

Credit was another structural constraint limiting agricultural productivity. Aggregate levels of financing to agriculture were insufficient to provide the necessary capitalization of the sector. Furthermore, small farmers received a disproportionately small share of credit, thus exacerbating technological backwardness and skewed land and income distribution. The principal financial institutions providing credit were the National Development Bank (Banco Nacional de Fomento—BNF), the Central Bank, and the Livestock Fund (Fondo Ganadero—FG), as well as about twenty-two commercial banks. The BNF was by far the largest lender to farmers, accounting for 45 percent of the sector's financing. Much of BNF lending did trickle down to short-term financing for small and medium farmers, but little BNF lending went to capital investment. The Central Bank offered approximately 25 percent of the sector's credit, followed by the commercial banks at 23 percent and the FG at 7 percent. Commercial bank lending went to large exporting farms to cover processing and marketing costs. Some smaller cotton and soybean farmers also received commercial bank credit to purchase necessary inputs. The majority of all lending to the livestock sector originated from the FG—the only agricultural government credit-lending institution that was expanding significantly in the 1980s.

Livestock

Raising and marketing livestock, a traditional source of livelihood in Paraguay, remained a major segment of agriculture and the economy at large during the 1980s. Livestock output accounted for roughly 30 percent of agricultural production and about 20 percent of the sector's exports. The raising of livestock represented more than a quarter of total land use and 80 percent of all capital investment in agriculture. Paraguay's vigorous livestock sector also was responsible for the country's high per capita production and consumption of meat and dairy goods. It was estimated that 40 percent of the country's land was especially suited for livestock and some 20 percent generally suitable. Endowed with plentiful grazing lands, Paraguay had vast potential for livestock development.

After the importation of 7 cows and a bull by the Spanish in the mid-1550s, the country's cattle herd swelled to some 3 million head by the time of the War of the Triple Alliance, the largest herd in the Southern Cone. As with every other sector of the Paraguayan economy, the war devastated the country's livestock sector, leaving only 15,000 head. It was not until World War I that domestic demand was met locally and significant exports left the country. By the end of World War II, beef exports had become a major foreign-exchange earner. Beef production and exports fluctuated considerably in the postwar period because of international price movements, weather conditions, government pricing policies, and other factors. In 1987 the country's cattle herd stood at about 8 million head with an annual slaughter rate of 1 million head. In that same year, 75 percent of the slaughter went to the domestic market and the remaining 25 percent to the export market.

Cattle, mostly beef cattle, were found throughout the countryside. The Chaco region was best known for its contribution to cattle raising because of its lack of crops and its sprawling ranches. Nevertheless, the cattle population density of Eastern Paraguay, 0.6 head per hectare, was actually higher than that of the Chaco region, 0.3 head per hectare.

The country's breeding stock was primarily Spanish criollo, although over the years considerable crossbreeding with English breeds and zebu cattle from Brazil had taken place. Although cattle were numerous in Paraguay, the country lacked a sufficient number of pure-bred breeding cattle. The livestock sector also suffered from a low calving percentage, a high mortality rate, and a long fattening period for steers. Artificial insemination was increasingly common. To a certain extent, cattle raising reflected the disparities in agriculture in general. There were numerous farmers who owned only a few head of relatively unproductive cattle that were slaughtered for the local market under relatively poor sanitary conditions. By contrast, extremely large cattle ranches typically were owned by expatriates and butchered more productive animals for both national and international markets.

Seventy slaughterhouses for the domestic market and eight for the export market operated in the 1980s. Local slaughterhouses often could not pass sanitary inspections, but government inspection efforts were focused on improving quality control of exports to meet the stringent regulations of foreign beef markets. The country's beef exports expanded until 1974, when Paraguay lost access

Driving cattle along the Trans-Chaco Highway
Courtesy Inter-American Development Bank

to European Economic Community (EEC) markets and lower world prices further stagnated output. Beef exports responded strongly but erratically in the 1980s as the government's minimum export price system and contraband activity undercut greater export efforts (see Monetary Policy, this ch.). For example, beef exports were a mere 3,100 tons in 1985, 48,000 tons in 1986, and 18,000 tons in 1987, the last being the more typical figure. The 1986 boom in beef exports was the direct result of beef shortages in Brazil caused by price controls under its "Cruzado Plan." Paraguay's principal export markets were Brazil, Peru, Chile, the EEC (specialty items only), Colombia, Uruguay, and Saudi Arabia. Missing from official 1987 data, however, was the unregistered sale of an estimated 300,000 head of cattle along the Brazilian border.

Official government policy favored strong cattle development and exports, a view articulated in national livestock programs since the early 1960s. A major policy tool to promote livestock growth was the FG. The FG was not only the major lender to the industry, but it also provided certain veterinary equipment and medicine, encouraged quality control in meat and dairy products, and operated a model farm in the Chaco.

Dairy cattle represented only a small fraction of the total herd. Most milk production occurred at an estimated 400 dairy farms in Asunción, Puerto Presidente Stroessner, Encarnación, and

Filadelfia. The best yields came from holstein-friesian dairy cattle followed by crossbreeds and criollo. High feed costs and the general inefficiency of small dairy farmers slowed the growth of the industry. The country produced approximately 180 million liters of milk a year in the late 1980s.

Other livestock activity including poultry farming and the swine industry. Some of the most productive poultry farming took place in the Mennonite colonies, in Japanese colonies in the eastern border region, and in the greater Asunción area. Observers estimated that there were over 14 million chickens, 400,000 ducks, 55,000 turkeys, and several other types of fowl. Egg production stood at 600 million per year in the late 1980s and was growing at about 4 percent a year. Pig farming was a relatively minor activity, engaged in mostly by small farmers. The pork industry's greatest structural problems were the high cost of feed and consumer preferences for beef. Government policy emphasized self-sufficiency in feed grown on small pig farms. Paraguay's swine population amounted to roughly 1.3 million in the late 1980s and had grown at a rate of 6 percent a year in the first half of the decade.

Forestry and Fishing

Forestlands constituted approximately one-third of Paraguay's total area. Utilized for fuelwoods, timber exports, and extracts, the country's wooded areas constituted a key economic resource. Approximately half of all woodlands contained commercially valuable timber. In the 1980s about 4 million hectares were being lumbered commercially. Forestry data were only broad estimates, however, as a full third of timber production was believed to be exported illegally to Brazil. Registered forestry exports accounted for about 8 percent of total exports during most of the 1980s. Forests have played an important role in the economy since the 1800s with the processing of yerba maté and the resilient quebracho. Because of a general decline in tannin exports, however, the quebracho played a correspondingly less important role in forestry.

Officially, Paraguay produced over 1 million cubic meters of lumber a year in the 1980s. Trees were processed at over 150 small, mostly outdated sawmills that produced wood products for the paper, cardboard, construction, and furniture industries and for export. Trees also fueled the country's railroad and largest steel mill. The country's woodlands contained over forty-five species of wood suitable for export, but fewer than ten species were exported in quantity. Paraguay was recognized as an exporter of fine timber, and its wood exports were internationally competitive. In 1987 lumber exports to Argentina, Brazil, and Mexico earned US$50 million in foreign exchange.

Despite the abundance of premium forests, deforestation was progressing at an alarming rate, about 150,000 to 200,000 hectares per year. The rapid depletion of Paraguay's woods was caused by the clearing of virgin forests associated with agricultural colonization, the farming practice of land-clearing and tree-burning, and the felling of trees for charcoal and the other fuelwoods that accounted for 80 percent of household energy consumption.

Although the country contained enormous installed energy capacity, fuelwood remained the most important domestic source of energy in the 1980s. In fact, Paraguay's per capita consumption of fuelwood was the highest in all of Latin America and the Caribbean and nearly three times the level of other South American countries. The deforestation question was complicated by the distribution of forestlands and population. Southeast Paraguay was being deforested the most rapidly. From the mid-1970s to the mid-1980s, that region's forestland decreased from just under 45 percent of all land to 30 percent. The Chaco maintained a large number of forestlands and shrubs, but they could not be economically exploited.

Government policy was slow to respond to deforestation because of the traditional abundance of forests as well as the generally laissez-faire dynamics of the land colonization process. In 1973 the government established a National Forestry Service under the Ministry of Agriculture and Livestock to protect, conserve, and expand the country's forests. The service, however, was hindered by a lack of resources, staff, serious government initiatives, and public education on the problem of deforestation. The planting of fast-growing trees and modernization of the lumber industry were recommended by the government, but only about 7,000 hectares of new forests were seeded annually in the mid-1980s. Given these levels of deforestation and reforestation, analysts estimated that few commercial lumbering lands would be available by the year 2020.

For landlocked Paraguay, fishing was only a minor industry. It focused on more than 230 freshwater fish species in the country's rivers and streams. Only fifty or so species of fish were eaten, dorado and pacú being the most popular. Some fishing companies, mostly family operations, maintained boats, refrigeration facilities, and marketing outlets.

Energy

Massive capital investments in hydroelectric projects along Paraguay's river borders with Brazil and Argentina in the 1970s and 1980s were the most salient characteristic of the country's energy sector and the economy at large. Although not a traditionally significant part of the national economy, the energy sector became an important contributor to the country's balance of payments as Paraguay prepared to become the world's largest exporter of electricity in the 1990s. The rapid growth in energy investment in the 1970s rippled throughout the nation's economy, stimulating the explosive growth of the eastern border region. The construction industry derived the greatest benefits from the hydropower projects, but the manufacturing, agricultural, and transportation sectors also gained from the sudden growth in the east. Paraguay was expected to surpass the United States in the mid-1990s as the world's leader in per capita installed electricity.

Commercial energy represented only one-third of total energy consumption, mostly imported petroleum for the transportation sector. Paraguay was 100 percent dependent on foreign oil. Oil exploration had taken place sporadically since the 1940s, but no significant petroleum deposits had been found by 1988. Paraguay, however, was the most unexplored country in South America in terms of petroleum. Paraguay was increasingly experimenting with renewable alternatives to fossil fuels, such as sugar-based ethanol, an octane enhancer (see Renewable Energy Resources, this ch.). Mining accounted for only 0.4 percent of GDP in 1986.

Electricity

The electricity subsector underwent fabulous growth in the 1980s, making it the most important segment of the energy sector. Once almost entirely dependent on thermal and diesel generation of electricity, the country by the late 1980s had shifted almost entirely to hydroelectricity. Electricity, gas, and water together accounted for 2.8 percent of GDP in 1986. The shift to hydropower started in 1968 upon the completion of the nation's first major hydroelectric plant, the Acaray plant, which supplied almost all of the country's electricity in the 1970s and most of the 1980s. Although the Acaray plant was expanded in the mid- to late 1970s, its role in the economy was overshadowed by the construction of two of Latin America's largest public-sector projects, the Itaipú and Yacyretá hydroelectric plants. In addition to these plants, the government had finalized plans with Argentina for another plant—Corpus— to be located between Itaipú and Yacyretá (see fig. 7). Other plants also were planned downstream of Yacyretá.

Despite the country's tremendous installed capacity and potential capacity for electricity, domestic demand and access to electricity lagged well behind supply and remained quite limited in the late 1980s. Not until the early 1960s did the government introduce the first serious energy policies to improve rural electrification. Electricity consumption increased 10 percent annually in the 1960s and upwards of 16 percent per year in the 1970s. General access to electricity improved from a low 11 percent in the 1970s to over 40 percent by the mid-1980s, but with considerable regional disparities. Approximately 62 percent of people living in the Central Department had electricity compared with only 37 percent of the eastern border region residents and fewer than 1 percent in the Chaco. Asunción accounted for nearly two-thirds of the nation's electricity consumption.

The electricity system was controlled by the National Power Company (Administración Nacional de Electricidad—ANDE), an autonomous, decentralized, public utility. Created in 1949, ANDE was reorganized in 1964 and made a financially independent entity attached to the Ministry of Public Works and Communications. Electricity was expensive for most Paraguayans, and power outages were common. Rapid growth in electrification added approximately 500 kilometers of electric lines per year to the grid in the 1980s, and reliability improved.

Only superlatives adequately describe the grandeur of the Itaipú hydroelectric power plant. Itaipú was the world's largest hydroelectric power plant, located on one of the world's five largest river systems. Itaipú's cost was estimated at US$19 billion, but no exact figure was calculated. The plant's dam, small compared to those at some hydroelectric plants, nonetheless required the diversion of the entire Río Paraná, including the permanent flooding of the spectacular Guairá Falls and of some 235,000 hectares of land. Over a 5-year period, the concrete poured each day would have been sufficient to construct a 350-story building. More importantly, the project created an "Itaipú euphoria" that brought jobs to 100,000 Paraguayans, instilled a renewed pride in the country, and strengthened the nation's image vis-à-vis its giant neighbor and largest economic partner, Brazil.

The Itaipú project began with the signing of the Treaty of Itaipú between Paraguay and Brazil on April 26, 1973. The treaty created a binational authority—Itaipú Binacional—to see that the two countries shared equally in the plant's operation. Itaipú provided Paraguay unprecedented employment opportunities and capital investment, but inadequate planning on the part of the government and the private sector hindered the country's ability to reap the project's full potential. Approximately 80 percent of the plant's construction was performed by local Paraguayan-Brazilian industry.

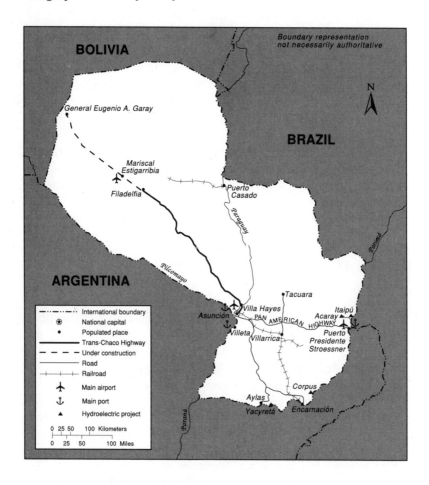

Figure 7. Transportation and Hydroelectric Facilities, 1988

Because the Paraguayan parliament demanded early on that Paraguay receive a fair share of the project's work, Paraguay was officially earmarked for 50 percent of all major contracts. In reality, Paraguay's small industrial sector was no match for Brazil's more technologically advanced industries. Observers believed that Brazilian companies actually rendered 75 percent of the total workload and provided almost all the key inputs such as steel, cement, machinery, and special technical expertise. Even housing materials for Paraguayan construction workers were smuggled in from Brazil.

After five years of labor, the Río Paraná was diverted, and from 1978 to 1982 key construction was completed on the plant, dam, and spillways. Brazil's serious economic problems in 1983 and 1984 slowed the completion of the dam, but overall delays were reasonable by regional standards. Electricity was first generated on October 25, 1984, more than a decade after the signing of the treaty.

Electrical operations were slowly developing at Itaipú in the late 1980s, and full capacity was not expected to be reached until 1992. Because of delays in Brazil's sixty-cycles-per-second system, the plant's fifty-cycle units were the first to produce commercially, and this electricity went to Paraguay. Itaipú was so colossal, however, that ANDE could process only about 30 percent of the output of one of Itaipú's eighteen generators at peak output. As stipulated in the treaty, Brazil and Paraguay bought their electricity from the binational power facility at predetermined rates. Because Paraguay was expected to use only a tiny fraction of its power for the foreseeable future, it sold most of its share back to Brazil, also at a predetermined rate, including normal compensation and royalties.

The major debate over Itaipú in the late 1980s revolved around the low prices that Paraguay had negotiated in the original treaty. What Brazil paid Paraguay for electricity was one-ninth what Paraguay was scheduled to receive from Argentina under the Treaty of Yacyretá, signed just seven months after Itaipú. After twelve years of indecision about how to adjust the Treaty of Itaipú, on January 25, 1985, Paraguay and Brazil signed five revisions to cover matters of financial compensation. Paraguay gained significantly from the 1985 revisions, but most analysts believed Paraguay deserved still greater compensation for its electricity. Further revisions were likely before the end of the century.

The Yacyretá project, although generally overshadowed by the colossal Itaipú project, was one of Latin America's major public-sector projects in the 1980s. Established hastily by Argentina's Peronist government on December 13, 1973, the Yacyretá project was stalled for years as a consequence of regional maneuvering, lobbying by the Argentine nuclear and oil industries, and political instability in Argentina. After ten years of delays, the first major engineering contract finally was awarded in June 1983. As with Itaipú, Yacyretá was hindered by the general lack of physical infrastructure at the dam site. Also as with Itaipú, Paraguayan firms did not receive equal work, despite stipulations in the initial agreement. Construction of the dam and the hydroelectric plant continued throughout the 1980s, but the major construction phase did not begin until the late 1980s, and numerous delays—mostly political—persisted. Yacyretá was not expected to become fully operational until the mid-1990s, more than twenty years after the treaty's signing and at a cost of as much as US$10 billion, five times the original calculation.

An early point of contention between Paraguay and Argentina was the percentage of each country's land that would be flooded for the project's dam; more than 1,690 square kilometers would be needed—a larger area than was flooded for Itaipú. It was agreed that flooding was to be just about equally divided. Another disagreement involved Paraguay's exchange-rate policies. Exchange rates determined the final price Argentina would pay for the plant's electricity. This issue continued to be negotiated in the late 1980s.

When completed, Yacyretá would be roughly one-quarter of the size of Itaipú, with an initial installed capacity of 2,700 megawatts and an annual generation capacity in excess of 17,500 gigawatt hours. Yacyretá's electricity per unit would be more expensive to generate than Itaipú's, and the unit price Paraguay would eventually receive was expected to be much greater. None of the electricity produced by Yacyretá was intended for use by Paraguayans; it was to be sold back to a binational body that would manage the plant. But the gearing up of key construction activity at Yacyretá in the late 1980s was expected to give a boost to the Paraguayan economy, which was suffering from what one observer termed the "post-Itaipú blues." Observers believed that the Argentine-Paraguayan project would provide renewed construction jobs, large capital inflows, and eventually badly needed foreign-exchange revenues. The binational project also would provide seriously needed bridges, highways, improved river transport at the port of Encarnación, and even increased irrigation potential for nearby rice fields.

Located midway between Itaipú and Yacyretá on the Río Paraná was the proposed site of the Corpus hydroelectric power plant. After years of preparation, Corpus remained in the planning stage in the late 1980s because of the slow progress at Yacyretá. Hydrologically linked with Itaipú and Yacyretá, the Corpus plant was designed to make optimal use of the falls at Itaipú and the currents of tributary rivers. In order to integrate and maximize the various projects along the Río Paraná, in October 1979 Paraguay, Argentina, and Brazil signed the Itaipú-Corpus Accord, which set specific regulations for the projects and improved communication among the countries. Although planning was still not final in 1988, Corpus was expected to be comparable in size to Yacyretá. When operable, Corpus would raise Paraguay's electricity output to an estimated 300 times its domestic demand. Beyond Corpus, Argentina and Paraguay also planned several smaller hydroelectric power plants downstream from Yacyretá,

including Itatí-Itá-Corá and others. Future hydroelectric development along the river would continue to be coordinated by the Combined Technical Commission for the Development of the Río
Paraná.

Petroleum

Paraguay imported 100 percent of its petroleum in the late 1980s.
Petroleum was imported primarily from Algeria because Paraguay's
only petroleum refinery was designed for "Saharan blend" oil. The
refinery, located at Villa Elisa, had a 7,500-barrels-per-day capacity,
very small by Latin American standards. Paraguay's refinery capability was limited in terms of products, causing the country to import
high-priced derivatives such as aviation fuel, premium gasoline,
and asphalt. The price of oil was high because of the complex transportation required through Argentina on the Río Paraná and
Río Paraguay. Paraguayan Petroleum (Petróleos Paraguayos—
Petropar)—owned 60 percent by the government and 40 percent
by the private firm Paraguayan Refinery (Refinería Paraguaya)—
imported all of the country's petroleum. Petropar was generally
viewed as a profitable and well-managed enterprise. Esso Standard
(Exxon), Paraguay Shell, and the Paraguayan company Copetrol
marketed all petroleum products to the public with the exception
of diesel and fuel oil, which were sold by Petropar.

Paraguay became increasingly concerned with its oil dependence
following the quadrupling of world oil prices in the autumn of 1973.
Although there was enough growth in other sectors of the economy
to offset the negative consequences, the crisis nonetheless rekin-
dled the interest of policy makers in oil exploration. As a result,
the legislature passed sweeping new regulations to promote oil
exploration by multinational companies. Despite having some of
the most liberal petroleum legislation in the world, Paraguay's
limited prospects and severe lack of infrastructure in the Chaco
dissuaded most companies from drilling, however. Indeed, from
1944 to 1986 only forty-three wells had been drilled in Paraguay.

Foreign firms conducted petroleum exploration under the
supervision of the Ministry of Public Works and Communications.
Most oil exploration in the 1980s took place in Carandayty Basin
on Paraguay's western border with Bolivia and in the Curupaity,
Pirity, and Pilcomayo basins bordering Argentina. Active exploration in Bolivia near its border with Paraguay and oil discoveries
in Argentina only fifteen kilometers from Paraguay's border heightened expectations of oil discoveries in Paraguay. Because of
Paraguay's complicated geology, however, oil exploration was more
difficult than originally anticipated and required sophisticated

Brazilian technology. With or without oil discoveries, the government was contemplating the construction of an oil pipeline to Brazilian ports to import oil, or, in the case of a large oil discovery, to transport oil exports.

Renewable Energy Resources

To reduce the nation's costly foreign-exchange expenditures on imported oil, the Paraguayan government in the 1980s experimented with a variety of nontraditional renewable energy resources. The most important of these experiments was a national plan for the use of ethanol, an octane enhancer and partial substitute for gasoline. The National Ethanol Plan mirrored efforts in Brazil to use sugar-based ethanol in vehicles, where most of Paraguay's petroleum was consumed. Ethanol policy was spearheaded by the National Commission on Fuel Alcohols and implemented by the government's Paraguay Ethanol Agency. In the 1980s, the policy was the subject of a national debate that examined the government's large role in the industry as a price fixer and promoter and weighed the industry's general inefficiency against its foreign-exchange savings.

Paraguay began producing ethanol in 1980. In the late 1980s, there were at least six fuel alcohol plants, and roughly ten more were planned into the 1990s. Most plants were located in cane-growing areas and used sugar or molasses to produce anhydrous alcohol, generally utilizing Brazilian technology. Hydrated ethanol, a complete gasoline substitute, also was produced for more than 7,000 specially made cars from Brazil. Ethanol production in the late 1980s exceeded 20 million liters. Analysts estimated that alcohol production substituted for 130,000 barrels of imported oil a year.

The government also experimented with other nontraditional energy resources. These included methanol, solar energy, wind energy, wood gasification, mini-hydroelectric plants, and gas generated from organic material.

Industry

Industry, especially the manufacturing sector, historically was linked to agricultural processing until the 1970s, when the construction of hydroelectric plants and new industrial incentives began to broaden the industrial base. Industry was composed principally of manufacturing and construction. Paraguay had no real mining sector, but the manufacture of construction materials included limited mining activity. Manufacturing and construction in the economy in the late 1980s remained dependent on developments in other sectors, such as agriculture and energy, for their growth.

Itaipú hydroelectric power plant
Courtesy United States Department of State

Although industry was becoming more visible in Paraguay in the 1980s, industry's share of GDP actually declined in the 1970s and 1980s because of more rapid growth in agriculture.

Manufacturing

Manufacturing accounted for 16.3 percent of GDP in 1986 and employed roughly 13 percent of the labor force, making Paraguay one of the least industrialized nations in Latin America. Manufactured exports, by most definitions, accounted for less than 5 percent of total exports; when semiprocessed agricultural products were included, however, that figure reached 77 percent. The growth of the country's manufacturing industries was hampered by numerous structural obstacles. These included a small internal market, limited physical infrastructure, costly access to seaports, a historical lack of energy production, and the openness of Paraguay's economy to the more industrialized economies of Brazil and Argentina. Another significant factor was the ubiquity and profitability of smuggling operations, which encouraged importing and reexporting rather than production.

Paraguay's earliest manufacturing industries processed hides and leather from its abundant cattle and tannin from quebracho trees (see Agriculture, this ch.). Small-scale manufacturing, especially textiles, flourished under the Francia dictatorship, when the

137

nation's borders were closed. The War of the Triple Alliance, however, devastated what little industry and infrastructure the country had, causing Paraguay to enter the twentieth century as an almost completely agricultural society. Land sales to foreigners stimulated increased agricultural processing in the early twentieth century, including meat packing and the processing of flour, oilseeds, sugar, beer, and pectin extract. After the early 1900s, small-scale manufacturing in all subsectors grew at a slow, but steady pace, with some of the fastest growth occurring because of the shortages during World War II.

The government's role in promoting industry increased in the postwar era, and in 1955 the Stroessner government undertook the country's first industrial census. Over the next twenty years, the government enacted a number of industrial incentive measures, the most important of which was Law 550. Law 550 promoted export-oriented industries or those that would save foreign exchange. It also provided liberal fiscal incentives for companies to develop specific areas of the country, especially the departments of Alto Paraguay, Nueva Asunción, Chaco, and Boquerón. Incentives for business were related mostly to import-duty exemptions, but they included a variety of tax breaks and placed no restrictions on foreign ownership. Approximately one-fourth of all new manufacturing investment from 1975 to 1985 was registered under Law 550. Most foreign investments originated from Brazil, West Germany, the United States, Portugal, and Argentina in that order of importance. The dynamic processes of agricultural colonization and hydroelectric development, combined with such attractive industrial incentives, caused manufacturing to grow at an unprecedented rate in the late 1970s and early 1980s.

Unlike many other Latin American governments, which followed an import-substitution industrial policy, the Paraguayan government had played a minimalist role in the economy through most of the postwar era, curtailing import tariffs and maintaining a realistic exchange rate. In the 1980s, however, Paraguay's exchange rate became overvalued and several state-owned heavy industry plants became operational.

In the late 1980s, the major subsectors of manufacturing were food, beverages, and tobacco; textiles, clothing, leather, and shoes; wood and related products; and chemicals, petroleum, and plastics. Despite some increases in heavy industry in the economy during the 1970s and 1980s, Paraguayan industry was generally small-scale. Manufacturing production remained focused on consumer goods, and capital goods comprised under 5 percent of industrial output. In fact, in the 1980s Paraguay did not contain even one of Latin America's 1,000 largest companies, at least some of which were found in most other countries in the region. Virtually every subsector of Paraguay's manufacturing was characterized by numerous small- to medium-sized firms and a few large firms, which often were foreign owned. Most companies operated well below their capacity.

The food, beverages, and tobacco subsector has been the core manufacturing activity throughout Paraguay's history. In the late 1980s, this subsector continued to dominate, accounting for about 45 percent of industrial activity, depending on agricultural output in a given year. Agro-processing involved a large number of small, inefficient, and often family-run firms as well as a small number of large, efficient, and usually foreign-owned firms. The larger firms produced only the most lucrative items, such as oilseeds, meats, and various beverages, often for export. Some of the most common small-scale producers manufactured milled items, baked goods, sugar and molasses, dairy products, candy, manioc flour, vinegar, coffee, and tobacco. Along with raw agricultural produce, processed and semiprocessed food generated nearly all of the country's exports in the late 1980s. But, as with other manufacturing subsectors, the profitability of the food subsector often was impaired by contraband items from Brazil and Argentina, such as flour, meat, or dairy products. Paraguayan goods crossed borders unofficially as well, thus lowering official exports.

The second most important manufacturing activity also relied on agricultural inputs for its base. Utilizing Paraguay's rich endowment of hardwood trees, the wood subsector represented about 15 percent of all industrial activity and contributed over 8 percent of exports in the 1980s. The most voluminous wood export was lumber, which was produced by hundreds of small sawmills throughout the central and eastern border regions. In addition to saw wood, mills also produced a variety of milled wood, plywood, chipboard, and parquet flooring. Although the country cut and processed only a fraction of its hundreds of species, Paraguayan wood was known for its quality. The country also contained several small paper companies and one large paper and cardboard factory located at Villeta.

Textiles, clothing, leather, and shoes comprised the third largest manufacturing subsector. These industries were traditional, grounded in the nation's abundance of inputs like cotton fibers, cattle hides, and tannin extract. The subsector accounted for about 10 percent of all manufacturing. The textile industry performed spinning, weaving, and dyeing operations and produced finished fabrics that amounted to over 100 million tons in 1986. Most fabrics were derived from cotton fibers, but a growing number of synthetic and wool fibers also were produced. Textile production provided inputs to approximately sixty clothing firms that operated under capacity and were generally inefficient. As with so many other manufacturers, clothing companies met stiff competition from widespread unregistered imports, which often originated in Asia and typically entered across the Brazilian border. The leather industry was characterized by 200 or so small tanneries dotting the Paraguayan countryside. In addition, many medium and two large tanneries fashioned leather goods. The leather industry operated at only about 40 percent of capacity, however. The shoe industry comprised a few hundred small workshops and a dozen or so medium-sized firms, which produced some 5 million pairs of leather and synthetic shoes a year.

The processing of petroleum, chemicals, and plastics represented an increasing activity. In the late 1980s, this subsector represented less than 5 percent of industrial activity, but its share of manufacturing output was expanding because of the growth of heavy industry in Paraguay, especially industry related to the energy sector. The country also produced fertilizers, industrial gases, tanning chemicals, varnishes, and detergents. In 1987 a group of Japanese investors was considering the construction of a new fertilizer plant with a 70,000-ton capacity per year. Since the early 1980s, ethanol was being produced in large quantities, and the government was considering producing methanol. Also processed were paints, soaps, candles, perfumes, and pharmaceuticals. One of Paraguay's fastest growing industries was the new, relatively modern plastics subsector, which supplied a wide variety of goods to the local market.

Construction

Construction was one of the fastest growing areas in the economy in the late 1970s and early 1980s because of hydroelectric dams, other infrastructure projects, and brisk growth in residential housing in Asunción. Many of the raw materials used in the construction industry, such as lime, sand, kaolin, gypsum, wood, and stones, were found and mined locally. Construction grew at a pace of over 30 percent per year from 1977 to 1980, but in the 1980s it fluctuated dramatically with changes in hydroelectric activity and general economic growth. Construction amounted to 5.9 percent of GDP in 1986.

One of the country's largest investments in construction and in industry in general involved the expansion and modernization of cement facilities. After years of undercapacity in cement production and an outdated wet-cement process, the government spent nearly US$200 million to expand the country's largest cement plant at Vallemí. Financed through a consortium of French banks, the National Cement Industry (Industria Nacional de Cemento—INC) was completed in 1986. Because this completion date followed the pouring of cement at Itaipú, however, virtually all cement for that project came from Brazil. Moreover, located 546 kilometers west of Asunción, INC was far removed from most industrial activity, particularly hydroelectric construction. As a result, in the late 1980s the plant operated at only 45 percent of capacity, and the plant's capital and operating costs formed a major part of the nation's debt burden in the 1980s. Increasing the plant's utilization by exporting to regional markets frequently was discussed but in the late 1980s remained an unlikely prospect. The financial burden of INC became a political issue as the country's debt burden mounted throughout the decade.

The metal industry was the other major industry serving construction activity. Although Paraguay possessed no commercially exploitable metallic minerals, it had three steel plants. The largest plant, Paraguayan Steel (Aceros Paraguayos—Acepar), was completely government owned. Fueled by large charcoal furnaces and fed with Brazilian iron ore, Acepar was capable of producing 150,000 tons of steel annually, or about five times the country's average demand in the 1980s. Acepar began operation in late 1986, having missed both the Itaipú construction boom and the opportunity to contract for Yacyretá. Acepar's 1987 output was under 50,000 tons and was not expected to increase substantially in the future. Acepar could not cover its own operating costs, and even with government subsidies its steel was five times as costly as steel from other producers. In addition to Acepar, Paraguay had plant with a capacity of 50,000 tons per year that produced competitively priced steel bars and other metal products; a marginal plant with only a 6,000-ton annual production capacity was also in operation.

Beyond steel production, the metal subsector comprised more than 1,000 small smiths and metal workshops. Paraguayan companies produced a wide assortment of consumer goods such as simple agricultural tools, general hardware items, and metal furniture. The subsector also contained several large metallurgical companies. For the first time in the 1980s, local metallurgical companies produced water tanks, fuel tanks, and grain silos. Paraguay also maintained two respected shipyards.

Services

Financial System

In 1986 the service sector contributed 51.3 percent of GDP. Of that total, commercial and financial services accounted for 30.3 percent, transportation and communications for 4.6 percent, and other services for 16.4 percent. The latter category included government services, informal services, and tourism.

The nation's financial system had a long history, but it did not undergo major changes until the rapid growth of the 1970s. Large increases in investment and accelerated growth brought on the swift monetization of the economy during the 1970s. National savings soared, as did the number of financial institutions, making Paraguay a budding financial center in the Southern Cone. Observers estimated that total financial activity increased more than sixty times from 1960 to the mid-1980s. But with the arrival of the 1982 regional recession, bank losses increased markedly, and by 1987 three major American banks had pulled out of the country.

The commercial banks were the most important component of the financial system after the Central Bank and held a third of the assets of that system. The commercial banking system in 1988 comprised twenty-two banks with forty-eight offices in Asunción and forty-seven branches outside the capital. Although Paraguay's oldest commercial bank was established in 1920, the system's growth was most pronounced in the second half of the 1970s when seven new banks were registered. The newer banks that arrived were large, multinational banks that entered Paraguay to manage the massive capital investment associated with hydroelectric projects, to finance rapidly expanding agricultural exports, to participate in the intense economic activity along the Paraguayan-Brazilian border, and to take advantage of the liberal banking laws. Three banks—the Brazilian Banco de Asunción, the Spanish Banco Exterior, and the American Citibank—held over half of all deposits. Despite the departure in 1987 of Bank of America, Chase Manhattan, and the Bank of Boston, Paraguay's commercial banking assets remained largely in foreign hands.

The National Workers' Bank (Banco Nacional de Trabajadores— BNT) was the country's only mixed bank, owned 90 percent by contributory members and 10 percent by the government. Established in 1973, the BNT was created to serve as a savings and loan, a development bank, and a provider of a variety of financial services. BNT's clients were individual workers, unions, federations, artisans, and cooperatives.

Asunción during the mid-day siesta
Courtesy Tim Merrill

Nonbanking institutions also were part of the burgeoning financial system. These included finance companies, insurance companies, and social security institutions. Most of these financial
intermediaries were opened in the 1970s as consumer savings
accumulated. The rapid growth of financial institutions was
epitomized by finance companies, at least twenty-six of which were
opened from 1975 to 1985. Unlike banks, most finance houses were
locally owned. The majority were located in Asunción, but at least
five operated in Eastern Paraguay. Representing approximately
6 percent of the financial system's assets, finance companies functioned mostly as short- to medium-term lenders for commercial
activity and consumer durables. Some finance companies operated
in conjunction with commercial banks, contrary to banking law.

By the late 1980s, Paraguay had forty insurance companies, the
overwhelming majority of which had been established since 1960
and were locally owned. Services varied considerably, but the companies tended to have a marginal role in the financial system. There
were also social security institutions, which offered health and retirement plans, but only one was in the private sector—a bank
employees' pension program that was an important lender for mortgages and consumer durables.

The financial system also encompassed an array of development
finance institutions, generally run by the government. Most notable

143

among these institutions was the BNF, the major lender to agriculture and a significant provider of credit to industry, commerce, and livestock activity (see Farming Technology, this ch.). The BNF contained 14 percent of national assets.

The major lender to livestock farmers was the government-operated Fondo Ganadero (FG), which also provided technical assistance to cattle raisers. The FG—established in 1969 with resources from the United States Agency for International Development (AID) and the World Bank—provided nearly 70 percent of the credit issued to livestock activity, usually in the form of medium- to long-term loans for fixed and working capital. The FG represented approximately 7 percent of the country's financial assets.

The Central Bank played an unusually active role in direct lending through a variety of mechanisms, most notably the Special Development Fund (Fondo Especial de Desarrollo—FED), which also was created with AID and World Bank capital. The FED operated two direct lending programs for rural enterprises and small farmers and a program for guaranteeing loans to rural enterprises. The FED accounted for roughly 2 percent of national financial assets.

A more minor government agency was the Agricultural Credit Agency (Crédito Agrícola de Habilitación—CAH), which had operated since 1943 providing credit and inputs to small farmers. CAH comprised only 1 percent of the country's assets.

The government also managed or participated in several other financial institutions. The most important were those that financed and mobilized savings for mortgages. Of these, the two major groups were the National System of Savings and Loans for Housing (Sistema Nacional de Ahorro y Préstamo para la Vivienda—SNAPV) and the Paraguayan Institute for Housing and Urban Development (Instituto Paraguayo de Urbanización y Vivienda—IPVU). The SNAPV was affiliated with private savings and loans, which together formed the National Bank of Savings and Loans for Housing (Banco Nacional de Ahorro y Préstamo para la Vivienda). With 4 percent of the country's assets, SNAPV served as a major issuer of mortgages. The IPVU, which contained only 1 percent of assets, fell under the umbrella of SNAPV activities and specialized in credit for low-income housing and urban development. The government also oversaw five public-sector entities that functioned as contributory social security agencies. These entities generally operated under the Social Insurance Institute (Instituto de Previsión Social—IPS), which provided health plans, workers' compensation, and unemployment insurance through a worker and employer contributory system.

Tourism

Tourism played a minor but expanding role in the economy in the 1980s. In 1986 the industry generated foreign-exchange earnings in excess of US$100 million. Most tourists came from neighboring Brazil and Argentina and stayed an average of three days. Tourist arrivals tripled from 1970 to 1986, although the number of tourists tended to reflect fluctuations of the value of the guaraní vis-à-vis other currencies in the region. Many tourists did not visit Paraguay for traditional sightseeing but rather to purchase the cheap consumer goods that constantly flooded Paraguay's contraband markets, especially along the Brazilian border.

Transportation

Inadequate physical infrastructure, which had been responsible for the economy's slow development, persisted in the late 1980s. Landlocked and underpopulated, Paraguay was often dependent on river systems as the principal means of transportation. In the 1980s, the country also enjoyed a rapidly growing road system and trucking industry. In the 1970s, Paraguay broke its long-time dependence on Argentina for access to the Atlantic Ocean when a major road system was completed, connecting the eastern border region with the Brazilian ports of Santos and Paranaguá. Along with new roads, the number of traffic lights in the capital increased, going from one in the early 1980s to over a dozen late in the decade.

Ports and Rivers

To reach Paraguay's major cities from the Atlantic Ocean, vessels must pass through nearly 1,500 kilometers of Argentine territory. Paraguay's river systems also connect the country with Bolivia and the Pacific Ocean as well as with Brazil, its largest trading partner. From the late 1880s, river transportation in Paraguay was dominated by Argentine and Brazilian shipping companies.

The Río Paraná and Río Paraguay are the country's two main waterways (see fig. 3). The Río Paraguay, with headwaters at Mato Grosso, Brazil, flows southward, converging with the Paraná in southwestern Paraguay, and then flowing to the Río de la Plata Estuary, the entrance for the great majority of ships servicing Paraguay's ports. Vessels over 5,000 tons can travel upriver only as far as Asunción during the high-water period (March to October). The Río Paraná, 4,500 kilometers in length, is one of the world's major rivers and the primary mode of transportation along Paraguay's eastern and southern borders. Also flowing southward, the Paraná throughout the 1980s was only navigable for most ships up to the port of Encarnación. The construction of the Yacyretá hydroelectric plant, however, was expected to raise the water levels at Encarnación, allowing ocean-going vessels to venture as far north as Puerto Presidente Stroessner.

As a result of the rapid growth in road construction since the 1970s, the transportation role of smaller rivers was declining, especially in terms of international trade. Still, these river systems comprised over 3,000 kilometers of inland waterways.

The port of Asunción was the nation's only truly modern port and handled most of the country's imports and exports (see fig. 7). Asunción sported modern berthing facilities and advanced cargo-handling equipment. Originally privately owned, the port was purchased by the government in 1940 and was managed by the Ministry of Public Works and Communications through the National Port Authority. In the 1980s, the government was striving to expand and upgrade the port's highly congested facilities. Because of congestion at Asunción, the government also was planning to build a new port thirty-seven kilometers south of the capital at Villeta. Asunción's future role as a port would be primarily to receive imports. In the late 1980s, Villeta already was handling a greater share of the country's agricultural and industrial exports. The fastest growing hub of commercial activity, however, was located at the port city of Puerto Presidente Stroessner, where Paraguay was connected with Brazil by the spectacular single-span Friendship Bridge. This growing city was also the site of the country's new international airport and generally served as the major way station for contraband trade. The country's other ports were generally small and less modern than Asunción; they included San Antonio, Encarnación, Concepción, Casado, Villa Elisa, Bahía Negra, Sajonía, Calera Cué, and Vallemí.

The government's Merchant Marine (Flota Mercante del Estado—Flomeres) handled approximately 25 percent of the country's annual cargo level. Although many of the country's ships were outdated, in the 1980s Flomeres purchased more modern ships from Japan through government financing from that nation. Paraguay also had a private-sector fleet of merchant ships and numerous small shipping enterprises. Argentine, Brazilian, Dutch, British, and American companies provided the balance of shipping services.

Roads and Vehicles

The lack of an adequate road system was one of the largest structural obstacles to more rapid and more evenly distributed development in the 1980s. As in the economy at large, Paraguay had made great strides in highway construction, increasing the road network from fewer than 1,000 kilometers after World War II to more than 15,000 kilometers in the late 1980s. Road construction, primarily the task of the Ministry of Public Works and Communications, increased steadily in the 1970s, representing about 25 percent of public-sector investment in that decade. But Paraguay still lacked an adequate network of paved roads. In the late 1980s, only 20 percent of the country's roads were paved, and the remaining 80 percent were mostly dirt roads, easily flooded and often impassible during inclement weather. Only three paved highways extended well into the interior from the capital.

In the 1980s, the completion of two major highway construction projects facilitated travel from Asunción to Argentina and Brazil. The other major thoroughfare in the country was the 700-kilometer Trans-Chaco Highway, one of the government's principal attempts to develop the Chaco region. Construction progressed slowly, however, and in the late 1980s only about half of the road had been paved. Most vehicles could not complete the trek to the Upper Chaco. The government was also building feeder roads to allow the transport of agricultural goods. Feeder road construction was very slow in many areas, and private agribusinesses sometimes built their own roads.

The number of registered vehicles quadrupled from 1975 to 1985 as a result of the growing road network, the strong performance of agriculture, and general economic growth. There were roughly 40,000 automobiles registered in Paraguay in the late 1980s, one-sixth of which ran on "alco-nafta," an ethanol-enhanced fuel. Other vehicles included 2,000 taxis, 3,000 buses, and more than 20,000 each of trucks, pickups, and motorcycles. Public transportation, including buses and streetcars, was widely used in Asunción, but service was limited in rural areas, especially in the Chaco. New bus terminals were built in the 1980s and bus routes expanded, particularly to accommodate the increased demand by bus-driven tourists. The trucking industry played an expanding role in the country's transportation. According to Paraguay's Chamber of Exporters, by 1982 about 62 percent of registered exports left the country on the road system, mostly by truck.

Rail System

Since 1965 the Paraguayan railroad has played a declining role in domestic transportation. One of South America's oldest rail systems, the President Carlos Antonio López Rail Line, was started in 1854. Swapped back and forth by the state and private companies several times, the railroad was nationalized in 1961. Offering twice-weekly service between Asunción and Encarnación, the 367-kilometer rail system was outdated, wood-powered, slow, and generally costly even with government subsidies. The amount of cargo carried on the railroad declined swiftly in the 1970s and 1980s as alternative roads and waterways became more efficient, but some agricultural goods did move by train. In Encarnación, the Paraguayan railroad system connected via ferry with the Argentine city of Posadas, which was connected by rail to Buenos Aires and the Uruguayan railroad. There also was a small ''soybean railroad'' near the Brazilian border. In the 1980s considerable debate revolved around the possibility of an electric urban transport system in Asunción or the electrification of the national railroad, drawing on the country's large installed electrical capacity.

Air Service

Air transport, like the country's road system, was still inadequate in the late 1980s but had grown considerably over the previous two decades. Estimates of the country's total number of airports were as high as 700. There were, however, only 400 registered airports, virtually all of which used dirt or grass runways. Few airports were used commercially and on a regular basis. The airports of several medium-sized cities, such as Concepción, Filadelfia, Encarnación, and Pilar, needed improved paving and lighting for runways.

In the late 1980s, Paraguay's only all-weather airports were at Asunción—which handled all international flights—and Mariscal Estigarribia. In April 1987, construction began on a second all-weather, international airport at Puerto Presidente Stroessner. Construction of the airport was undertaken by a Spanish firm using Japanese equipment and financing. The high cost of the project—upwards of US$100 million—and the prominent role of Japanese consultants and equipment stirred controversy.

Paraguay was one of the last countries in the Western Hemisphere to establish commercial air service. The first service was offered in 1929 by an Argentine firm, and not until 1938 was regular air service available. The country's international flag carrier was Paraguayan Airlines (Líneas Aéreas Paraguayas—LAP). Government owned and under the administrative control of the air force, LAP carried approximately 70 percent of the country's air passengers in the late 1980s. The air force's Military Air Transport (Transporte Aéreo Militar) and the National Transport Airlines (Líneas Aéreas de Transporte Nacional) offered domestic service. Numerous foreign carriers also serviced the country: Braniff, Eastern, Varig (Brazil), Iberia (Spain), Aerolíneas Argentinas, LAN-Chile, and Bolivian Airlines being among them.

A trolley in Asunción
Courtesy Tim Merrill

Communications

Although Paraguay was the first nation on the South American continent to enjoy telegraph services, its communications system developed slowly. In the 1980s, only one in forty-nine Paraguayans owned a television, one in twenty a radio, and one in fifty-two a telephone. In each category, Paraguay ranked last in South America, well behind lesser developed countries such as Bolivia and Guyana.

Telephone services were solely owned by the state's National Telecommunications Company (Administración Nacional de Telecomunicaciones—Antelco). Domestic telephone service was outdated and sometimes unreliable. Consumers typically waited six months to have service installed and were charged a very high price. Long-distance service was available from most major cities and was generally more dependable than local service because it used a microwave and satellite transmission system. Telex services also were available through Antelco. Communication services in the Chaco remained very deficient in the 1980s.

External Sector

External Trade

In the 1980s, Paraguay was a rather open economy, in which foreign trade played a large role. Registered imports as a percentage of GDP in 1986 were approximately 28 percent; when unregistered imports were included, however, that figure exceeded 50 percent, showing the Paraguayan economy to be very open. With the exception of the Francia regime, international trade had been an important component of economic activity in Paraguay since independence. In the 1980s, the composition of trade was essentially the same as it had been for decades: raw and semiprocessed agricultural exports and imported fuels, capital goods, and manufactured items. Paraguay's dependence on just a few exports, mostly soybeans and cotton, made its export base sensitive to weather conditions and international commodity prices. As a result of low prices for agricultural exports, poor weather conditions, and an overvalued exchange rate, which reduced the international competitiveness of the nation's exports, Paraguay experienced unprecedented trade deficits in the 1980s. A sharp rise in imports—the legacy of the boom years of the 1970s—also exacerbated chronic trade deficits that persisted in the late 1980s.

Import data varied widely, and economists viewed the statistics cautiously, more as a general barometer than a specific indicator. In 1986 official imports were estimated at US$518 million. Unregistered imports in the same year were believed to have reached US$380 million, or 42 percent of total imports. Unregistered trade figures were generally calculated by comparing Paraguay's official trade data with those of its major trading partners. Computing the total trade deficit, including estimates for unregistered imports and exports, the country's trade deficit stood at an unprecedented US$527 million in 1986 (see table 7, Appendix). Some 62 percent of all imports were manufactured goods, and 38 percent were primary commodities. Manufactured products, capital goods, and fuels accounted for 81 percent of all imports. Food, metals, minerals, and other raw materials made up the balance.

Government import policies were liberal, characterized by low tariffs and by import taxes on luxury consumer goods, a significant source of government revenues. Special import exemptions were extended to certain industries, such as those established under Law 550 (see Manufacturing, this ch.). The government's import policies favored import-substitution strategies only where feasible and favored capital imports to accelerate the capitalization of the private sector.

Despite the industrial nature of the country's import basket, most imports originated from developing countries. Developing countries contributed approximately 48 percent of imports, followed by industrial countries, with 38 percent, and undisclosed countries, with 14 percent. Registered Brazilian exports, 28 percent of the market, were more than double those of any other nation exporting to Paraguay. Considering the brisk smuggling activity along the border, Brazil was clearly the main economic force influencing Paraguay. Other major importers, in order of importance, were the United States, Argentina, Algeria, Japan, Britain, and West Germany. Algerian crude oil was sometimes bartered for the country's agricultural exports.

One of the greatest challenges that Paraguay faced in the late 1980s was controlling its domestic consumption. Imports had swelled in the 1970s at a time when unprecedented exports and capital inflows offset the negative consequences of high import levels. These fortunate circumstances were not present in the subsequent decade.

Export data also varied and were generally less credible than import data. Estimates of registered exports in 1986 stood at US$233 million, but when adjusted for unregistered exports that figure reached US$371 million. The percentage of illicit exports fluctuated greatly in the 1980s. Analysts believed that illegal exports represented 37 percent of total exports in 1986, but that they had made up as much as 89 percent of total exports in 1981.

The structure of Paraguay's export basket displayed one of the hemisphere's highest concentrations on a few cash crops. Although Paraguay's exports were historically all agricultural, they had included a variety of products, including beef, timber, cash crops, and processed agricultural goods. That pattern changed in the early 1970s, however, as the price of soybeans and cotton soared (see Crops, this ch.). The percentage of total exports attributed to cotton and soybeans rose from 1 percent in 1960 to 6 percent in 1970, 60 percent in 1981, and 63 percent in 1987. Beef, wood, quebracho, and oilseeds represented a decreasing percentage of exports. The fragility of the export structure was apparent in the 1980s, as poor weather conditions and prices greatly hindered the pace of export expansion and economic growth.

In contrast to the concentration of products exported, Paraguay maintained well diversified export markets. Unlike most Latin American economies, Paraguay exported extensively to European markets and only marginally to the United States. Trade with Latin America was also vibrant. Some 55 percent of all the nation's exports went to industrial countries, particularly members of the EEC. In the late 1980s, the Netherlands, purchaser of 22 percent of Paraguay's exports, became its number-one recipient of registered exports, mostly processed oils. Following the Netherlands among industrialized countries trading with Paraguay were

Paraguay: A Country Study

Switzerland (10 percent), West Germany (5 percent), Belgium and Luxembourg (5 percent), Spain (4 percent), and Italy (4 percent). The United States purchased only 3 percent of Paraguay's goods in 1986. Developing countries, all in the Western Hemisphere, received 26 percent of Paraguay's registered exports. Brazil received 15 percent, Argentina 9 percent, and Uruguay 2 percent. These figures, however, did not include contraband, which, if added, made Brazil the number-one market overall and Argentina probably the second. Other markets took 19 percent of exports. Although not recorded in government data, observers believed that in the mid-1980s Paraguay made limited sales of cotton and grain to the Soviet Union despite the fact that the countries did not maintain diplomatic relations.

Since the first National Economic Plan of 1965, the government's trade policy had explicitly promoted exports. The extraordinary growth in exports in the 1970s, and to a limited degree in the 1980s, however, was more the direct response of Paraguay's free-market economy to international price movements than the result of government policy. One of the reasons for Paraguay's declining level of exports after 1982, besides lower prices, was the government's exchange-rate policies. A five-tiered exchange rate system and generally overvalued guaraní generated less competitive exports and slowed their expansion. Export taxes and foreign-exchange taxes also discouraged exports, particularly registered exports. Another growing disincentive for certain exporters was the Central Bank's Aforo system (see Monetary Policy, this ch.).

Balance of Payments and Debt

In 1982 Paraguay experienced its first balance-of-payments deficit in twelve years, which was followed by at least five years of consecutive deficits. Balance-of-payments deficits were the direct result of the mushrooming merchandise trade deficit and the decreased level of private capital investment, both the legacy of the 1970s, when large surpluses on the capital account more than made up for current-account deficits. The balance-of-payments situation became quite fragile in the late 1980s. Expectations of rectifying the country's international accounts centered around a reversal of the declining terms of trade, increased electricity exports, continued devaluations of the guaraní, and renewed capital inflows associated with Yacyretá.

Chronic deficits on the current account, primarily trade deficits, were the prime reason for the poor performance of the country's balance of payments. The nation's trade deficit grew from US$10 million in 1970 to US$57 million in 1975 and US$527 million in

Construction work on the Trans-Chaco Highway
Courtesy Inter-American Development Bank

1986. Over the same period, debits on the services portion of the
current account were negative but to a lesser extent. Growth in
tourism in particular served to lower the services deficit after 1982.
Net transfers played only a minimal role in the current account.

Large surpluses on the country's capital account offset current
account deficits until 1982, when exports and capital inflows began
to slow. Most capital inflows in the 1970s and 1980s were related
to Itaipú and later Yacyretá, and their special role earned them
separate entries on the balance of payments. Capital account surpluses in the 1970s and early 1980s increased Paraguay's international reserves to a high of US$781 million in 1981, or roughly
seven months of imports. The country's largest balance-of-payments
deficit occurred in 1982. This was financed from accumulated
reserves, as were the five years of deficits that followed. In 1986,
during the post-Itaipú recession period, reserves declined to US$377
million, the equivalent of less than four months of imports. Unlike
many Latin American countries in the 1980s, however, Paraguay
had amassed sufficient reserves in the 1970s to finance its balance-
of-payments deficits. Paraguay did not have to draw on IMF or
other external resources to weather its deficits.

Foreign direct investment in Paraguay in the 1970s and 1980s,
the source of capital account surpluses, was mostly in hydroelectric development, banking, and Law 550 companies. The most

153

striking feature of foreign investment was the growing dominance of Brazil, which represented one-fifth of all foreign investment and 72 percent of Latin American investment inParaguay. The Banco do Brasil became one of the country's leading creditors, financing 80 percent of Itaipú, 100 percent of the steel company Acepar, and considerable agribusiness investment in the eastern border region. West Germany followed Brazil and was particularly involved in banking and Yacyretá. The United States was the third largest foreign investor, with a portfolio of banking, petroleum exploration, and agribusiness. United States capital was dominant among Law 550 firms. Other major foreign investors included Argentina, Japan, France, and Italy.

Paraguay weathered the Latin American debt crisis of the 1970s rather well. As the fastest growing economy in Latin America for most of the 1970s, Paraguay prospered while many of its neighbors struggled. Paraguay's debt grew from under US$200 million in 1972 to US$842 million by 1980, but with rapid growth in GDP, debt as a percentage of GDP remained approximately 15 percent. Unlike many neighboring economies in the 1970s, which borrowed to compensate for balance-of-payments deficits or inefficient state-owned enterprises, Paraguay's minimal lending generally went toward productive investment in infrastructure, hydroelectricity, and agriculture. Because Brazil carried the overwhelming share of the debt burden of Itaipú, even that large investment did not greatly indebt the country. Furthermore, about 80 percent of Paraguay's debt was with official creditors, not commercial banks, allowing for greater flexibility and more favorable terms of loan repayment. Latin America as a region, by contrast, owed more than 70 percent of its debt to commercial banks in 1987.

Paraguay's debt, however, grew rapidly in the 1980s, at the second fastest rate in Latin America. From 1980 to 1987, the country's indebtedness more than doubled, to roughly US$2 billion. Because of Paraguay's slow economic growth during that period, debt as a percentage of GDP spiraled to above 50 percent. Over the same period, Paraguay's debt-service ratio—total debt-service payments as a percentage of exports of goods and services—swelled from 19 percent to 37 percent. Paraguay's rapidly growing debt in the 1980s mirrored that of its neighbors for the first time in the sense that loans were destined primarily to cover the capital and operating costs of state-owned enterprises. The central government and state-owned enterprises were responsible for almost equal shares of nearly 90 percent of the country's external debt in the 1980s. In 1986 the government was unable to make its payments on a debt to Banco do Brasil; rescheduling this debt blemished

Paraguay's previously untarnished credit rating. In the late 1980s, analysts expected Paraguay's national indebtedness to grow.

Foreign Assistance

Most of Paraguay's foreign assistance came in the form of concessional loans from multilateral development banks, particularly the World Bank and the IDB. These sources of assistance accounted for the high percentage of the country's debt with official creditors. From 1946 to 1982, the World Bank provided Paraguay US$1.3 billion, the IDB, US$409 million, and United Nations agencies, US$30 million. Paraguay received no money from the IMF in the 1980s. Multilateral bank lending went toward energy, agriculture, transportation, communications, public health education, rural electrification, and support activities, such as statistics gathering. In addition, the IDB also made loans to smaller projects benefiting low-income farmers and small-scale enterprises in Asunción's large informal sector.

The United States was traditionally the largest bilateral donor in Paraguay, but in the 1980s Japan and West Germany surpassed the United States in bilateral economic assistance. From 1946 to 1987, the United States provided US$212 million to Paraguay, 61 percent in the form of project-specific funding, 18 percent through the "Food for Peace" program, and 20 percent for other programs, including narcotics interdiction. The last year of major United States funding was 1981. From 1982 to 1987, United States assistance was under US$12 million. During the 1980s, AID classified Paraguay as an "advanced developing country" and offered that as one reason for its declining economic assistance. Other reasons were political (see Relations With The United States, ch. 4). Despite the dwindling financial support of AID, the United States maintained a large Peace Corps volunteer program. The Inter-American Foundation also remained active in Paraguay.

*   *   *

After decades of sparse research and publishing on the Paraguayan economy, in the 1980s there appeared unprecedented documentation of the rapidly changing economy. Most of the research and publication efforts inside Paraguay took place at the Paraguayan Center for Sociological Studies (Centro Paraguayo de Estudios Sociológicos). This institute published numerous valuable articles in its journal, *Revista paraguaya de sociología*. Outside the Center, the Central Bank published the most comprehensive data

through its Department of Economic Studies, including the *Boletín estadístico* (monthly) and *Cuentas nacionales* (annual).
One of the most encyclopedic studies on the Paraguayan economy in the 1980s was Guillermo F. Peroni and Martin Burt's *Paraguay: Laws and Economy*. Two more critical essays were Ricardo Rodríguez Silvero's *La deformación estructural: Reflexiones sobre el desarrollo socio-económico en el Paraguay contemporáneo* and Anibal Miranda's *Desarrollo y pobreza en Paraguay*. The most in-depth book concerning Itaipú was *Itaipú: Dependencia o desarrollo* by Ricardo Canese and Luis Alberto Mauro. As of 1988, there was no book published in the United States that examined in detail the Paraguayan economy of the 1970s and 1980s. Two of the best journal articles published in the United States were written by Werner Baer and Melissa Birch: "Expansion of the Economic Frontier: Paraguayan Growth in the 1970s" and "The International Economic Relations of a Small Country: The Case of Paraguay."
In general, data on the economy varied greatly, and no single source was definitive as of 1988. The most reliable data were produced by the IMF, the World Bank, the IDB, and the Economist Intelligence Unit. (For further information and complete citations, see Bibliography.)

Chapter 4. Government and Politics

Presidential offices at the Government Palace, Asunción

ON FEBRUARY 14, 1988, General Alfredo Stroessner Mattiauda was elected for his eighth consecutive term as president of the Republic of Paraguay. Stroessner, the candidate of the National Republican Association-Colorado Party (Asociación Nacional Republicana-Partido Colorado), officially won 88.7 percent of the vote. At the time of the election, the president was seventy-five and in his thirty-fourth year of rule. He had held power longer than any other Paraguayan and was five years ahead of Cuba's Fidel Castro Ruz for longevity in office in the hemisphere. Among contemporary international leaders, only Kim Il Sung of the Democratic People's Republic of Korea (North Korea) and Todor Zhivkov of Bulgaria had been in power longer. When Stroessner first took office in August 1954, Juan Domingo Perón was president of Argentina, Getúlio Dornelles Vargas was president of Brazil, and Dwight D. Eisenhower was president of the United States.

Stroessner's enduring power was based on the twin pillars of the armed forces and the Colorado Party. The former—from which he emerged and in which he maintained positions as commander in chief of the armed forces and commander in chief of the army—provided the institutional base for order and stability. The latter, of which he wrested control in the mid-1950s, furnished the links with large sectors of society, provided for mobilization and support, and allowed him to legitimate his rule through periodic elections. The overall system, based on these two institutional pillars, functioned through a combination of coercion and cooptation involving a relatively small sector of the population in the slightly industrialized and partly modernized country.

As Stroessner and the enduring small group of supporters around him aged, the regime was increasingly unable to respond to popular demands to begin a transition toward democracy, despite much speculation in the mid-1980s that change was in the air. The demands for change originated from a variety of sources, both foreign and domestic. As the neighboring republics of Argentina, Bolivia, Brazil, and Uruguay underwent political transitions from authoritarian to democratic regimes in the early 1980s, Paraguay was often considered with Chile, on the far side of the Andes, the only remaining analogous regime in South America. Pressure from these new democracies for a similar transition in Paraguay was low; however, in the 1980s the United States was clearly in favor of a political opening for a peaceful transition in the post-Stroessner era. Support for democracy with broad participation, as well as a pointed critique of the Stroessner regime's human rights policies, also were prominent in the speeches of Pope John Paul II during his visit to Paraguay in May 1988.

In addition to the external isolation and foreign pressure, there were important internal pressures for a transition. After very high rates of economic growth in the 1970s, Paraguay's economy stagnated in the 1980s. In addition, the external debt nearly doubled during the same period. Within Paraguay the major opposition political parties, which had formed a National Accord (Acuerdo Nacional) in 1979, began to promote public demonstrations in April 1986. This growing, heterogeneous movement was joined in its opposition by other organizations and movements, including the Roman Catholic Church and sectors of business, labor, and university students.

Despite these pressures, Stroessner was once again nominated by the Colorado Party for the 1988 election, although the nomination split the party into a number of competing factions. The state of siege declared by Stroessner in 1954 was finally lifted in April 1987, but opposition politicians and leaders of movements were arbitrarily arrested, meetings broken up, and demonstrations violently repressed. With the closing of the daily *ABC Color* in March 1984, the weekly *El Pueblo* in August 1987, and Radio Ñandutí in January 1987, of the independent media, only the Roman Catholic Church's Radio Cáritas and its weekly *Sendero* remained. Under these conditions, most opposition parties advocated abstention or blank voting in the elections. The church also registered its reservations on the validity of the elections by admitting the acceptability of blank voting.

Paraguay had had barely two years of democratic rule by law in its entire history. It lacked any tradition of constitutional government or liberal democracy to serve as a reference point. Traditionally, out-of-power groups had proclaimed their democratic commitment but repressed their opponents when they took over the reins of power. Thus, a transition to democracy for Paraguay would not mean a return to a previous status, as in the case of its neighbors, but rather the creation of democracy for the first time.

The Governmental System

Constitutional Development

The Republic of Paraguay is governed under the Constitution of 1967, which is the fifth constitution since independence from Spain in 1811. The Constitutional Governmental Regulations approved by Congress in October 1813 contained seventeen articles providing for government by two consuls, José Gaspar Rodríguez de Francia and Fulgencio Yegros. The framers also provided for a legislature of 1,000 representatives. Recognizing the importance of the military in the embattled country, the framers gave each consul the rank of brigadier general and divided the armed forces and arsenals equally between them. Within ten years, however, both Yegros and the legislature had been eliminated, and Francia ruled until his death in 1840 (see El Supremo Dictador, ch. 1).

In 1841 Francia's successor, Carlos Antonio López, asked the legislature to revise the constitution. Three years later, a new constitution granted powers to López that were as broad as those under which Francia had governed. Congress could make and interpret the laws, but only the president could order that they be promulgated and enforced. The constitution placed no restrictions on the powers of the president beyond limiting his term of office to ten years. Despite this limitation, Congress subsequently named López dictator for life. He died in 1862 after twenty-one years of unchallenged rule (see Carlos Antonio López, ch. 1).

At the end of the disastrous War of the Triple Alliance (1865-70), a constituent assembly adopted a new constitution in November 1870, which, with amendments, remained in force for seventy years. The constitution was based on principles of popular sovereignty, separation of powers, and a bicameral legislature consisting of a Senate and a Chamber of Representatives. Although its tenor was more democratic than the two previous constitutions, extensive controls over the government and the society in general remained in the hands of the president.

In 1939 President José Félix Estigarribia responded to a political stalemate by dissolving Congress and declared himself absolute dictator. To dramatize his government's desire for change, he scrapped the constitution and promulgated a new one in July 1940. This constitution reflected Estigarribia's concern for stability and power and thus provided for an extremely powerful state and president. The president, who was chosen in direct elections for a term of five years with reelection permitted for one additional term, could intervene in the economy, control the press, suppress private groups, suspend individual liberties, and take exceptional actions for the good of the state. The Senate was abolished and the Chamber of Representatives limited in power. A new advisory Council of State was created, modeled on the experience of corporatist Italy and Portugal, to represent group interests including

161

business, farmers, bankers, the military, and the Roman Catholic Church. The military was responsible for safeguarding the constitution.

After taking power in 1954, President Stroessner governed for the next thirteen years under the constitution of 1940. A constituent assembly convoked by Stroessner in 1967 maintained the overall framework of the constitution of 1940 and left intact the broad scope of executive power. Nevertheless, it reinstated the Senate and renamed the lower house the Chamber of Deputies. In addition, the assembly allowed the president to be reelected for another two terms beginning in 1968.

The Constitution of 1967 contains a preamble, 11 chapters with 231 articles, and a final chapter of transitory provisions. The first chapter contains eleven "fundamental statements" defining a wide variety of topics, including the political system (a unitary republic with a representative democratic government), the official languages (Spanish and Guaraní), and the official religion (Roman Catholicism). The next two chapters deal with territory, civil divisions, nationality, and citizenship. Chapter four contains a number of "general provisions," such as statements prohibiting the use of dictatorial powers, requiring public officials to act in accordance with the Constitution, and entrusting national defense and public order to the armed forces and police, respectively.

Chapter five, with seventy-nine articles, is by far the longest section of the Constitution and deals in considerable detail with the rights of the population. This chapter purportedly guarantees the population extensive liberty and freedom, without discrimination, before the law. In addition to the comprehensive individual rights, spelled out in thirty-three articles, there are sections covering social, economic, labor, and political rights. For example, Article 111 stipulates that "The suffrage is the right, duty, and public function of the voter. . . . Its exercise will be obligatory within the limits to be established by law, and nobody can advocate or recommend electoral abstention." The formation of political parties is also guaranteed, although parties advocating the destruction of the republican regime or the multiparty representative democratic system are not permitted. This chapter also specifies five obligations of citizens, including obedience to the Constitution and laws, defense of the country, and employment in legal activities.

Chapter six identifies agrarian reform as one of the fundamental factors for the achievement of rural well-being. It also calls for the adoption of equitable systems of land distribution and ownership. Colonization is projected as an official program involving not only citizens but also foreigners.

The Legislative Palace, site of meetings of the National Congress
Courtesy Tim Merrill

Chapters seven through ten concern the composition, selection, and functions of the legislature, executive, judiciary, and attorney general, respectively. Chapter eleven discusses provisions for amending or rewriting the Constitution. The final chapter contains transitory articles, the most important of which states that for purposes of eligibility and reeligibility of the president, account will be taken of only those terms that will be completed since the presidential term due to expire on August 15, 1968. The only constitutional amendment, that of March 25, 1977, modifies this article to allow the president to succeed himself without limit.

The Executive

The Constitution of 1967 states that government is exercised by the three branches in a system of division of powers, balance, and interdependence. Nonetheless, in the late 1980s the executive completely overshadowed the other two, as had historically been the case in Paraguay. The president's extensive powers are defined in Article 180. He is commander in chief of the armed forces and officially commissions officers up to and including the rank of lieutenant colonel or its equivalent and, with the approval of the Senate, the higher ranks. The president appoints, also with the Senate's consent, ambassadors and other officials posted abroad and members of the Supreme Court. Judges at other levels also are named by the president following the Supreme Court's approval. The president selects the attorney general after consulting the Council of State and with the approval of the Senate. The president also

163

appoints lower level public officials, including the rector of the National University, the heads of the Central Bank and the National Development Bank, and the members of the Rural Welfare Institute (Instituto de Bienestar Rural—IBR) and the National Economic Council. The Constitution has no provision for impeachment by the National Congress of either the president or his ministers.

Only the president can appoint and remove cabinet ministers and define functions of the ministries that they head. The Constitution does not limit the maximum number of ministries but stipulates that there must be at least five. In 1988 there were ten ministries. These were—ranked according to total expenditures for 1987—national defense; education and worship; interior; public health and social welfare; public works and communications; agriculture and livestock; finance; foreign relations; justice and labor; and industry and commerce.

The president also names the members of the Council of State, the nature of which is defined under Articles 188 through 192 of the Constitution. The Council of State is composed of the cabinet ministers, the archbishop of Asunción, the rector of the National University, the president of the Central Bank, one senior retired officer from each of the three services of the armed forces, two members representing agricultural activities, and one member each from industry, commerce, and labor. The last five members are selected from within their respective organizations and their names submitted to the president for consideration. All are appointed and removed by the president. The Council meets periodically during the three months that the National Congress is in recess and can meet at other times should the president so request. Its function is to render opinions on topics submitted by the president, including proposed decree laws, matters of international politics or of an economic or financial nature, and the merits of candidates proposed for the position of attorney general. Nonetheless, the Council is generally not consulted on important policy decisions.

In addition to the powers already stipulated, the president has the right to declare a state of siege as defined in articles 79 and 181. The state of siege provision, which was also part of the constitution of 1940, empowers the president to abrogate constitutional rights and guarantees, including habeas corpus, in times of internal or external crises. Within five days of a state of siege, the president must inform the National Congress of the reasons for it, the rights that are being restricted, and its territorial scope, which may include the whole country or only a part. Article 79 stipulates that the state of siege can be only for a limited period. Nonetheless, when Stroessner came into power in 1954, he declared a state of siege and had it renewed every three months for the interior of the country until 1970 and for Asunción until 1987.

The National Congress also granted Stroessner complete discretion over internal order and the political process through supplemental legislation, including the Law for the Defense of Democracy of October 17, 1955, and Law 209, "In Defense of Public Peace and Liberty of Person," of September 18, 1970. The latter, formulated in response to perceived guerrilla threats, significantly strengthens the executive's hand in dealing with political challenges (see Security and Political Offenses, ch. 5).

In addition to the powers derived from the Constitution, the president also has the right of ecclesiastical patronage. Under the terms of a concordat with the Vatican, the state is expected to maintain the property of the Roman Catholic Church and support the clergy, in return for which the president nominates candidates for all clerical offices, including parish priests. Although the president's nominations are not strictly binding on the Holy See, historically there has been little tendency to ignore his preferences.

In order to be eligible for the presidency, an individual must be a native Paraguayan, at least forty years of age, Roman Catholic, and characterized by moral and intellectual features qualifying him for the position. The president is chosen for a five-year term in direct general elections that must be held at least six months before the expiration date of the incumbent's term. The term of office begins on August 15, with the first term having begun in 1968. There is no provision for a vice president. In the event of the president's death, resignation, or disability, Article 179 provides for convocation of the National Congress and Council of State within twenty-four hours to designate a provisional president. If at least two years of the term have elapsed, the provisional president serves out the full term of five years. If fewer than two years have elapsed, elections are to be held within three months, and the successful candidate is to complete the five-year term of office.

The Legislature

The National Congress is a bicameral legislature, consisting of a popularly elected Senate and Chamber of Deputies. The Constitution stipulates that the Senate have at least thirty members and the Chamber of Deputies sixty, plus alternates. In the 1988 general elections, thirty-six senators and twenty-one alternates were elected as well as seventy-two deputies and forty-two alternates. The alternates serve in the place of the senators or deputies in the case of death, resignation, or temporary disability. The two houses meet in regular sessions every year from April 1 to December 20.

Special sessions may be convened outside this period by the president, who may also extend the regular sessions. Members of both houses must be native-born Paraguayans; whereas deputies need be only twenty-five years of age, senators must be at least forty. Members of the clergy and armed forces officers on active duty may not be elected to the National Congress. Also prohibited are those affiliated with a commercial enterprise that operates a public service or has obtained a concession from the government. Members of both houses are elected for five-year terms coinciding with terms served by the president. There is no restriction concerning reelection.

The functions of the National Congress are stipulated in the twenty-one items of Article 149 and include the following: the enactment, amendment, and repeal of laws; the establishment of political divisions of the country and municipal organizations; the authorization for contracting loans in connection with banking, currency, and exchange matters; the annual enactment of the national budget; the approval or rejection of treaties, conventions, and other international agreements; the granting of amnesty; the formulation of electoral laws; and the approval, modification, or refusal of decree laws. The Senate and Chamber of Deputies have different specific functions. The former deals primarily with the ratification of treaties and national defense, the approval of nominations to other organs, and, on the initiative of the Chamber, the judgment of members of the Supreme Court of Justice for possible removal from office. The Chamber is concerned primarily with fiscal or tax issues and bills concerning electoral and municipal matters.

The Constitution, in articles 168 through 170, provides for a Standing Committee of the National Congress. Before adjourning in December, the National Congress appoints from among its members six senators and twelve deputies to act until the following session as the Standing Committee. This committee elects its own officers and may conduct a valid session with the presence of a simple majority of its members. The Standing Committee has the power to ensure that the Constitution and its laws are observed; to receive the returns on the election of the president, senators, and deputies and pass them on to the National Congress; to convoke sessions to examine election returns on senators and deputies so that the National Congress may meet at the proper time; and to exercise any other powers assigned to it by the Constitution.

All bills submitted to the National Congress by the executive are discussed and acted upon in the same session, unless they have been returned because of lack of time to consider them. If the

Stroessner campaign posters, Asunción
Courtesy Tim Merrill

executive objects to a bill or part of a bill, it is returned to the chamber of origin, which studies the objections and states its judgment. When this action has been taken, the bill is sent to the other chamber for the same purpose. If both chambers uphold the original sanction by an absolute majority vote, the executive branch must promulgate it. If the two chambers disagree on the objections, however, the bill is not reconsidered in that session of the National Congress. Any bill completely rejected by the executive may be considered again at the same session of the National Congress only by an affirmative vote of a two-thirds majority of both chambers. In that case, the bill is reconsidered, and, if an absolute majority is obtained again in the two chambers, it is promulgated by the executive. If a bill that has been approved by one chamber is totally rejected by the other, it returns to the former for reconsideration. If the chamber of origin ratifies it by an absolute majority, it goes again to the chamber that reviews it, and that body can reject it again only by a two-thirds absolute majority. If such a majority has not been obtained, the bill is considered sanctioned. If the chamber that reviews a bill approved by the chamber of origin does not act upon it within three months, that chamber is considered to have given the bill a favorable vote, and it is forwarded to the executive to be promulgated.

In practice, the legislature is controlled tightly by the executive. The president sets the legislative agenda and provides most of the bills considered by the National Congress. When the National Congress passes one of the bills submitted by the executive, it does so in general terms as a broad grant of power, leaving it to the executive to "issue rules and instructions" for the law's application. In addition, an executive that encounters a hostile legislature can dissolve it by claiming a constitutional crisis. Although the president must call for new elections within three months, in the interim he can rule by decree. During the congressional recess, the executive also rules by decree, although the National Congress subsequently may review the president's actions. The president also may extend the congressional session or call an extraordinary session. In addition, the president's annual budget takes priority over all other legislation; it must be debated within one month, and it can be rejected only by an absolute majority of both houses.

In addition to constitutionally based limits on the National Congress, the legislature also was constrained by Stroessner's tight control of the ruling Colorado Party. Stroessner supervised personally the selection of the party's legislative candidates. Because the Colorado Party won a majority of votes in each of the five elections between 1968 and 1988, it received a two-thirds majority of congressional seats under the governing electoral law, thus ensuring a compliant legislature for Stroessner. Although opposition parties could use the National Congress as a forum to question and criticize Stroessner's policies, they were unable to affect the outcome of government decisions.

The Judiciary

Article 193 of the Constitution provides for a Supreme Court of Justice of no fewer than five members and for other tribunals and justices to be established by law. The Supreme Court supervises all other components of the judicial branch, which include appellate courts with three members each in the areas of criminal, civil, administrative, and commercial jurisdiction; courts of first instance in these same four areas; justices of the peace dealing with more minor issues; and military courts (see The Criminal Justice System, ch. 5). The Supreme Court hears disputes concerning jurisdiction and competence before it and has the power to declare unconstitutional any law or presidential act. As of 1988, however, the court had never declared invalid any of Stroessner's acts.

Supreme Court justices serve five-year terms of office concurrent with the president and the National Congress and may be reappointed. They must be native-born Paraguayans, at least thirty-five years of age, possess a university degree of Doctor of Laws, have recognized experience in legal matters, and have an excellent reputation for integrity.

Local Government

Paraguay is a centralized republic with nineteen departments, fourteen of which are east of the Río Paraguay and the remainder in the Chaco region (see fig. 1). The capital, Asunción, is located in the Central Department. The central government exerts complete control over local administration. The departments are headed by government delegates (*delegados de gobierno*) who are appointed by the president and report to the minister of interior. Their duties are concerned primarily with public order and internal security. The departments are divided into municipalities—the local government unit—of which there were 200 in 1988.

A municipality consisted of a town or village and the surrounding rural area. In order to qualify as a municipality, an area had to have a minimum population of 10,000 in 1988, a central town or village with a defined geographical area, and sufficient financial resources to pay for its municipal needs.

There is no separate town or city government apart from the municipality. The municipality is limited in jurisdiction; it has no control over education, police, and social welfare matters or over public health except for urban sanitation. Each municipality has a presidentially appointed mayor (*intendente*) who acts as executive agent of the municipality. In addition, each municipality has a board (*junta municipal*) elected by local residents for a five-year term of office. A rural municipality is supervised by a local company police sergeant (*sargento de compañía*) who reports both to the government delegate and the minister of interior.

The Electoral System

Regulations pertaining to the electoral system, voting, and political parties were found in the Electoral Statute, Law No. 886 of December 11, 1981. The statute's 21 chapters and 204 articles provided minute detail on virtually all aspects concerning elections. Article 1 stipulated that "the suffrage is the right, duty, and public function of the elector. Its exercise is elaborated according to this Law." Article 8 specified that the political party obtaining a majority of votes would receive two-thirds of the seats in the Congress, with the remaining one-third divided proportionately among the minority parties. According to Article 20, a party must obtain 10,000 signatures of citizens to be registered. Article 25 proscribed parties of communist ideology or those that sought to overthrow the regime and its principles. Article 26 prohibited subordination to or alliance of parties with parties in other countries, whereas Article 27 banned parties and other political organizations from receiving external financial support. Article 49 made voting obligatory. Articles 158 and 159 defined the functions and composition, respectively, of the Central Electoral Board, the body responsible for implementing and interpreting the provisions of the Electoral Statute. As with the composition of the National Congress, the majority party held two-thirds of the seats of the Central Electoral Board.

Political Dynamics

In the late 1980s, Paraguay was an authoritarian regime under the personalistic control of Stroessner. Whereas Francia took the title of The Supreme Dictator (El Supremo Dictador), Carlos Antonio López The Most Excellent One (El Excelentísimo), and Francisco Solano López The Marshall (El Mariscal), Stroessner called himself The Continuer (El Continuador). Indeed, not only did Stroessner continue the authoritarian tradition of these three nineteenth-century dictators and the twentieth-century examples of Estigarribia and Higinio Morínigo, he also remained in office for more than three decades. Stroessner assumed power following a more open but highly unstable period in Paraguay's history.

The political instability of the immediate postwar period, culminating in the civil war in 1947, offered important lessons for most Paraguayans. As Riordan Roett and Amparo Menéndez-Carrión put it: "Paraguayans have thus learned to equate open politics with weakness and authoritarian politics with strength." The personalistic nature of Stroessner's regime, which is known as the Stronato, is evident in the names of the capital's airport (President Alfredo Stroessner International Airport), the second largest city (Puerto Presidente Stroessner), and in a prominent neon sign on top of a building in the central square of Asunción that flashes: "Peace, Work, Well-being with Stroessner." Stroessner's enduring, active, and highly involved control completely determined the workings of the structure of government. Not only does the Constitution of 1967 grant the president extensive powers in relationship to the other institutions, but the powers of the central government far outweigh those of other levels. Furthermore, Stroessner personally picked all important civilian and military personnel.

Despite the authoritarian nature of his rule, Stroessner argued in his speeches that the country had a functioning democracy, pointing with pride to the multiparty character of the legislature and the constitutional requirement of separation of powers. At the same time, however, Stroessner insisted on an "authentically Paraguayan democracy." Such a democracy required, in Stroessner's view, a strong government in order to ensure the state of law. Paraguayan democracy also meant freedom and security without anarchy and terrorism.

The Twin Pillars of the Stroessner Regime

Although the Colorado Party emerged triumphant from the civil war of 1947, an ongoing struggle among its factions hindered governmental continuity. Between 1948 and 1954, six persons occupied the presidency. Stroessner, who had become commander in chief of the armed forces, was an active participant in the political intrigue of that era and eventually led his troops in a successful coup in May 1954 against President Federico Chaves. Two months later, Stroessner was selected as a compromise candidate by the Colorados, who considered his presidency only a temporary interlude, and he ran in elections from which other parties were excluded. Relying on his control of the armed forces, and with considerable shrewdness and the constant work for which he was famous, Stroessner gained control over the factions of the Colorados and subordinated the party to his interests. By 1967 all within the party had become supporters of Stroessner (see Consolidation of the Stroessner Regime, ch. 1). In addition to the control of the government itself, the major institutional bases of his rule, and thus of the Paraguayan political system, were the armed forces— including the national police, a paramilitary force that was under the jurisdiction of the Ministry of Interior but was headed by army officers—and the Colorado Party.

The Armed Forces

Historically in Paraguay, as in virtually all Latin American republics, no president has been able to remain in power without the support of the armed forces. Between 1936 and 1954, the army was the instrument for every change of government. Stroessner brought the armed forces under control, thereby reinforcing his rule; yet he also skillfully counterbalanced the armed forces with the Colorado Party.

In the late 1980s, the armed forces and the Roman Catholic Church were the only national institutions that had maintained continuity since independence. Because of the violent upheavals that characterized its history, Paraguay had the most uncompromisingly martial history of any country in Latin America. It resisted the Triple Alliance of Argentina, Brazil, and Uruguay for almost five years and collapsed only when more than one-half of its total population and almost all of its men had been killed (see The War of the Triple Alliance, ch. 1). During the 1932–35 Chaco War, Paraguay took on a country having three times its human resources and many times its economic resources. Paraguay won a resounding military victory but at the cost of 8 percent of its total male population and subsequent economic ruin (see The Chaco War and the February Revolution, ch. 1; The History and Development of the Armed Forces, ch. 5). This violent history hindered the development of a genuine aristocracy, thus allowing the officer corps to emerge as a social and, to a large extent, an economic elite.

In addition to his constitutional role as commander in chief of the armed forces, Stroessner retained his position as commander in chief of the army. A professional soldier recognized for outstanding service during the Chaco War, Stroessner took his duties as armed forces commander particularly seriously. He devoted one day a week exclusively to military matters at the headquarters of the general staff and made frequent visits to military commands throughout the country. Stroessner personally determined all promotions and transfers, from lieutenant to chief of staff. His long and intense involvement with the armed forces, combined with the small size of the country and the armed forces, made it possible for him to know intimately the officer corps.

Stroessner's control was also enhanced by the senior structure of the armed forces. The chief of staff, an army general, formally commanded all the troops in the name of the president and was directly subordinate to Stroessner. In fact, the chief of staff's position was actually that of a liaison officer. The minister of national defense was not in the direct chain of command and dealt mainly with administrative matters, including budgets, supplies, and the military tribunals (see The Armed Forces in the National Life, ch. 5).

Through his domination over the appointment and budgetary processes of the armed forces, Stroessner sought to prevent the emergence of an independent profile within the military. Public pronouncements of the armed forces were generally limited to pledges of unwavering support for the president and commitments to fight international communism. High-ranking officers did express their concerns regarding the divisions that emerged within the Colorado Party in the mid-1980s over the issue of presidential succession; nevertheless, these officers all called on Stroessner to seek another term in 1988.

Adrian J. English, an expert on Latin American militaries, concluded that the organization of the Paraguayan army appeared to be based more on political than military considerations. Stroessner ensured the loyalty of the officer corps by offering them well-paid positions and extensive benefits, such as family allowances, health care, pensions, and loans. Many officers also acquired wealth through control of state enterprises, such as public utilities, ports, transportation, meat packing, and alcohol distribution. Substantial information also linked elements in the military to smuggling and drug trafficking (see Relations with The United States, this ch.).

The Colorado Party

Two conflicting political movements—the Colorado Party and the Liberal Party (Partido Liberal—PL)—emerged following the departure of Argentine and Brazilian forces in 1876 (see Liberals Versus Colorados, ch. 1). The Colorados dominated politics between 1876 and 1904, whereas the Liberals governed between 1904 and 1940. Following the dictatorship of Morínigo and the resulting civil war, the divided Colorados returned to power in 1948.

Upon assuming office in 1954, Stroessner turned the Colorado Party into a key element of his rule. Unusual in the Latin American context, the party was a highly organized, omnipresent, and important instrument for the control of society and the functioning of government. The Colorado Party served the interests of the Stroessner regime in a number of ways. First, the party sponsored numerous rallies and demonstrations, thereby promoting identification of the population with the regime. Speakers at such rallies generally employed the language of nationalism, a particularly important theme in a small, landlocked country surrounded by more powerful neighbors. Second, the party mobilized electoral support for government-sponsored candidates. Third, the extensive party media, including the daily newspaper *Patria* and the radio program "La Voz del Coloradismo," promoted the government's view of national and international events. In addition, the party employed its ancillary organizations, which included professional associations, veterans' groups, women's federations, peasants' groups, cultural societies, and students' clubs, to maintain contact with virtually all sectors in the country.

The Colorado Party's control of jobs in the public and semipublic sectors, a particularly important situation in an underdeveloped country short of opportunities in the private sector, also enabled it to co-opt all potentially significant elements into the regime. Party membership was considered necessary for success. Civilian employees of the central and local governments, including teachers and workers in state hospitals, were recruited from within the ranks of the party, and party dues were deducted from their salaries. Officers in the armed forces also were obliged to join the party; indeed, admission to the officer corps was restricted to children of Colorados. In the late 1980s, the party claimed a membership of 1.4 million, or approximately 35 percent of the total population.

173

Colorado local committees (*seccionales*) were found in every community, dispensing jobs and favors to party members. These committees, of which there were 243 in 1988 (including 26 in Asunción), met at least once a week and had executive committees of 9 members and 6 alternates who served 3-year terms of office. The local committees, which also had more specialized units for laborers, peasants, youth, and women, served as the party base and collected intelligence. The party also had a rural militia, the *py nandí*, or "barefoot ones," which was estimated to number 15,000. The *py nandí* were especially active in the 1960s in pursuing guerrilla bands.

In theory, the highest body in the Colorado Party was the National Convention, which convened regularly every three years or could be convoked more frequently in the case of crises or to nominate slates for elections. The party was actually run, however, by the National Committee of the Colorado Party (Junta de Gobierno), which consisted of thirty-five members and sixteen alternates elected at the National Convention. The National Committee maintained contact with the party's ancillary organizations and supervised the local committees. The committee also elected its own executive consisting of a president, three vice presidents, and other officials. The National Committee president set the party's agenda, chaired executive meetings, presented the budget, called emergency sessions, and represented the party before the government or other organizations.

Given the importance of the Colorado Party in defending the Stroessner regime, the National Committee attempted to avoid at all costs the emergence of contested leadership lists in local committees. When such lists did appear in the mid-1980s, however, they ironically reflected cracks that had developed within the National Committee itself. The committee split into two main camps: militants (*militantes*) and traditionalists (*tradicionalistas*). Militants, also known as Stronistas, favored Stroessner's regime and wanted little or no change. They generally felt more loyalty to Stroessner personally than to the party. Their leaders included those who particularly benefited from the system and perceived it as good for themselves and the country. Traditionalists favored a transition to a less authoritarian regime. They believed Paraguay was moving toward a more open system and wanted the party to play a role in the process. Traditionalists stressed the original content of Colorado ideology and further emphasized democracy and social justice. Many of their leaders were from families who had played a major role in the party since the 1940s.

Both militants and traditionalists were subdivided into several factions. Militants broke into two camps: the orthodox (*ortodoxo*)

*A school in Limpio constructed by the
"Colorado government of President Stroessner"
Courtesy Inter-American Development Bank*

and institutionalists (*institucionalistas*). The orthodox favored having Stroessner remain in power until he died, after which his son, Air Force Lieutenant Colonel Gustavo Stroessner Mora, would succeed. The institutionalists were somewhat more pragmatic. One well-known advocate of this position, the minister of public health and social welfare, Adán Godoy Jiménez, proposed that Stroessner stay in power until he died or resigned, at which time a civillian or military figure with the same orientation would assume power.

Traditionalists were even more fragmented than were militants. The traditionalist group closest to the regime, at least prior to the rupture of 1987, was led by Juan Ramón Chaves, the octogenarian president of the party for twenty-five years and president of the Senate, who symbolized the link to the pre-Stroessner period. The ethicals (*éticos*) coalesced around National Committee member Carlos Romero Arza, the son of Tomás Romero Pereira, architect of the party's alliance with Stroessner in 1954. In a September 1985 speech, Romero Arza called attention to the lack of political ethics in the party. He denounced corruption and bad management, blaming opportunists who had joined the party during the Stroessner regime as a way to enrich themselves. Romero Arza urged a return to the traditional values that inspired previous Colorado governments and called for political dialogue between the party and the political opposition.

Two additional factions formed in 1987. One—the Movement for Colorado Integration (Movimiento de Integración Colorado—MIC), also called the Group of Thirty-four—was composed of long-standing Colorados who had retired from public life. Led by Edgar L. Ynsfrán, a former minister of interior, the MIC advocated a reassertion of the authority of the National Committee and a restructuring of the party to confront the opposition in a more open system. Another faction—the National and Popular Movement (Movimiento Nacional y Popular)—was led by congressman and Colorado intellectual Leandro Prieto Yegros and proposed to act as a bridge between the traditionalists and the militants.

Colorado Party factionalism broke into public prominence following elections in late 1984 for members of the National Committee. Mario Abdo Benítez, a militant and Stroessner's private secretary for twenty years, had expected to be elected the first vice president in recognition of his support of the Stronato. After Abdo Benítez was unexpectedly defeated at the National Convention, his followers carried on their fight at the local committee level. Conflicts became public in some towns, with rival groups of Colorados accusing each other of rigging the party elections and appealing for support from different members in the National Committee.

The conflict took a dramatic turn in early 1986 when the ethicals publicly opposed Stroessner's bid for yet another term of office and openly called for a civilian Colorado Party candidate in the 1988 elections. They were later joined by the MIC in this appeal. This action represented the first time since 1959 that an organized sector of the party openly opposed Stroessner. In April 1986, Stroessner acknowledged the divisions in the party and denounced the ethicals and the MIC as "deserters." In retaliation for the ethicals' stance, Stroessner fired Romero Arza from his position at the National Development Bank and forced him to resign from the Council of State. Those around him became politically isolated and had to stand on the sidelines at the regular National Convention in August 1987.

In May 1987, the militants presented their slate of four candidates for the presidency and three vice presidencies of the National Committee. The slate was headed by Sabino Augusto Montanaro, minister of interior since 1968, and also included Benítez, Godoy, and José Eugenio Jacquet, minister of justice and labor. In 1976 Montanaro had been excommunicated by the Roman Catholic Church for allowing the police to torture church workers who were involved in rural protests. Although the militants had captured control of a majority of the local committees and thus appeared headed for a solid victory at the National Convention, Montanaro decided to leave nothing to chance. A few hours before the convention was to begin, the police arrived at the building where it was to be held and restricted access to the militants and those from the National and Popular Movement, who by then had endorsed the militants' slate. Although Chaves, who was still the party's president and was the nominee of the traditionalists, declared the proceedings invalid, the militants went ahead with the convention and captured the four leadership posts and all other seats on the National Committee. Within two weeks, Stroessner had endorsed the militants' victory and claimed that it was a legitimate expression of the Colorado majority.

The militants' victory at the National Convention was repeated in November 1987, when the party held a nominating convention for the presidential and congressional election scheduled for February 1988. The 874 militant delegates unanimously chose Stroessner to be the Colorado Party standard-bearer and drew up a slate of congressional candidates that excluded traditionalists. These victories were achieved, however, at the cost of aggravated divisions in the party, itself a key component of the regime's infrastructure.

By mid-1988 Stroessner had given no indication of choosing a likely successor. Observers assumed that the party, in conjunction with the armed forces, would play a vital role in the succession process. Yet although Stroessner clearly supported the militant wing of the party, most observers believed that the militants lacked close contacts with the armed forces.

Opposition Parties

The existence of many factions within the Colorado Party did not indicate real pluralism but rather the fragmentation of an old political movement that had enjoyed both the benefits and the stresses of supporting a personalized authoritarian rule. By the same token, the existence of opposition political parties could not be considered evidence of true representative democracy.

Opposition parties faced formidable obstacles in attempting to challenge Colorado Party control. For example, the Colorado Party's virtual monopoly on positions and patronage made it difficult for other parties to obtain the necessary numbers of signatures for legal recognition. In addition, the Colorados held a two-thirds majority on the Central Electoral Board. At the same time, however, the government needed the political participation of at least some opposition parties in order to support the posture of democracy. The Constitution reserves one-third of the congressional seats for opposition parties, regardless of their share of the vote. Even so, most of the opposition did not participate in elections; indeed, only three opposition parties—the PL, the Radical Liberal Party (Partido Liberal Radical—PLR), and the Febrerista Revolutionary Party (Partido Revolucionario Febrerista—PRF)—had legal recognition in the late 1980s.

Between 1947 and 1962, the Colorado Party was the only legal party. With the consolidation of Stroessner's power and the prodding of the administration of United States president John F. Kennedy, however, in 1962 the general granted legal standing to a Liberal splinter group, the Renovation Movement (Movimiento Renovación). The Renovationists participated in the 1963 elections; as the president's loyal opposition, they began to enjoy some of the privileges formerly reserved only for the Colorados. In 1967, after two decades in exile, the PLR accepted Stroessner's offer of legal participation and returned to participate in elections. In 1976 the two Liberal factions unsuccessfully sought to form a single party; the Renovation Movement then changed its name to the Liberal Party. The other legal party, the PRF, was organized following Colonel Rafael Franco's overthrow of the Liberal Party in 1936. The PRF, more commonly known as the Febreristas, received legal recognition in 1965. The Febreristas affiliated with the Socialist International in 1965 and claimed to have 50,000 active members in 1986.

In the early 1970s, the Febreristas and the bulk of the PLR withdrew from elections following their refusal to endorse the constitutional amendment allowing Stroessner to stand for unlimited reelection. The breakaway faction of the PLR lost its legal status and renamed itself the Authentic Radical Liberal Party (Partido Liberal Radical Auténtico—PLRA). Thus, the PLR and the remaining wing of the PL were the only challenges to the Colorado Party in the elections of 1973, 1978, 1983, and 1988 (see table 8, Appendix). The PLR and PL thereby were entitled to occupy one-third of the seats in the National Congress, although their combined average vote in the elections was only 10 percent. Neither had the organization, finances, or human resources to oppose the Colorados effectively.

In addition to the PLRA, other nonlegal parties included the Christian Democratic Party (Partido Demócrata Cristiano—PDC) and the Colorado Popular Movement (Movimiento Popular Colorado—Mopoco). The PDC was founded in 1960. The government allowed the legalization of parties in the early 1960s but required new ones to have 10,000 members. Although the PDC lacked the necessary members, it claimed that it was exempt from

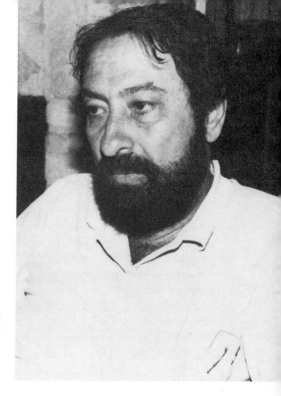

PLRA leader Domingo Laíno
Courtesy Richard S. Sacks

the new law because the party had already existed before the law was passed. The government rejected this argument, however, contending that the law was based on a 1959 decree law. The government's contention was upheld by the Supreme Court.

Mopoco was founded in 1959 by Colorados who had served in the administration of Federico Chaves, Stroessner's predecessor. The party leadership was forced into exile because of continued opposition to Stroessner and did not return to Paraguay until 1981 under an amnesty provision. The leaders discovered subsequently, however, that the amnesty did not truly reflect a change in government policy, as they became subject once again to harassment and imprisonment. In addition, because Mopoco was not a legally recognized political party, it could not communicate with the electorate.

In 1979 the Febreristas, PLRA, PDC, and Mopoco founded the National Accord. All claimed to be center left and reformist, and they were carefully and vocally anti-Marxist. The Accord's fourteen-point platform stressed the need for nonradical but basic reforms, including an end to the state of siege, freedom for political prisoners, amnesty for exiles, respect for human rights, elimination of repressive legislation, and a broadly representative government that would prepare society for free elections within two years. Specifically to further free elections, the Accord called for the abolition of the Electoral Statute. Despite government

179

attempts to destroy the momentum of the Accord by expelling PLRA leader Domingo Laíno in December 1982, the Accord held together.

The Accord benefited from the legal status of the Febreristas. As a legally recognized party, the Febreristas could hold meetings and rallies, offer an umbrella to the other members of the Accord, and publish—until 1987—a weekly newspaper, *El Pueblo.* Nonetheless, the police often used force to break up Accord rallies and arrest its leadership. The human rights organization Americas Watch charged that eighty-four Accord political activists had been arbitrarily arrested between early 1985 and March 1986. In addition, component parties of the Accord were often divided not only among themselves but also internally (see Political Developments Since 1986, this ch.). In July 1987, a new party, the Popular Democratic Movement (Movimiento Democrático Popular—MDP), was formed. The MDP strongly criticized the regime, oriented itself toward the lower classes, and offered a program to the left of the National Accord parties.

The Paraguayan Communist Party (Partido Comunista Paraguayo—PCP) was less significant than other opposition political parties, was excluded from the National Accord, and had been isolated historically from other parties, even in exile. It was proscribed by the 1955 Law for the Defense of Democracy, Law 209 of 1970, and the Electoral Statute. The tight control of the political environment and the presence of the Colorado Party local committees in even small communities virtually prohibited the radical left's penetration in Paraguay (see Security and Political Offenses, ch. 5).

Political Developments Since 1986

The splits in the Colorado Party in the 1980s and the conditions that led to this—Stroessner's age, the character of the regime, the economic downturn, and international isolation—provided an opportunity for demonstrations and statements by the opposition prior to the February 1988 general elections. In addition, the official attitude to human rights benefited somewhat as Stroessner attempted to improve his image abroad. In March 1986, for example, Stroessner met with an Americas Watch delegation, the first time he had ever received a human rights group. Two years earlier, another Americas Watch delegation had been arrested and expelled from the country upon arrival. The state of siege was also allowed to lapse in Asunción in April 1987.

The PLRA leader Laíno served as the focal point of the opposition in the second half of the 1980s. The government's effort to isolate Laíno by exiling him in 1982 had backfired. In fact, Laíno received considerable international attention during five unsuccessful attempts to return to Paraguay. On his fifth attempt, in June 1986, Laíno returned on a Uruguayan airliner with three television crews from the United States, a former United States ambassador to Paraguay, and a group of Uruguayan and Argentine congressmen. Despite the international contingent, the police violently barred Laíno's return. The police action dashed hopes that Stroessner's meeting three months earlier with the Americas Watch representatives presaged a substantial liberalization of government policy.

In response to increased pressure from the United States, however, the Stroessner regime relented in April 1987 and permitted Laíno to arrive in Asunción. Laíno took the lead in organizing demonstrations and diminishing somewhat the normal opposition party infighting. The opposition was unable to reach agreement on a common strategy regarding the elections, with some parties advocating abstention and others calling for blank voting. Nonetheless, the parties did cooperate in holding numerous lightning demonstrations (*mítines relámpagos*), especially in rural areas. Such demonstrations were held and disbanded quickly before the arrival of the police.

The elections of 1988 provided the opportunity for two organizational innovations. The first was the establishment of the MDP (see Opposition Parties, this ch.). In addition, the Accord groups, which now expanded to include the Colorado ethicals and some labor and student movements, organized a National Coordinating Committee for Free Elections to monitor the political situation, expose what they termed the "electoral sham," and encourage either abstention or blank voting.

Obviously stung by the upsurge in opposition activities, Stroessner condemned the Accord for advocating "sabotage of the general elections and disrespect of the law" and used the national police and civilian vigilantes of the Colorado Party to break up demonstrations. A number of opposition leaders were imprisoned or otherwise harassed. Hermes Rafael Saguier, another key leader of the PLRA, was imprisoned for four months in 1987 on charges of sedition. In early February 1988, police arrested 200 people attending a National Coordinating Committee meeting in Coronel Oviedo. Forty-eight hours before the elections, Laíno and several other National Accord members were placed under house arrest.

During the six weeks of legal campaigning before the elections, Stroessner addressed only three Colorado rallies. Despite limited campaign activities, the government reported that 88.7 percent of the vote went to Stroessner, 7.1 percent to PLR candidate Luis

María Vega, and 3.2 percent to PL candidate Carlos Ferreira Ibarra. The remaining 1 percent of ballots were blank or annulled. The government also reported that 92.6 percent of all eligible voters cast their ballots. The National Coordinating Committee rejected the government's figures, contending that abstention was as high as 50 percent in some areas. In addition, election monitors from twelve countries, including the United States, France, Spain, Brazil, and Argentina, reported extensive irregularities.

Shortly after the elections, researchers from the Catholic University of Our Lady of Asunción and the West German Friedrich Naumann Foundation released the findings of a public opinion poll that they had conducted several weeks earlier. The poll, which measured political attitudes of urban Paraguayans—defined as those living in towns with at least 2,500 residents—suggested that the Colorado Party had considerable support, although nowhere near the level of official election statistics. Asked for whom they would vote in an election involving the free participation of all parties and political movements, 43 percent named the Colorado Party; the PLRA, which finished second in the poll, was mentioned by only 13 percent of all respondents. (The two ''official'' opposition parties, the PLR and the PL, trailed badly with only 2.9 percent and 2.7 percent, respectively.) Stroessner's name also topped the list of those political leaders considered most capable of leading the country; indeed, after Laíno, who finished second in the list, Colorado traditionalists, militants, and ethicals captured the next five positions.

Although contending that these results reflected the Colorados' virtual monopoly of the mass media, opposition politicians also saw several encouraging developments. Some 53 percent of those polled indicated that there was an ''uneasiness'' in Paraguayan society. Furthermore, 74 percent believed that the political situation needed changes, including 45 percent who wanted a substantial or total change. Finally, 31 percent stated that they planned to abstain from voting in the February elections.

Relations between militants and traditionalists deteriorated seriously in the months following the elections. Although Chaves and his followers had not opposed Stroessner's reelection bid, Montanaro denounced them as ''legionnaires''—a reference to those Paraguayan expatriates who fought against Francisco Solano López and who were regarded as traitors by the original Colorados (see The Postwar Period, ch. 1). Prominent traditionalists, among them the head of the Central Electoral Board and the minister of foreign relations, lost their government positions. Luis María Argaña left his post as chief justice of the Supreme Court following the

The poster reads "Stroessner: Peace and Progress, 1988–1993"
Courtesy Richard S. Sacks

completion of his five-year term and was replaced by a militant. Argaña attempted to distance himself somewhat from his traditionalist colleagues by claiming that he had not authorized his name to appear on a traditionalist list prior to the August 1987 convention; nonetheless, most observers thought that he was the most likely candidate to succeed Chaves as head of the movement. By late 1988 the only major agencies still headed by traditionalists were the IBR and the National Cement Industry (Industria Nacional de Cemento). In September 1988, traditionalists responded to these attacks by accusing the militants of pursuing "a deceitful populism in order to distract attention from their inability to resolve the serious problems that afflict the nation." Traditionalists also called for an end to personalism and corruption.

The Colorado Party was not the only political group confronted by internal disputes in the late 1980s. The PLRA had two major currents; Laíno headed the Liberation for Social Change (Liberación para Cambio Social), whereas Miguel Abdón Saguier led the Popular Movement for Change (Movimiento Popular para el Cambio). Despite the efforts of PDC founder Luis Alfonso Resck, a bitter leadership struggle erupted within that party in late 1988. Finally, the PRF found itself in the middle of an acrimonious battle between the Socialist International and the Latin American Socialist Coordinating Body.

Interest Groups

The Roman Catholic Church

Social life in Paraguay had always been closely tied to religion, but politically the Roman Catholic Church traditionally had remained neutral and generally refrained from commenting on politics. In the late 1960s, however, the church began to distance itself from the Stroessner regime because of concerns over human rights abuses and the absence of social reform. The Auxiliary Bishop of Asunción, Aníbal Maricevich Fleitas, provided an early focus for criticism of the regime. With the growth of the Catholic University and the influx of Jesuits from Europe, especially Spain, the church had a forum and a vehicle for reform as well as a dynamic team of spokespeople. Some priests moved into the poor neighborhoods, and they, along with others in the rural areas, began to encourage the lower classes to exercise the political rights guaranteed in the Constitution. These priests and the growing Catholic Youth movement organized workers and peasants, created Christian Agrarian Leagues and a Christian Workers' Center, and publicized the plight of the Indians. As part of the program of education and awareness, the church founded a weekly news magazine, *Comunidad,* and a radio station that broadcast throughout the country.

In April 1968, the regime reacted against this criticism and mobilization by authorizing the police to invade the university, beat students, arrest professors, and expel four Jesuits from the country. Although the Paraguayan Bishops' Conference (Conferencia Episcopal Paraguaya—CEP) met and issued a blistering statement, the regime was not deterred from continuing its crackdown on the church. The Stroessner government arrested church activists, shut down *Comunidad,* disbanded Catholic Youth rallies, outlawed the Catholic Relief Service—the church agency that distributed assistance from the United States—and refused to accept Maricevich as successor when Archbishop Aníbal Mena Porta resigned in December 1969.

The following January, the government and church reached an agreement on the selection of Ismael Rolón Silvero as archbishop of Asunción. This resolution did not end the conflict, however, which resulted in continued imprisonment of university students, expulsions of Jesuits, and attacks on the Christian Agrarian Leagues, a Catholic preparatory school, and even the offices of the CEP. Rolón stated that he would not occupy the seat on the Council of State provided by the Constitution for the archbishop of Asunción until the regime restored basic liberties.

In the 1970s, the church, which was frequently under attack, attempted to strengthen itself from within. The church promoted the establishment of peasant cooperatives, sponsored a pastoral program among students in the Catholic University, and endorsed the creation of grassroots organizations known as Basic Christian Communities (Comunidades Eclesiásticas de Base—CEBs). By 1986 there were 400 CEBs consisting of 15,000 members. These organizational efforts, combined with dynamic regional efforts by the church symbolized in the Latin American Episcopal Conference (Conferencia Episcopal Latinoamericana—Celam) meeting in Puebla, Mexico, in 1979, resulted in a renewed commitment to social and political change. Following the Puebla conference, the Paraguayan Roman Catholic Church formally committed itself to a "preferential option for the poor," and that year the CEP published a pastoral letter, "The Moral Cleansing of the Nation," that attacked growing economic inequalities and the decline of moral standards in public life. In 1981 the CEP released a detailed plan for social action. Two years later, the bishops issued a pastoral letter denouncing increasing evictions of peasants.

By the early 1980s, the church had emerged as the most important opponent of the Stroessner regime. The CEP's weekly newspaper, *Sendero,* contained not only religious information but also political analysis and accounts of human rights abuses. The church's Radio Cáritas was the only independent radio station. Church buildings and equipment were made available to government opponents. In addition, the bishops joined with leaders of the Lutheran Church and Disciples of Christ Church to establish the Committee of the Churches. This committee became the most important group to report on human rights abuses, and it also provided legal services to those who had suffered such abuse.

Keeping an eye on the post-Stroessner political situation and concerned to bring about a peaceful democratic transition, the CEP began in 1983 to promote the idea of a national dialogue to include the Colorado Party, business, labor, and the opposition parties. This concept was endorsed by the National Accord, which demanded constitutional reforms designed to create an open, democratic, pluralist, and participatory society. The Colorado Party rejected the calls for dialogue, however, on the grounds that such action was already taking place in the formal structures of government at national and local levels.

In the late 1980s, the church was better able to respond in a united manner to criticism and repression by the regime than had been the case in the late 1960s and early 1970s. Five days after the suspension of the state of siege in Asunción in 1987, police broke up

185

a Holy Week procession of seminarians who were dramatizing the predicament of peasants who had no land. Rolón denounced this police action. In October 1987, the clergy and religious groups of Asunción issued a statement that condemned the preaching of hatred by the Colorado Party's radio program "La Voz del Coloradismo," demanded the dismantling of assault squads made up of Colorado civilians, and called for respect for civil rights and a national reconciliation. Later that month, the church organized a silent march to protest government policies. The march, which attracted between 15,000 and 30,000 participants, was the largest public protest ever staged against the regime and demonstrated the church's impressive mobilization capabilities.

Critical statements by the church increased with the approach of the 1988 general elections and with the government's continued refusal to participate in the national dialogue. In January 1988, the CEP issued a statement on the current situation, calling attention to the government's use of corruption, violence, and repression of autonomous social organizations. The bishops warned of increasing polarization and violence and indicated that blank voting in the upcoming elections was a legitimate political option, a position frequently denounced by Stroessner and the Colorado Party. The archbishopric of Asunción followed up in February by issuing a document rejecting the government's accusations of church involvement in politics and support for opposition parties. Immediately after the elections, Rolón granted an interview to the Argentine newspaper *Clarín*, in which he blamed the tense relations between church and regime on the government's use of violence. He criticized the government for its disregard of the Constitution, harassment of political opponents, and refusal to participate in the national dialogue, and he charged that the elections were farcical.

In the confrontational atmosphere after the elections, the visit by Pope John Paul II to Paraguay in May 1988 was extremely important. The government rejected the church's plans to include Concepción on the papal itinerary, claiming that the airport runway there was too short to accommodate the pope's plane. Maricevich, who now headed the diocese of Concepción, charged, however, that the city had been discriminated against throughout the Stroessner era as punishment for its role in opposing General Higinio Morínigo in the 1947 civil war. The pope's visit was almost cancelled at the last moment when the government tried to prevent John Paul from meeting with 3,000 people—including representatives from unrecognized political parties, labor, and community groups—dubbed the "builders of society." After the government agreed reluctantly to allow the meeting, the Pope arrived in

*Graffiti in Asunción: "Ten o'clock at the cathedral.
Enough of the repression. We demand liberty."
Courtesy Richard S. Sacks*

Asunción and was received by Stroessner. Whereas Stroessner spoke of the accomplishments of his government and the recent free elections, the Pope called for a wider participation in politics of all sectors and urged respect for human rights. Throughout his three-day trip, John Paul stressed human rights, democracy, and the right and duty of the church to be involved in society. His visit was seen by observers as supporting the Paraguayan Roman Catholic Church's promotion of a political transition, development of grassroots organizations, and defense of human rights.

Business

The business sector was a relatively weak interest group and generally supported the government. The local business community was quite small, reflecting both the country's low level of industrialization and the presence of many foreign-owned financial institutions and agro-processing firms. Although local businessmen traditionally supported the Liberal Party, the political and monetary stability of the Stronato appealed to business leaders and made them cooperate closely with the Colorado Party and the government. Furthermore, businesses that strongly supported the government accrued considerable financial benefits, whereas those who were uncooperative placed their businesses in jeopardy. In an effort to increase its influence over the business sector, the government encouraged the formation of associations of businessmen and industrialists. The two leading business associations—the Federation of Production, Industry, and Commerce (Federación de la Producción, la Industria, y el Comercio—Feprinco) and the Paraguayan Industrial Union (Unión Industrial Paraguaya—UIP)—each had seats on the Council of State. The Colorado Party also maintained relations with the business sector through its ancillary organizations.

The business sector began to define some independence from the government, however, following the country's economic slump in the early and mid-1980s and a perceived lack of government response to the problem. For example, Feprinco president Alirio Ugarte Díaz spoke out against the government's economic policies, asking for action in reviving the economy and eliminating corruption. Although neither the Feprinco nor the UIP participated in the national dialogue in 1987, both submitted requests to the government for major policy changes to reverse the economic slump.

Urban Labor

Labor has not been an organized, tightly knit, autonomous force in Paraguay. The firms have traditionally been small, workers were not politically active, and personal relationships between employers and employees prevailed. As in other Southern Cone (see Glossary) countries, the paternal state anticipated demands of a growing labor force, granted some benefits, and impeded the formation of strong labor organizations. When Stroessner came to power, most of organized labor belonged to the Paraguayan Confederation of Workers (Confederación Paraguaya de Trabajadores—CPT), an unstructured amalgam of trade unions. Despite its loose association with the Colorado Party, the CPT declared a general strike in 1958. Stroessner crushed the strike, dismissed the CPT leadership, and appointed a police officer as its head. Consistent with these actions, the government, and not the workers, continued to determine the confederation's leadership in the late 1980s.

The CPT remained the only legally recognized large labor organization; it contained 60,000 members and claimed to represent 90 percent of organized labor. The CPT's refusal to endorse strikes after 1959 reflected the government's dominance over it. In 1985 the CPT lost its membership in the International Labour Organisation (ILO) after an ILO delegation to Paraguay determined that the CPT was neither independent nor democratic. Nonetheless, the CPT's existence allowed the labor force some access to government officials.

The first attempt to reform the labor movement came in 1979 with the emergence of the Group of Nine trade unions. The group, which included bank workers, a sector of construction workers, and the outlawed journalists' union, unsuccessfully attempted to take control of the CPT in March 1981. Several unions of the group subsequently broke away from the CPT and in 1982 led a successful national boycott of Coca Cola in order to reinstate trade union members at the bottling plant. From this effort emerged the Inter-Union Workers Movement (Movimiento Intersindical de Trabajadores—MIT) in 1985. The MIT received recognition from both the International Confederation of Free Trade Unions and the Latin American Central Organization of Workers (Central Latinoamericana de Trabajadores—Clat), both of which sent representatives to express their support for the new movement. In the late 1980s, the MIT remained small, and its members were subject to harassment and imprisonment; nevertheless, it was still the only independent labor movement since Stroessner took power.

Rural Labor

For most of the Stronato, the government could rely on a supportive peasantry. Linked through the local committees of the Colorado Party, many peasants participated in the land colonization programs of the eastern border region that were sponsored by the government's IBR. Others bypassed the IBR altogether and participated independently in the settlement of the area (see Land Reform and Land Policy, ch. 3). In any event, the availability of land served to alleviate somewhat the frustration of peasants who were in a poor economic situation.

In the 1970s and early 1980s, a number of factors contributed to a dramatic reduction of land in the eastern border region. First, an estimated 300,000 to 350,000 Brazilians crossed into Paraguay in search of cheap land (see Immigrants, ch. 2). Second, many squatters were forced off their lands by new agribusinesses that were much more efficient than the previous operators of estates. In addition, the completion of the Itaipú hydroelectric project resulted in high unemployment of construction workers, many of whom were former peasants. As a result, an estimated 200,000 families lacked title to their land or had no land at all.

In about 1980, landless peasants began to occupy land illegally. Although some settlements were smashed by the government, others eventually received formal recognition by the IBR. A number of rural organizations also sprang up after 1980 to promote the interests of peasants. Although one of these organizations—the Coordinating Committees of Agricultural Producers (Comités de

Coordinación de Productores Agrícolas)—was sponsored by the government, its leaders sometimes assumed positions not in line with official policy. Associations of peasants sponsored by the Roman Catholic Church were formed to establish cooperatives and commercialize crop production. A variety of rural organizations loosely grouped themselves into the Paraguayan Peasant Movement (Movimiento Campesino Paraguayo—MCP) in 1980. The MCP included associations of peasants and landless workers as well as the Permanent Commission of Relatives of the Disappeared and Murdered, which dealt with victims of repression in the rural areas.

Although small, the MCP was quite successful in mobilizing the rural poor. For example, in July 1985, it brought together more than 5,000 landless peasants in Caaguazú, where they established the Permanent Assembly of Landless Peasants (Asamblea Permanente de Campesinos sin Tierra—APCT). Despite government harassment, the APCT claimed to be the nation's largest independent mass organization with a membership of 10,000 families. Its objectives were spelled out in a thirteen-point program advocating a radical transformation of society.

Students

In recent decades, public education has been tightly controlled by the government, and private educational institutions also had to conform. Public-sector educational personnel, from the minister of education and worship down to the primary-school teachers, had to belong to the Colorado Party. The Catholic University, although subject to pressure and even invasion by the police, enjoyed a somewhat more open environment for teaching and research than did the National University.

For most of the Stronato, students at the public and Catholic universities were represented by the government-sponsored University Federation of Paraguay (Federación Universitaria del Paraguay—FUP). In June 1985, however, several hundred law students demonstrated publicly in favor of freedom of the press and an end to corruption. Following the death of a law student, violent confrontations erupted with the police in April 1986. The student movement removed itself from the control of the National Committee of the Colorado Party, and the FUP was disbanded. In April 1987, a new organization, the Federation of University Students of Paraguay (Federación de Estudiantes Universitarios del Paraguay—FEUP) was formally launched at a meeting attended by 5,000 students. The FEUP participated in the national dialogue although the union was not legally recognized.

The Media

Although there was some improvement in the human rights situation in Paraguay in the late 1980s, the same cannot be said regarding the media. The Stroessner regime did not hesitate to silence newspapers and radio stations that became too independent and critical. The only media that remained critical and were allowed to function belonged to the Roman Catholic Church.

In 1988 there were five progovernment daily newspapers in Asunción: *El Diario de Noticias, Hoy, La Tarde, Última Hora, and Patria. Última Hora* demonstrated somewhat more independence from the regime than the other four. Weekly newspapers included one published by the Colorado Party, *Mayoría*, and another, more or less independent, *Nande,* which practiced self-censorship. There was one opposition weekly, *Sendero,* published by the Roman Catholic Church. It had a limited circulation and was often confiscated off the streets. In addition, Mario Medina, bishop of Benjamín Aceval, published a monthly journal, *Nuestro Tiempo,* that focused on land problems, human rights issues, and problems with freedom of the press. Because of government harassment, the journal was printed in Brazil. Consequently, getting it into Paraguay was difficult; the maximum circulation of 300 copies was either hand delivered or mailed in disguised envelopes.

In the early 1980s, *ABC Color* was the largest selling daily newspaper, having a circulation of 85,000. The newspaper was founded in 1967 by Aldo Zuccolillo—a wealthy businessman and confidant of Stroessner and others in his inner circle—and was originally supportive of the regime. The paper began to focus on polemical issues, however, including corruption among senior government officials and the negative aspects of the Treaty of Itaipú with Brazil, and included interviews with opposition politicians. Its circulation increased, and it became the most important source in Paraguay for independent information. In May 1983, *ABC Color's* offices were surrounded by troops, and Zuccolillo was arrested. Following further harassment, the newspaper was shut down in March 1984 by order of the minister of interior. Despite resolutions in the United States Congress, protests by the United States embassy in Asunción, and protest visits by the Inter-American Press Association, as of 1988 *ABC Color* remained closed.

In the late 1980s, there were two semi-official television stations and fifty-two radio stations, only three of which were independent. One of the latter was Radio Cáritas of the Roman Catholic Church. Until it was closed in January 1987, the most important independent station was Radio Ñandutí. The station's popular live phone-in

191

program frequently aired complaints about corruption and the lack of democracy. In July 1983, however, Radio Ñandutí's director, Humberto Rubín, was arrested several times; in April and May 1986, the station was attacked by Colorado vigilantes. After months of jamming and other harassment, Radio Ñandutí was finally forced off the air.

Although little free media existed in the late 1980s, there was, nevertheless, a certain amount of critical reporting on political and social events and themes in the progovernment dailies. Occasionally reported, for example, were activities of and statements by unrecognized political parties, labor organizations, and community organizations; critical statements by the Roman Catholic Church and the Inter-American Commission on Human Rights; harassment and imprisonment of opposition politicians; and repression of peasants. Self-censorship was predominant, but there was more reporting on critical topics than might have been anticipated under a tightly controlled political system. Most reports did not, however, touch directly upon the president except to praise and esteem him.

Foreign Relations

Since gaining independence, Paraguay's fortunes have been largely determined by its relationships with its immediate neighbors. Like Uruguay to the south, it is a buffer state separating Brazil and Argentina—the two largest countries in South America—and, like Bolivia to the west, it is landlocked. The circumstance of being landlocked has historically led the country alternately into isolationism and expansionism; its buffer status has underwritten its sovereignty. Paraguay's foreign policy has traditionally aimed at striking a balance between the influence of its two large neighbors.

Foreign policy under Stroessner was based on two major principles: nonintervention in the affairs of other countries and no relations with countries under Marxist governments. The only exception to the second principle was Yugoslavia. Paraguay maintained relations with Taiwan and did not recognize China. It had relations with South Africa but not with Angola or Mozambique. Paraguay broke diplomatic relations with Cuba in 1959 after the Castro government provided support to Paraguayan radicals. It terminated relations with Nicaragua in 1980 after the assassination in Asunción of Anastasio Somoza Debayle, the deposed Nicaraguan dictator. It was a member of the United Nations (UN), the Organization of American States (OAS), and the Latin American Integration Association, and a signatory of the 1947 Inter-American Treaty of Reciprocal Assistance (Rio Treaty).

National headquarters of the Colorado Party, Asunción
Courtesy Richard S. Sacks

Argentina and Brazil

Paraguay had traditionally been aligned with Argentina, as the port of Buenos Aires provided the only access to external markets, thus determining the direction of Paraguayan trade. Paraguay depended heavily on Argentina for trade throughout the twentieth century, although many Paraguayans chafed at their dependence. Even before taking power in 1954, Stroessner criticized Argentine hegemony. Soon after becoming president, Stroessner joined with sectors in the Colorado Party and the armed forces to explore ways to limit the influence of Buenos Aires in Paraguayan affairs.

Stroessner's interests coincided with those of Brazil, which desired to increase its influence at the expense of Argentina and to establish transportation linkages with countries to the west. In the 1950s, Brazil funded the construction of new buildings for the National University in Asunción, granted Paraguay free-port privileges on the Brazilian coast at Paranagua, and built the Friendship Bridge over the Río Paraná, thereby linking Paranagua to Asunción. The signing of the Treaty of Itaipú in April 1973 symbolized that Paraguay's relationship with Brazil had become more important than its ties with Argentina.

The Stroessner regime benefited politically and economically from its relationship with Brazil, and the diplomatic and moral support given to Stroessner enhanced his prestige. Because of the tremendous infusion of money and jobs associated with Itaipú, the Paraguayan economy grew very rapidly in the 1970s. Brazilians moved in massive numbers into the eastern border region of Paraguay, where they helped change the nature of export crops to emphasize soybeans and cotton. Observers reported that 60 percent of Paraguayan economic activities derived from agriculture, industry, commerce, and services were in the hands of Brazilians, working as partners with Paraguayans. Brazilian tourism and purchases of contraband and other goods at Puerto Presidente Stroessner also brought in substantial revenue. Military equipment and training in the 1980s also were provided overwhelmingly by Brazil. In addition, Brazilian banks financed a growing share of Paraguay's external debt in the 1980s (see Balance of Payments and Debt, ch. 3).

The intimacy of Paraguayan-Brazilian relations generated a variety of problems. First, Paraguayan opposition groups charged that Brazil had become Paraguay's colonial warder. For example, PLRA leader Laíno wrote a book denouncing Brazil's designs on Paraguay. The opposition pointed to Paraguay's mounting debt problem in the late 1980s and attributed much of it to unnecessary and inefficient Brazilian construction projects. Some US$300 million of this debt resulted from the controversial Paraguayan Steel (Aceros Paraguayos—Acepar) mill that the Brazilians financed and built. Acepar was completed after the demand from Itaipú had passed, its steel could not be consumed by Paraguay, it imported raw materials from Brazil, and its product was too expensive to be sold abroad. The Itaipú project itself also represented a source of embarrassment for the Stroessner regime. *ABC Color,* among others, pointed out that the Treaty of Itaipú authorized Paraguayan sales of excess electricity to Brazil at a price highly advantageous to Brazil. Opposition pressure forced a renegotiation of the rate in 1986 (see Electricity, ch. 3).

For its part, Brazil also objected to several actions of the Stroessner government. In the late 1980s, a number of public and private Paraguayan institutions failed to pay their debts to Brazilian creditors. As a result, Itaipú electricity payments were withheld, and several Paraguayan accounts were frozen in Brazil. Brazil also contended that Paraguayan officials were involved in smuggling a wide array of products into or out of Brazil. In 1987 analysts estimated that US$1 billion of electronics equipment was smuggled into Brazil, primarily through Puerto Presidente Stroessner. In the same year, Brazilian farmers reportedly smuggled over US$1 billion of agricultural products into Paraguay for reexport, thereby avoiding payments of Brazilian taxes. Analysts also estimated that up to half of all automobiles in Paraguay were stolen from Brazilian motorists. Brazilian teamsters threatened to block the Friendship Bridge between Brazil and Paraguay to protest the alleged murders of truckers whose vehicles were taken to Paraguay.

Despite Brazil's transition to a civilian government in 1985 and the appointment in 1987 of its first nonmilitary ambassador to Asunción in twenty years, Paraguayan-Brazilian relations remained good. Given its substantial investments in Paraguay, Brazil valued the political stability offered by the Stroessner regime. Brazilian officials refrained from criticizing Stroessner publicly and generally avoided specific pressures for a political transition in Paraguay. In 1986, however, the president of Brazil met with his counterpart from Argentina to discuss increasing commercial and industrial cooperation in the Río de la Plata region. The presidents made it clear that only democratic countries were eligible to join this new regional economic integration program. Thus Bolivia, democratic but distant from the Plata, could participate, whereas Paraguay was excluded. Although participation in this program could help the Paraguayan economy, Stroessner was not prepared to change the nature of his regime in order to gain membership. Indeed, Stroessner did not hesitate to challenge Brazil if he believed that Paraguayan internal stability was at stake. In 1987, for example, police attacked several visiting Brazilian congressmen who were meeting in Asunción with National Accord leaders.

Diplomatic relations between Paraguay and Argentina were somewhat strained in the late 1980s. During the 1983 Argentine presidential elections, PLRA leader Laíno actively campaigned among the thousands of Argentine citizens of Paraguayan descent for the Radical Civic Union (Unión Cívica Radical—UCR) ticket headed by Raúl Alfonsín Foulkes. With the election of Alfonsín, Laíno's party was accorded considerable prestige by the Argentine government. Although Alfonsín refrained from public criticism of Stroessner, he did send letters of support to opposition politicians, including the imprisoned Hermes Rafael Saguier of the PLRA. In addition, Alfonsín allowed Laíno to stage anti-Stroessner rallies in Argentina. A PLRA demonstration in 1984 in the Argentine border town of Formosa resulted in the Paraguayan government's decision to close that border crossing for three days.

In the late 1980s, Paraguay refused to respond to Argentina's requests for extradition of former Argentine officers accused of human rights abuses during the so-called Dirty War of the late 1970s. Paraguay also ignored queries regarding the illegal adoption of children of disappeared Argentines. As a result, the

Argentine ambassador was recalled for three months. Argentine congressmen also visited opposition politicians in Paraguay to demonstrate their support.

Paraguayan opposition leaders expressed dismay at the selection of Carlos Menem as the Peronist candidate for the May 1989 Argentine presidential elections. During the campaign for his party's nomination, Menem met with Stroessner and reminded voters that the Paraguayan president had given asylum to Juan Perón after the 1955 military coup in Argentina. In late 1988, Menem held a wide lead in the polls over his UCR opponent.

The United States

Between World War II and the late 1970s, foreign relations between Paraguay and the United States were largely conditioned by a complementarity of security interests, United States interest in trade and investment, and Paraguay's desire for development assistance. Stroessner, believing his government to be threatened by subversive communist elements from inside and outside Paraguay, was one of the staunchest supporters of United States security policies in the hemisphere. On security issues that were raised in the OAS and the UN, Paraguay voted with the United States more consistently than did any other South American country.

In the late 1970s, however, the relationship began to falter as a result of human rights abuses and the absence of political reform. The United States concern with these issues became public after President Jimmy Carter appointed Robert White as ambassador to Asunción and persisted through the administration of Ronald Reagan. Ambassador Arthur Davis (1982–85) often invited prominent members of the National Accord to official embassy functions. He also cancelled performances by a United States Army band and a parachute team at the May 1984 Independence Day celebration as a personal protest against the closing of *ABC Color*.

Concern over political developments in Paraguay continued to be manifested during the tenure of United States ambassador Clyde Taylor (1985–88). Taylor met frequently with members of the opposition, protested the continued shutdown of *ABC Color*, the harassment of Radio Ñandutí, and the exile of Domingo Laíno. Taylor was criticized by Paraguayan officials, including Minister of Interior Sabino Montanaro, and other members of the Colorado Party. On February 9, 1987, Taylor was teargassed while attending a reception in his honor sponsored by Women for Democracy, an anti-Stroessner group.

The United States strongly supported the evolution of a more open political system with freedom of the press and expression and the participation of all democratic parties. In June 1987, Assistant Secretary of State for Inter-American Affairs, Elliott Abrams, noted that there were some indications of an improving political climate, which, if continued, could benefit relations between the two countries. He urged the government of Paraguay to institute democracy in order to avoid a rift with the United States and unrest within Paraguay itself. Abrams also was criticized by members of the Colorado Party. The Congress of the United States actively supported the Reagan administration's position on human rights and Paraguay's transition to democracy.

Foreign relations between the United States and Paraguay were also adversely affected by the involvement of some members of Stroessner's government in narcotics trafficking (see Crime, ch. 5). A 1986 report to the United States House of Representatives stated that there was evidence of military collaboration and even active participation in the operation of cocaine laboratories. In 1987 Taylor, a former deputy assistant secretary of state for international narcotics matters, stated that the level of narcotics trafficking in Paraguay could not have been reached without official protection. In its 1988 annual narcotics report, the United States Department of State also concluded that Paraguay was "a significant money-laundering location for narcotics traffickers due to lax government controls." An investigative story by Cox Newspapers in October 1988 charged that Gustavo Stroessner collected payoffs from all narcotics traffickers conducting business in Paraguay.

In accordance with the Foreign Assistance Act of 1961, the Reagan administration certified to Congress in 1988 that the Paraguayan government was fully cooperating with United States drug enforcement efforts. The administration based this certification, however, more on its own national interests than on specific actions of the Paraguayan government. Three factors motivated the administration to issue the certification. First, the administration believed that it needed additional time to test the sincerity of Stroessner's professed willingness to cooperate in controlling drugs. In 1987 the United States provided Paraguay with a US$200,000 grant to train and equip an antinarcotics unit. The following year the United States Drug Enforcement Administration reopened a station in Asunción after a seven-year absence. Second, the administration feared that decertification could jeopardize the Peace Corps' substantial presence in Paraguay. In 1987 US$2 million was earmarked to support Peace Corps activities in Paraguay. Finally, the administration contended that certification enhanced the ability of the United States to encourage democratic reform in Paraguay.

Economic relations between the United States and Paraguay were minimal in the late 1980s. The United States invested only a small amount in Paraguayan banking and agriculture and conducted little trade (see External Trade, ch. 3). In January 1987, by an executive order of President Reagan, Paraguay was suspended from receiving benefits through its membership in the Generalized System of Preferences. Although Paraguay still belonged to the system, it could no longer take advantage of the preferential tariff treatment for its exports to the United States. Despite the relatively low level of its exports, observers regarded the suspension as symbolically important. As of mid-1988, the suspension remained in effect.

At the end of 1988, both continuity and change marked the Paraguayan political system. The government continued to take a strong stand against political dissidents, and PLRA leaders were periodically detained to prevent them from staging rallies. The PDC suspended its planned national convention after the minister of interior refused to authorize it. Students belonging to the MDP were arrested for putting up the movement's posters. Police arrested five former priests from Western Europe, accused them of belonging to an extremist organization, and deported them to Argentina. At the same time, however, signs of political change appeared. A silent protest march sponsored by the Roman Catholic Church attracted an estimated 50,000 participants, making it the largest opposition event of the Stroessner era. When Chilean voters rejected the bid by Augusto Pinochet Ugarte to extend military rule well into the 1990s, the prospect of a civilian president in Chile by 1990 only served to further isolate Stroessner from the democratic trend sweeping South America. Finally, the seventy-six-year-old general's cancellation of public appearances in September because of health problems caused many to speak openly of a post-Stroessner Paraguay.

* * *

There is little available literature in English on politics in contemporary Paraguay. The best recent book is Paul H. Lewis's *Paraguay Under Stroessner,* which covers the period up to the late 1970s. Somewhat more information is available in chapter or article form. The chapter, "Paraguay," in Adrian J. English's *Armed Forces of Latin America* is a good overview of this topic with some political background. R. Andrew Nickson's "Tyranny and Longevity: Stroessner's Paraguay" is the best recent overview of the political situation, and Thomas G. Sanders's *Prospects for Political Change in Paraguay* is equally good but slightly dated. More dated is Riordan Roett and Amparo Menéndez-Carrión's "Authoritarian Paraguay: The Personalist Tradition." Also very useful are the articles published periodically by John Hoyt Williams in *Current History* and by Williams and J. Eliseo da Rosa in *The Latin America and Caribbean Contemporary Record.* (For further information and complete citations, see Bibliography.)

Chapter 5. National Security

Francisco Solano López

IN MID-1988 THE ARMED FORCES continued to act as a major source of support for the authoritarian regime of President Alfredo Stroessner Mattiauda. Stroessner had used them, along with the police and the ruling National Republican Association—Colorado Party (Asociación Nacional Republicana—Partido Colorado), as the primary instruments to maintain his regime since coming to power in a coup d'état in 1954. Under the Constitution, the president is designated the nation's commander in chief. Stroessner, himself a general in the Paraguayan army, had chosen to fill this role actively, retaining command authority over the defense forces and involving himself personally in day-to-day decision making related to them. Stroessner was able to keep the military under his control, rather than vice versa, through his cultivation of ties of personal loyalty, his direction of assignments and promotions, and his reliance on a system of checks and balances within and among the defense forces, the police, the Colorado Party, and elite forces under his own control. Military members had also been given a substantial stake in Stroessner's regime, which granted them special privileges and power through salary, benefits, and opportunities for patronage and graft.

Paraguay had a strong military tradition, and the nation took great pride in its performance against Argentina in 1811, in the 1865–70 War of the Triple Alliance, and in the Chaco War of 1932–35 against Bolivia. The military tradition remained a valued one, even though the country had faced little if any external threat since the Chaco War. Instead, the armed forces under Stroessner were chiefly occupied in preserving internal security and supporting the regime. The military was also charged with guarding Paraguay's borders and protecting against insurgency, which had been limited to the 1959–64 period and was largely ineffective. In addition, the armed forces devoted a large portion of their resources to civic action and rural development. In keeping with the limited external threat, the military was equipped mainly to meet public order and internal security assignments. Reflecting the nation's troubled economy and the absence of significant threats, defense spending in the 1980s had not kept up with inflation. Most military equipment had thus grown more and more outdated.

For administrative purposes, the armed forces fell under the purview of the Ministry of National Defense. Operational command of the approximately 17,000-member military was held directly by the president and exercised through the armed forces general staff. The army was the largest and most influential of the three services. It was equipped mainly as a light infantry force. Army officers, usually retired from active service, held positions in other branches of government and as managers of state-run economic, social, and political organizations. The navy was a riverine force that included a battalion of marines. The small air force flew mainly transport planes and helicopters, but also had a small number of counterinsurgency aircraft and a paratroop battalion.

The country enjoyed unprecedented internal security under Stroessner, and conditions of public order could generally be characterized as peaceful. This level of order came about, however, largely as a result of the government's willingness to use whatever means it deemed necessary to quell disorder and suppress dissent. From 1954 until April 1987, the government ruled almost continually under state-of-siege provisions. These provisions suspended in the name of security civil rights guaranteed in the Constitution. The government justified the extraordinary security measures as the price of peace in a "democracy without communism," even though the nation had not faced a credible communist threat since at least the mid-1960s.

The government's harsh internal security measures ensured that opposition to the regime remained muted throughout the 1970s and early 1980s. A slight relaxation in the government's response to domestic dissent, combined with the inspiration of Argentina's return to civilian democratic rule in 1984, emboldened some members of the opposition in the mid-1980s. Members of the press, the political opposition, and labor groups, as well as students, peasants, and representatives of the Roman Catholic Church, began to express dissatisfaction with Paraguay's political system and the economic hardship that followed the end of the construction of the Itaipú hydroelectric project (see Growth and Structure of the Economy, ch. 3). In 1985 and increasingly in 1986, unprecedented demonstrations were mounted in Asunción and elsewhere. Most of these were peaceful until they were violently dispersed by police and other security personnel. The lapse of the state of siege in April 1987 was followed by a short interval of greater official tolerance toward dissent. This tolerance ended abruptly in late 1987, however, when a faction of the Colorado Party describing itself as militant, pro-Stroessner, and combative, took control of the Colorado Party. As of late 1988, the government's return to harsh repression had not abated.

Criminal justice was the responsibility of the national government. The national judiciary, headed by the five-member Supreme

Court of Justice, administered the country's criminal courts. All penal and procedural statutes were issued by the central government. Paraguay's police force was also a national force, organized under the Ministry of Interior. Police were divided into one force that served the capital area and another that served the rest of the country in divisions assigned to each of the nation's eighteen other departments. Public confidence in the criminal justice system was undermined because, although the judiciary was formally a coequal branch of government, in practice it was clearly subordinate to the executive branch. Moreover, both the judiciary and the police were widely viewed as susceptible to political and economic influence.

The History and Development of the Armed Forces

The nation's military tradition is rooted in the colonial past, when armed groups in what is now Paraguay fought against royal Spanish armies and Jesuit-led Indian forces. Elements of these Paraguayan armed groups were organized into a force of approximately 3,000 members that in 1811 repelled an invasion by Argentine forces seeking to annex Paraguay. As a result of that victory, Paraguay declared its independence (see Struggle with the Porteños, ch. 1).

The modern army and the navy owe their origins to forces built up under José Gaspar Rodríguez de Francia, who ruled as a dictator from 1814 to 1840 (see El Supremo Dictador, ch. 1). After heavily purging existing forces to ensure their loyalty to him, Francia imposed strict discipline within the ranks. Under his direction, army and naval strength was increased to deter Argentina from further attacks on Paraguay and to act as the infrastructure for his own autocratic rule. Francia instituted a program of conscription to meet the military's manpower requirements. He also placed landholdings confiscated from his opponents under the control of the army, which until the late 1980s partially fed and supported itself by either working the land directly or leasing it out.

The army and navy were further improved by President Carlos Antonio López, who ruled from 1841 to 1862. Like Francia, López used the military both to maintain his rule and to deter invasion by the nation's larger neighbors (see Carlos Antonio López, ch. 1). López was succeeded by his son, Francisco Solano López, an army general who had studied military matters in Europe. The younger López completely reorganized the 7,000-member army he had inherited and began a program of rapid military expansion. By 1864 the army numbered 30,000 and comprised 30 infantry battalions, 23 cavalry regiments, and 4 artillery regiments. The navy was also strengthened, acquiring the world's first steamship built intentionally as a warship.

The buildup reflected López's aspirations to increase his influence in the region. Attempts to do so led to the 1865–70 War of the Triple Alliance, in which Paraguay faced Argentina, Brazil, and Uruguay in a bloody confrontation that eventually drastically reduced the national population (see The War of the Triple Alliance, ch. 1). Paraguay began the war with an extensive military establishment, but its opponents, especially Brazil, had far greater economic and manpower resources. Paraguay's military was able to make up some of the imbalance through its fierce fighting and its determination to accept total destruction rather than surrender. As the war progressed, however, even López's harsh methods of compelling devotion to battle proved insufficient, and the nation was reduced to conscripting boys down to the age of twelve, but boys as young as ten could volunteer. By the war's end, the army was made up of a few hundred men—most of whom were wounded, old, or very young. Brazil's soldiers were stationed in Paraguay as an army of occupation until 1876.

The next few decades were spent in rebuilding the devastated nation, so there was little money for the military. Although the army remained small, it emerged as a center of political power and a primary source of national political leaders. General Bernardino Caballero became a national leader, governing first directly as president and later behind the scenes as the head of the armed forces (see The First Colorado Era, ch. 1). He also founded the National Republican Association—which adopted red as its symbolic color and came to be known as the Colorado Party.

The bitter competition between the Colorados and their Liberal Party (Partido Liberal—PL) opponents extended into the armed forces. The late 1800s saw the beginning of what came to be a pattern of army intervention in national politics, rebellions by army factions, and assumption of power by army leaders. The military saw action both in putting down armed revolts and in mounting them. Elements of the army fought on both sides when exiled PL members launched an invasion of Paraguay with the tacit support of Argentina in 1904, eventually deposing the Colorado government. The military again divided into warring groups between 1922 and 1924 when civil war broke out among PL factions. By that time, the army had become the chief source of political power and the most frequent instigator of political change.

Growing tension with Bolivia over a long-disputed boundary in the Chaco fueled a secret program of rearmament in the late 1920s (see fig. 3). A major clash between the two countries occurred in 1928; both nations then began to prepare for war, building up their military capability and stationing growing numbers of troops in the Chaco. After war broke out in July 1932, Paraguay rapidly mobilized and brought troop strength up to 24,000. The army succeeded several times in outflanking the more numerous Bolivian forces, cutting their supply lines and access to water. Paraguayan forces also benefited from the fact that Bolivian troops—mostly Indians from the Andes Mountains—were not used to the climate and low altitude of the Chaco. The Chaco War was the bloodiest war in the Western Hemisphere during the twentieth century. By the time a truce was signed in 1935, about 36,000 Paraguayans and an estimated 44,000 Bolivians were dead. The nation was also left economically devastated (see The Chaco War and the February Revolution, ch. 1).

In keeping with the terms of the armistice with Bolivia, Paraguay reduced its army to under 5,000 soon after the war's end. The military had captured a large quantity of light arms, mortars, and artillery in the Chaco War. These made up a substantial portion of the army inventory for some fifteen years, because little new equipment was acquired in the 1940s. In the early 1950s, however, the military establishment expanded, and the army beefed up its artillery, infantry, and engineer forces. During the same period, Argentina and Brazil began to compete for military influence in Paraguay, each presenting the nation with its excess second-hand equipment, most of which had been manufactured in the United States. A small quantity of aircraft and other items were also turned over by the United States, so that by the 1950s most of the nation's military inventory was of United States manufacture.

Although the years following the Chaco War had been a period of stagnation for the armed forces in the purely military sphere, the same could not be said of the political sphere. Paraguayans had viewed the war as a defense of their homeland, and military service was seen as a matter of great pride and prestige. As had been the case after the War of the Triple Alliance, military figures who had made their reputation in the war emerged very soon as the nation's political leaders. The first of these leaders was the popular war hero Colonel Rafael Franco, who came to power in a 1936 coup against a PL government. He was supported by veterans dissatisfied with the settlement with Bolivia and with their remuneration for service, as well as by students, intellectuals, and members of organized labor seeking various reforms. Franco's supporters formed the Febrerista Revolutionary Party (Partido Revolucionario Febrerista—PRF), more commonly known as Febreristas, named after the month in which the coup had occurred. Although Franco was deposed in a military revolt a year later, the Febreristas continued to be an active source of government opposition in the next two decades. Six of the eleven regimes during the 1935–54 period were headed by army officers, ending with the regime of General Stroessner. In addition, all of the five civilian presidents came to power with army backing and/or were deposed under army pressure (see Morínigo and World War II, ch. 1).

The defense forces continued to be divided internally along political lines. Tension among factions that aligned with different parties sometimes resulted in open conflict. For instance, army units rose in revolt during World War II, when Paraguay, like most South American countries, declared war on the Axis powers. The most serious conflict came in 1947, however, after President Higinio Morínigo, an army general who had ruled since 1940—primarily with the support of the army rather than a particular party— appeared to give increasing power to the Colorado Party. In reaction, civil war broke out after the air force and army broke into factions, most of the military supporting a coalition of Febrerista, PL, and communist elements. The rebel forces, joined by virtually the entire navy, were put down only with great difficulty by the government. Morínigo's cause was helped significantly by the fact that Stroessner—then a lieutenant colonel—committed his artillery regiment to the government side.

Because up to 80 percent of the military had joined the rebel side during the civil war, the government initiated a widespread purge of the armed forces, and the marines were disbanded entirely until the 1950s. As a result, the defense forces became almost completely an organization of the Colorado Party. Stroessner's own impressive performance in the war was responsible for his emergence as one of the nation's leading military figures in the late 1940s. Stroessner and fellow Colorado Party members viewed with particular bitterness the communist role in the civil war. After that time, the suggestion of a potential communist threat was sufficient to promote an immediate negative reaction by the government.

Transforming the armed forces into an organization composed almost exclusively of Colorado personnel did not rid them of factionalism. Warring elements within the party took part in coup attempts in 1948 and 1949, and Stroessner was a main player in each attempt. At one point, he was forced to flee to Brazil to escape reprisal for his role in an unsuccessful revolt. He was back in the country within a few months, however, after taking part in a successful coup in 1949. As a reward for his role, he was given a series of rapid promotions, rising to commander in chief of the armed forces in 1951. Stroessner himself came to power as president in an army-backed coup in 1954 (see The 1954 Coup; Consolidation of the Stroessner Regime, ch. 1).

The Virgin of Asunción
at the National Pantheon of Heroes, Asunción. The Virgin
holds the honorary rank of marshal of the Paraguayan Army.
Courtesy Tim Merrill

Stroessner inherited a military establishment still ridden by factionalism, as well as an economy damaged by civil war and political instability. After forces loyal to him forestalled a planned coup in 1955, he followed up by purging dissident elements the next year. During the late 1950s, opposition to Stroessner flared over austerity measures imposed by his government, and strikes and student demonstrations followed. The opposition drew inspiration and some funds from foreign sources. A government crackdown in 1958 and 1959 included another purge of the armed forces. After that time, virtually all members of the officer corps were either associated with a pro-Stroessner wing of the Colorado Party or personally loyal to or dependent upon Stroessner.

Opposition to Stroessner's rule was purely internal until 1959, when guerrillas that were allied with elements of Febrerista, PL, and communist opponents mounted sporadic and largely ineffective raids from bases in Argentina and Brazil. Never of sufficient size to threaten the government or seriously upset public order, these insurgencies were easily quelled by the military, which relied on intelligence provided by Colorado Party members throughout the country. Using the armed forces and the police, the government also cracked down on internal opposition, branding many of its opponents as communist. Guerrilla activity died out by 1964 as a result of harsh government reprisals, lack of support within Paraguay, and moves by Argentina and Brazil to close guerrilla bases in their countries.

By late 1988, in the absence of any external or insurgent threat, the armed forces continued to help enforce the government's tight control over the domestic political scene. The military leadership appeared to accept that national economic conditions dictated that the government's rhetorical support for the defense forces could not be matched by sufficient material support to replace or update the aging armed forces inventory. Although the military appeared to remain completely loyal to Stroessner, his government, and the Colorado Party, its personnel were not immune to factionalism within the Colorado Party. This factionalism manifested itself in political violence in the mid-1980s (see The Twin Pillars of the Stroessner Regime; Political Developments Since 1986, ch. 4). As of late 1988, however, political factionalism within the armed forces did not appear to have seriously affected operations of any of the three services.

The Armed Forces in the National Life

The ideal of an apolitical military force that is shielded from domestic political debates, kept out of domestic decision making, and kept under firm civilian control has not been relevant to the Paraguayan experience. The nation's military, particularly the army as the dominant service, traditionally has been the most powerful institution in the nation, exercising an heroic military role in times of external threat and exerting a strong political and economic presence in peacetime. Many military officers have aspired to national political leadership, and several have achieved it.

In turn, political leaders—whether in power or in the opposition—historically have sought to exert their personal influence over the internal operations of the armed forces and to use the military as an instrument of their own regimes. Such efforts have fallen squarely within the Paraguayan cultural tradition, which stresses the importance of personal ties and personal loyalty over abstract ideology or institutionalism. In such a small country, military, economic, social, and political elites frequently shared ties of kinship or personal affinity. Therefore, institutional barriers have not been strong enough to prevent the intrusion of political or other considerations into purely military matters. On one level, the lack of separation between political and military affairs has resulted in decisions on such matters as promotions and assignments being based on considerations other than merit or satisfaction of qualifying factors.

On another level, this lack of separation has had grave consequences for national stability. It is true that under the strong and efficient management of Francia, the Lópezes, and Stroessner, the military remained internally unified and acted as the main instrument of authoritarian rule. For most of the rest of the nation's history, however, political turmoil in the national leadership was reflected in divisiveness within the armed forces. The resulting factionalism frequently erupted into violence that itself threatened public order and political stability. Supporters of the Stroessner regime have justified his authoritarian rule in part by noting the correlation between periods of national stability and the presence of strong rulers able to exert control over the military and the political process.

In late 1988, the military's most significant role in the national life was its apparently unified backing for the Stroessner regime. Such backing resulted from Stroessner's efforts first to achieve and then to maintain military support. By 1959 he had completely purged the officer corps of all persons who were not members of the pro-Stroessner wing of the Colorado Party. Thereafter, candidates for service were screened for loyalty to the party. Factionalism within the Colorado Party persisted, however, and also surfaced in the 1980s in the officer corps. In 1986, for instance, the head of the army's First Cavalry Division was reported to have been replaced on political grounds by an officer closely identified with the "traditionalist" faction of the Colorado Party—the faction also favored by the army's powerful First Corps commander, Major General Andrés Rodríguez. In late 1988, it was unclear how deeply the party factionalism had affected officer morale or how this factionalism had affected relations between the military and the Colorado Party leadership, which was taken over by the "militant" faction in late 1987.

Despite its influence in national political affairs, the Colorado Party did not control the military, and the armed forces had no political officers serving alongside military officers. Instead, party loyalty served as a litmus test of trustworthiness and loyalty to the regime. The Colorado Party, which was highly organized, block by block in towns and cities, also served as a channel of information on military matters and the actions of military personnel. In addition, the party was a potential check on the power of the armed forces.

Stroessner played an active role in overseeing military affairs. The president chaired the promotion boards held twice a year and oversaw all important assignments. He devoted one day each week to military matters and attended numerous ceremonies and parades. He took time to cultivate junior officers, especially those in direct command of troops, and made sure that conditions of service were good enough to keep the military content. In addition to relying on personal loyalty and oversight, Stroessner relied on the structure of the military establishment to maintain control over the armed forces. He held command personally through the armed forces general staff, dividing command and support duties between the general staff and the Ministry of National Defense. Stroessner also maintained his own well-armed and well-trained security force, the Presidential Escort Regiment.

Missions

The nation faced no foreseeable external threat in late 1988 and took care to maintain workable diplomatic relations with its large neighbors, Brazil and Argentina. Relations with Bolivia, which had sometimes been slightly strained over issues related to the shared border in the Chaco, had not been viewed as a serious threat to national security since the Chaco War. The threat of insurgent activity appeared low, and no incidents of guerrilla activity had been reported since a limited number of minor incursions took place in the early 1970s. Consequently, the external defense mission of the armed forces was essentially limited to monitoring the nation's borders.

The internal security mission was far more significant. Military units frequently were called out to control demonstrations or handle other manifestations of unrest. The military also maintained checkpoints in the sparsely populated Chaco region as part of the government's administration of the area.

All three branches of the armed forces were involved in civic-action projects. The army's engineer battalions were responsible for road construction and the maintenance of transportation routes. The engineers also built schools and public buildings for rural communities, did excavation work, constructed water tanks, and provided bricks and tiles for local building projects. The navy performed ship repair for the merchant fleet, and naval vessels transported goods to needy communities at no cost. The air force provided transportation services and helped build schools and landing fields in isolated areas. Medical personnel from all three services operated rural clinics and offered free emergency medical treatment. The army's veterinary unit was the nation's only public veterinary service. All three services were active in disaster relief efforts.

Manpower

In mid-1988 the total strength of the armed forces was estimated at 19,500 persons. This number represented a ratio of approximately 4.4 military personnel for every 1,000 Paraguayans, down from more than 9 per 1,000 in the late 1960s. This level was slightly below the average for Latin American countries, a falloff since the early 1970s, when Paraguay's ratio was more than twice the average. An estimated 55 percent of armed forces personnel were conscripts.

Conscription had a long history in the nation. During the nineteenth century, the practice of "press-ganging" Indians and peasants into the military was common in Paraguay. The current system of conscription, however, was rooted in 1908 when a formal program of compulsory universal military service was instituted for males. In mid-1988 the system of conscription had its legal foundation in Article 125 of the Constitution, which states: "Every Paraguayan citizen is obliged to bear arms in defense of the nation and this Constitution. Military service is compulsory for male citizens, and those who have completed military service shall remain in the reserves. Women shall not render military service except in case of necessity during an international war, and not as combatants." In accordance with Article 125, women were not subject to the draft in the 1980s, and very few served in the armed forces.

Males were liable for two years of service upon reaching eighteen years of age. College students fulfilled their obligations by spending three summers in military training, which led to reserve officer commissions. Those males exempted from service were required to pay a military tax. Conscription was strictly enforced, but the number judged physically fit to serve was generally greater than actual manpower requirements, and only about half of those eligible were actually called to serve. The number of men required annually to replace those completing service did not adversely affect the labor force.

Conscripts came from all segments of Paraguay's population, which was relatively homogeneous in ethnic, social, and cultural makeup. Entry was greatly facilitated by personal or family ties to the Colorado Party. Military service generally was viewed as a patriotic duty, and service for conscripts was not particularly rigorous. In fact, for many conscripts, fulfilling their military obligation represented an opportunity to acquire skills valuable in finding later employment, including training in mechanics, carpentry, and all types of construction. Many conscripts learned to read and write during their period of service, and most learned to drive.

After meeting their service obligations, conscripts entered an organized reserve, serving nine years. They were then liable for ten years of service in the National Guard, followed by service in the Territorial Guard until the age of forty-five. Officers, noncommissioned officers (NCOs), and enlisted personnel also incurred reserve obligations after leaving service. In practice, the National Guard and the Territorial Guard seemed to exist primarily as paper organizations in 1988.

Entry into the officer corps was highly competitive. In practice, successful candidates had family or personal connections with the Colorado Party. Officer candidates came both from the Francisco López Military College in Asunción and from the reserve officer-training program for college students. Conditions of military service were very good, especially for senior officers. Salaries, when combined with allowances and medical and pension benefits, compared favorably with those of the civilian population. Military personnel also enjoyed special privileges, including access to private military stores and clubs. Members of the armed forces were exempt from car-licensing fees. Officers also had access to favorable business and real estate loans.

Senior officers lived particularly well. The nation, like most Latin American countries, had a strong tradition of patron-client relations, and senior officers were especially well placed to aid friends, relatives, and associates. They influenced decisions related to the allocation of public and private employment, the choice of political appointees, the award of public and private business contracts, and the outcome of judicial and legal decisions. Retired officers provided a pool from which the executive filled management

214

positions in government and in public-sector enterprises. A small number of very senior officers had sufficient influence to render their actions virtually immune to investigation by law enforcement officials or to scrutiny by the domestic press.

Paraguay had one of the largest officers corps in Latin America. Officers in command of many of the most influential positions were members of the "old guard," who had supported Stroessner in his rise to power and had held command ever since. For a number of years, these long-serving generals had blocked promotions for middle-ranking officers, but resentment over this issue did not appear to be a serious problem during the 1980s.

The rank structure of the armed forces generally conformed to that used in the United States, except that Paraguay had two ranks equivalent to the United States army and air force first lieutenant and navy ensign and did not employ all of the ranks found in the United States military. The army had ten officer ranks ranging from second lieutenant to general. The eight air force officer ranks were identical to those of the army in level from second lieutenant to brigadier general, but did not include higher general officer ranks. Army and air force enlisted personnel had nine grades ranging in level from private first class to sergeant major, but naval enlistees had seven grades from the equivalent of seaman to master chief petty officer. The navy had nine officer ranks from ensign to vice admiral (see fig. 8).

Rank insignia for officers of the army and air force were indicated by a series of five-pointed stars on shoulder boards. Insignia for general, major general, and brigadier general consisted of four, three, and two gold stars, respectively, surmounted at the outer end by an embroidered wreath. Field-grade officers wore gold stars, and company-grade officers wore silver stars on shoulder boards. For parades, full dress, and special occasions, the shoulder boards were exchanged for gilt epaulettes. Naval officer ranks were indicated by gold-colored bands on the lower sleeve of the shirt. Army enlisted personnel wore yellow stripes and/or yellow bars on a red background; navy enlisted personnel wore black stripes on white background; and air force enlisted personnel wore light blue stripes on a blue background (see fig. 9).

The armed forces had both summer and winter uniforms. The three services had full dress, dress, and service uniforms for officers and parade, garrison, service, and field uniforms for enlisted personnel. The army winter service uniform was dark green, the navy's dark blue, and the air force's light blue. Navy officers wore all-white summer dress uniforms; army and air force officers wore a white shirt with summer dress uniforms for special occasions.

Service	1	2	3	4	5	6	7	8	9
ARMY — Paraguay Rank	SUBTENIENTE	TENIENTE/TENIENTE PRIMERO	CAPITÁN	MAYOR	TENIENTE CORONEL	CORONEL	GENERAL DE BRIGADA	GENERAL DE DIVISIÓN	GENERAL DE EJÉRCITO
U.S. Rank Titles	2D LIEUTENANT	1ST LIEUTENANT	CAPTAIN	MAJOR	LIEUTENANT COLONEL	COLONEL	BRIGADIER GENERAL	MAJOR GENERAL/LIEUTENANT GENERAL	GENERAL
AIR FORCE — Paraguay Rank	SUBTENIENTE	TENIENTE	TENIENTE PRIMERO	CAPITÁN	MAYOR	TENIENTE CORONEL	CORONEL	GENERAL DE BRIGADA	
U.S. Rank Titles	2D LIEUTENANT		1ST LIEUTENANT	CAPTAIN	MAJOR	LIEUTENANT COLONEL	COLONEL	BRIGADIER GENERAL	
NAVY — Paraguay Rank	GUARDIA MARINA	TENIENTE DE CORBETA	TENIENTE DE FRAGATA	TENIENTE DE NAVÍO	CAPITÁN DE CORBETA	CAPITÁN DE FRAGATA	CAPITÁN DE NAVÍO	CONTRALMIRANTE	VICE-ALMIRANTE
U.S. Rank Titles	ENSIGN	LIEUTENANT JUNIOR GRADE		LIEUTENANT	LIEUTENANT COMMANDER	COMMANDER	CAPTAIN	COMMODORE ADMIRAL	REAR ADMIRAL

Figure 8. Officer Ranks and Insignia, 1988

	SOLDADO	CABO SEGUNDO	CABO PRIMERO	SARGENTO SEGUNDO	VICE-SARGENTO PRIMERO	SARGENTO PRIMERO/ SARGENTO AYUDANTE	SUB-OFICIAL/ SUB-OFICIAL MAYOR	SUB-OFICIAL PRINCIPAL
PARAGUAY RANK / ARMY	NO INSIGNIA							
U.S. RANK TITLES	BASIC PRIVATE	PRIVATE 1ST CLASS	CORPORAL	SERGEANT	STAFF SERGEANT	SERGEANT 1ST CLASS/ MASTER SERGEANT	FIRST SERGEANT/ SERGEANT MAJOR	COMMAND SERGEANT MAJOR
PARAGUAY RANK / AIR FORCE	SOLDADO	CABO SEGUNDO	CABO PRIMERO	SARGENTO SEGUNDO	VICE-SARGENTO PRIMERO	SARGENTO PRIMERO/ SARGENTO AYUDANTE	SUB-OFICIAL/ SUB-OFICIAL MAYOR	SUB-OFICIAL PRINCIPAL
AIR FORCE insignia	NO INSIGNIA							
U.S. RANK TITLES	AIRMAN BASIC	AIRMAN 1ST CLASS	SERGEANT	STAFF SERGEANT	TECHNICAL SERGEANT	MASTER SERGEANT	SENIOR MASTER SERGEANT	CHIEF MASTER SERGEANT
PARAGUAY RANK / NAVY	DRAGONEANTE	CABO SEGUNDO	CABO PRIMERO	MAESTRE	SUB-OFICIAL DE SEGUNDA	SUB-OFICIAL DE PRIMERA	SUB-OFICIAL MAYOR	SUB-OFICIAL PRINCIPAL
NAVY insignia	NO INSIGNIA							
U.S. RANK TITLES	SEAMAN RECRUIT	SEAMAN	PETTY OFFICER 3D CLASS	PETTY OFFICER 2D CLASS	PETTY OFFICER 1ST CLASS	CHIEF PETTY OFFICER	SENIOR CHIEF PETTY OFFICER	FLEET FORCE MASTER CHIEF PETTY OFFICER

Figure 9. Enlisted Ranks and Insignia, 1988

217

Defense Spending

According to the latest available government figures, the defense budget for 1985 was 13.9 billion guaraníes (for the value of the guaraní—see Glossary). That figure represented approximately 10.1 percent of the total expenditures of the central government, down from the 13- to 14-percent levels sustained in the early 1970s. When measured in current guaraníes, military spending increased more than fivefold during the 1972–82 period. The most rapid growth occurred in the 1979–81 period, when revenues from the Itaipú project were at their highest (see Fiscal Policy, ch. 3). When factoring in inflation during the ten-year period, growth was a more modest, but still respectable, 80 percent. The sharp dropoff in revenues from Itaipú was reflected in defense expenditures after 1982; when measured in current guaraníes, military spending fell by 10 percent in 1983, thereafter rising relatively sharply. These increases were insufficient to match high levels of inflation during the period, however. When measured in constant 1980 guaraníes, defense spending fell almost 30 percent during the 1982–85 period.

When compared with other Latin American countries, the portion of the national budget devoted to defense was about average. The military's percentage of the gross national product (GNP—see Glossary) was about 1 percent in 1985, a low percentage for Latin American nations. The level of military expenditures per soldier was among the lowest in the hemisphere.

A breakdown of the defense budget was not publicly available in late 1988, but the army, as the largest service, was known to account for the biggest portion. A large part of army spending went to fund civic-action projects. It must therefore be assumed that the purely military operations of the army, as well as those of the navy and air force, were affected adversely by budget constraints during the mid-1980s. Any modernization of the military's relatively obsolete inventory would require a significant increase in defense spending.

The domestic defense industry was very limited in scope, and the nation imported almost all of its military equipment. The Directorate of Military Industries, an agency subordinate to the Ministry of National Defense, maintained a complex in Asunción that produced explosives and repaired and maintained military vehicles. Under the auspices of the army quartermaster, such items as field kitchens and uniforms were manufactured locally. The navy also maintained repair workshops and a naval shipyard.

The army, which had owned large tracts of land since the 1800s, ran a number of ranches and farms. The produce from these operations helped to supply the military's food requirements. In conjunction with these operations, the army also operated a slaughterhouse and a meat-packing concern.

Armed Forces Organization, Training, and Equipment

Article 180 of the Constitution names the president as commander in chief of the armed forces and provides that actual command may be delegated to a general officer. As of late 1988, however, President Stroessner had not exercised this option, but rather had retained direct command over the armed forces since 1954.

The president was assisted by the minister of national defense, who was by tradition an active-duty or retired army general officer. The minister of national defense was not in the direct chain of command, and the ministry's duties were limited to administrative matters, including finance, military justice, and inspection (see fig. 10). The ministry also had responsibility for defense industries, civil aviation, and the National War College.

The president exercised command through the armed forces general staff, the chief of which was always an army general officer. The general staff office had sections that handled and coordinated matters concerning the army, the navy, and the air force.

The Presidential Escort Regiment also came under the direct command of the president. Personnel assigned to this elite unit numbered some 1,500 in 1988, all of whom were screened for personal loyalty to the president. The unit's headquarters and assets were located in the capital. Administratively part of the army, the regiment was primarily an infantry element, but was also equipped with a small motorized police unit. It was assigned to protect public officials, including the president.

Below the chief of the armed forces general staff were the commanders of the army, navy, and air force. These three commanded all tactical and support units of their respective service. Each service had its own staff made up of the usual sections: personnel, intelligence, operations, and logistics.

The nation was divided geographically into six military regions. The first military region had its headquarters at Asunción and covered the Central, Cordillera, and Paraguarí departments (see fig. 1). Within it were located the headquarters of all three services, the Presidential Escort Regiment, and most training establishments and combat support units. The bulk of naval and air force assets were also located there, as were historically powerful cavalry and infantry divisions and artillery battalions. The second military region, headquartered at Villarrica, comprised the departments of Guairá, Caazapá, and Itapúa. The third,

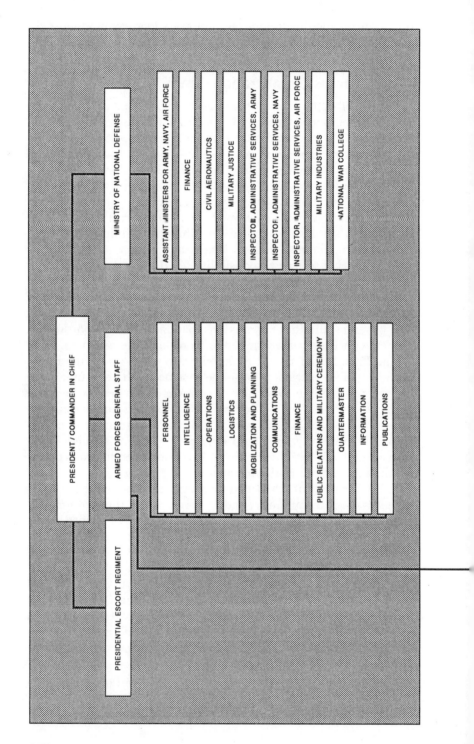

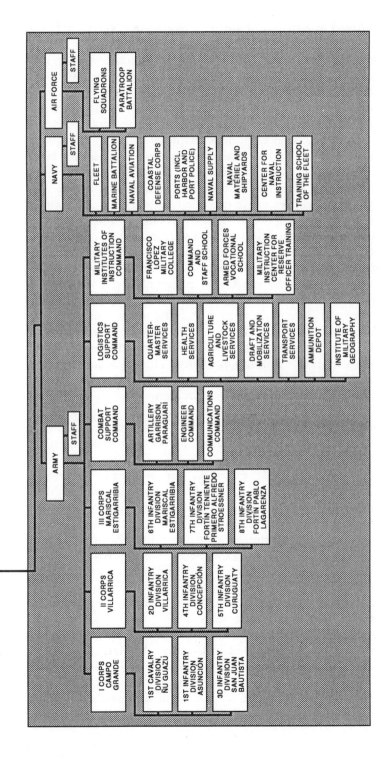

Figure 10. Organization of the Armed Forces of Paraguay, 1988

headquartered at San Juan Bautista, covered the Ñeembucú and Misiones departments. The fourth military region included the Amambay, San Pedro, and Concepción departments and was headquartered at Concepción. The fifth had its headquarters at Puerto Presidente Stroessner and covered the Caaguazú, Alto Paraná, and Canendiyú departments. The sixth military region, headquartered at Mariscal Estigarribia, encompassed the departments of Presidente Hayes, Boquerón, Nueva Asunción, Chaco, and Alto Paraguay.

The armed forces had an extensive training program for both officers and NCOs. The senior school for officers of all three branches was the National War College, which was run by the Ministry of National Defense. Established in 1968, it offered courses designed to prepare officers for command of larger units. The curricula also included the study of political, social, economic, and military problems of national importance. Located in Asunción, the National War College also admitted senior civil servants.

Two army-run establishments also trained officers from all three branches. The first was the Command and Staff School at Asunción. Long-held plans to establish a separate naval command and staff school continued to be frustrated by financial constraints as of 1988. The army also ran the Francisco López Military College, the nation's triservice military academy. The academy offered a four-year program of military studies and graduated commissioned officers. Entrance to the academy was by examination and, because of the opportunities available to military officers, competition for acceptance was keen. Many cadets attended a four-year military preparatory school, the Liceo Militar, before matriculating to the academy.

Reserve officers of all three services were trained at the army's Armed Forces Officer Training School. The army also ran the Military Instruction Center for Reserve Officer Training, where military personnel from all three branches, as well as civilian officials, received instruction in internal security and public-order issues.

Because most of the lower ranks were filled by two-year conscripts, the necessity for a highly trained cadre of career NCOs was well recognized. Most NCOs were trained primarily in their respective service, although specialists in a few fields, including medicine, studied at triservice schools.

Conscripts, who were trained in their respective service, received much of their basic instruction in Guaraní, the language of the indigenous Guaraní Indians (see Indians, ch. 2). About 95 percent of the nation's population was of mixed Guaraní and Spanish descent, and an estimated 90 percent of the population spoke Guaraní. The military's use of the language was believed to have strategic value because during the Chaco War, the Bolivian military could not understand messages sent in Guaraní.

Since the mid-1950s, the armed forces establishment has been most strongly influenced by Brazil and Argentina, both of which maintained military missions in the nation and supplied most of the country's military equipment. The United States also maintained a military attaché in Asunción, but United States military influence was limited. During the 1980s, United States military assistance was confined to grants under the International Military Education and Training program, under which Paraguayan officers studied in various United States military schools. Paraguayan military officers also regularly attended the Inter-American Defense College in Washington, D.C. During the 1980s, Paraguay purchased a small quantity of military equipment from the United States under the Foreign Military Sales program. This matériel consisted principally of communications equipment and spare parts intended to be used for disaster relief, search and rescue, and the interdiction of narcotics traffic.

Paraguay joined the Inter-American Defense Board in 1942, which maintained a headquarters and staff in Washington, D.C., and acted as a military advisory group to the Organization of American States, of which Paraguay was also a member. The nation also joined with the United States and twenty other Latin American nations in 1945 to sign the Act of Chapultepec, in which each agreed to consult on any aggression against a cosignator. In 1948 Paraguay became a signatory to the Inter-American Treaty of Reciprocal Assistance (Rio Treaty), in which the United States and other Latin American and Caribbean countries committed themselves to work toward the peaceful settlement of disputes and collective self-defense in the Americas. Paraguay was also a signatory to the 1967 Treaty for the Prohibition of Nuclear Weapons in Latin America (Tlatelolco Treaty). In 1970 it signed the Treaty on the Non-Proliferation of Nuclear Weapons and in 1975 accepted the Biological Weapons Convention, which prohibits the development, production, or stockpiling of such weapons.

The Army

The Paraguayan army has existed since independence in 1811, when it consisted of two infantry battalions backed up by a militia. It was built up under Francia to include cavalry and artillery elements and was also backed by a reserve force. The army continued to occupy an important position under the presidencies of both Lópezes, who devoted considerable resources to training, organization, and weaponry. During the 1860s, under the younger López, the army grew to be the largest in Latin America, maintaining fixed artillery positions around Asunción and in other fortresses in the country. In 1864 during the lead-up to the War of the Triple Alliance, the army was large enough to invade Argentina and Brazil, one invasion force numbering as high as 25,000. Eventually, a force estimated at 50,000 was mobilized during the war—far more than the nation was able to train or arm adequately. The army was overwhelmed by the larger and better equipped armies of its opponents, which by the war's end in 1870 had reduced the Paraguayan army to a few remnants.

The army was reestablished after the Brazilian occupation ended in 1876, but until the turn of the century it consisted mainly of small units assigned to defend the frontiers or to act as ceremonial forces in the capital. Less a professional institution than a collection of forcibly conscripted troops, the army during the late 1800s came under the shifting commands of officers allied with whatever government was currently in power.

Efforts to improve matters met with uneven results. Most of the new equipment acquired during the 1895–1904 period was lost in 1904 during the Liberal revolt (see The First Colorado Era, ch. 1). The Liberals were backed by a well-equipped armed force, the personnel and equipment of which were then incorporated into a 2,000-strong army reorganized by the new government. The army again underwent reorganization after the 1922 civil war. It grew only slightly until the late 1920s, when tensions with Bolivia prompted a mobilization, and new battalions were formed. Approximately 140,000 men saw service during the three-year Chaco War, after which the army was reduced dramatically to little more than its prewar level.

The factional split of the army during the 1947 civil war was followed by a large turnover in personnel. After operations were "regularized," the army was expanded. The greatest buildup came in the engineer arm, which began to be used extensively in civic-action work. A cavalry division was also organized.

After Stroessner became president in 1954, he enlarged the army again, the most important new element being the Presidential Escort Battalion (later expanded to a regiment). The army inventory grew more slowly. A small quantity of light and medium tanks, armored personnel carriers, and armored cars were acquired during the 1960s and 1970s, mostly from the United States and Brazil. These acquisitions barely kept pace with deletions of obsolete and broken-down equipment, however.

In 1982 the government announced a new army tactical organization that incorporated existing units into three corps. At the same time, two new infantry divisions were formed.

As of late 1988, army strength stood at 12,500, including members of the Presidential Escort Regiment; about 8,100 army personnel were conscripts (see table 9, Appendix). Army combat arms included infantry and cavalry divisions and artillery and engineer battalions. Logistics services branches included signals, transport, administration, war matériel, medical, and veterinary elements that were dispatched in support of combat units.

The army's main tactical units included eight infantry divisions and one cavalry division (see table 10, Appendix). At full strength, the infantry divisions were each designed to comprise a headquarters, three infantry regiments, and a logistics support battalion that included transport and medical units. In peacetime, however, the divisions were actually made up of a single, sometimes ''skeletonized'' infantry regiment. The cavalry division included mechanized elements as well as men on horseback.

The eight infantry divisions and the cavalry division were organized tactically into three army corps. The First Corps was headquartered at Campo Grande near Asunción and included the First Cavalry Division, which was located at Ñu Guazú and comprised four cavalry regiments. The First Corps also contained the First Infantry Division and the Third Infantry Division, headquartered respectively at Asunción and San Juan Bautista. The Second Corps contained the Second, Fourth, and Fifth Infantry Divisions. The Second Infantry Division, along with the Second Corps headquarters, was located at Villarrica. The Fourth Infantry Division was headquartered at Concepción, the Fifth at Curuguaty. The Third Corps also had three infantry divisions. The Sixth Infantry Division and corps headquarters were located at Mariscal Estigarribia in the Chaco. The Seventh and Eighth Infantry Divisions were headquartered at Fortín Teniente Primero Stroessner and Mayor Pablo Lagarenza, respectively.

Three other major elements also rounded out this tactical organization. The first was the Combat Support Command, which comprised an artillery garrison consisting of three artillery battalions, an engineer command composed of six engineer battalions, and a communications command made up of a signals and transport battalion. The artillery battalions were garrisoned at Paraguarí and were attached to the infantry divisions on an ad hoc basis. The engineer battalions were dispatched as needed throughout the country and assigned to military and civilian construction projects as well as other civic-action tasks. The second major support element was the Logistics Support Command, which encompassed a variety of service elements, including quartermaster, medical, veterinary, and transport services. This command also oversaw the army's ammunition depot, draft and mobilization program, and surveying and mapping unit. The army's training establishments, including the Francisco López Military College, came under the Military Institutes of Instruction Command—the third major army support element.

Major ground force arms were heterogeneous in origin. Much was obsolete United States equipment, most of which was obtained thirdhand from Argentina and Brazil. The small armor inventory consisted of twelve M-4A3 medium and twelve M-3A1 light tanks. It was unclear how many of the United States-made tanks were operable. The army also had twelve United States-made M-8 and M-3 armored cars; twenty Brazilian-made Cascavel armored vehicles; three United States-made M-2 armored personnel carriers (APCs), and ten Brazilian-made Urutu APCs. Artillery pieces included 75mm and 105mm howitzers of French and Swedish manufacture, plus six British-made 152mm coastal guns. The army used French-made 81mm and United States-made 107mm mortars and United States-made 75mm antitank guns. Also in the army's inventory were eight light transport aircraft and three helicopters.

The army's conscripts were trained initially in the unit to which they were assigned. A variety of specialty schools, including the Armaments School, the Signals School, and the Engineer School, offered advanced training.

The Navy

Paraguay's naval forces were first developed under Francia, who kept a fleet of eleven vessels. Under the presidencies of both Lópezes, the navy was expanded to include both a marine battalion and a naval artillery element. The navy played a significant role in the early part of the War of the Triple Alliance. Using the steam warship *Tacuarí,* naval forces in early 1865 helped capture the Argentine city of Corrientes, then battled an attacking Brazilian fleet, first losing and then regaining control of the city. After finally forcing the Brazilian fleet to withdraw to Riachuelo, the Paraguayan navy attacked again in one of the world's largest riverine naval engagements. Although the battle was inconclusive, the navy's losses forced it to withdraw upriver. Thereafter, the navy fought a series of holding actions until 1868, when its forces had been almost completely destroyed.

For the fifty years following the end of the occupation by Brazilian forces in 1876, the navy remained very small. In response to tensions with Bolivia, however, it was upgraded in the late 1920s, adding a small air arm in 1929 and acquiring new vessels in 1931. The fleet's role in the Chaco War, however, was limited largely to carrying troops and supplies on the first leg of the journey into the Chaco and to supplying antiaircraft cover for the army. Some naval officers also saw service as ground force commanders. In addition, the naval air arm carried out important reconnaissance and support missions and undertook in 1934 the first night air raid in the Western Hemisphere.

After the Chaco War, the navy inventory grew slowly; the primary acquisitions were patrol boats donated by the United States in 1944. The naval aviation arm benefited from donations by the United States and Argentina in the 1950s. The fleet was augmented in the 1960s and early 1970s by three United States-manufactured minesweepers acquired from Argentina. During the same period, the United States transferred or leased to Paraguay a variety of craft, including launches, landing craft, tugs, and support vessels. These were purchased outright during the 1975–77 period. The only major acquisition during the 1980s was a Brazilian-built river gunboat commissioned in 1985.

As of late 1988, naval personnel numbered some 3,150, of whom approximately one-third were conscripts. These included personnel assigned to the fleet, to naval aviation, and to a battalion of marines, as well as members of the coast guard and the harbor and port police.

The ship inventory consisted of six river defense vessels, seven patrol craft, and three amphibious vessels, in addition to various support, transport, and cargo vessels (see table 11, Appendix). The bulk of the fleet was antiquated: five of the six river patrol vessels were laid down in the 1930s; the newest was of 1980s vintage. One large patrol craft had a wooden hull and first saw service in 1908.

The main naval base was located in the capital at Puerto Sajonía and included a dockyard and the naval arsenal. Secondary bases were located across the Río Paraguay at Chaco i and at Bahía Negra and Puerto Presidente Stroessner.

The 500-strong marine battalion included both a regular and a commando regiment. It was headquartered at Puerto Sajonía, but most personnel were stationed on the upper Paraguay at Bahía Negra and Fuerte Olimpo.

The small naval air arm had only some fifty-five personnel assigned to it. It flew primarily utility and training aircraft as well as a few helicopters. Most equipment was located at Chaco i, although the helicopters sometimes were detached to two vessels that had helicopter platforms.

The navy was also responsible for the coast guard, which maintained navigational aids and guarded major river crossings. Some 250 naval personnel manned four batteries of coastal defense guns on the upper part of the Río Paraguay. The harbor police, which regulated the merchant fleet, was also under the navy's control.

After training at the military academy in Asunción, naval officers were sent to Argentina for advanced training in Argentine naval schools and on the Argentine fleet vessels. Enlisted personnel received basic and advanced naval training at Puerto Sajonía; some were also sent to Argentina to train.

The Air Force

The history of aviation in Paraguay began in 1912 when an army officer was sent to France to train and returned with a monoplane. Both were lost in a crash a few years later. For several years, economic considerations prevented further development of military aviation, although aircraft flown by mercenary pilots were used by both sides in the 1922 civil war.

A small air element, under army control, was first developed in the mid-1920s, when a flying school also was established. By 1932 the army's air arm had twenty aircraft and was organized into a fighter and a reconnaissance squadron. It was no match for the Bolivian air force, however, and during the Chaco War, the air arm was used primarily for logistic and transport duties.

The air force was established as an independent defense force in 1946. It split into two factions the next year, each bombing the forces of the other side in the 1947 civil war. After regular operations were restored in the late 1940s, the force began to be expanded with the delivery of the first of a number of transports provided by the United States. A paratroop unit was added in 1949. During the 1950s and 1960s, the nation acquired surplus aircraft from Argentina and Brazil. After 1975, however, Brazil emerged as the principal source. The only exception came in 1983 when the air force purchased trainers that the Chilean air force was retiring from service; however, these were also of Brazilian manufacture.

As of late 1988, air force strength was approximately 1,400, half of whom were estimated to be conscripts. The air force was organized into three squadrons. The first was a composite squadron headquartered at Campo Grande. It flew the nation's only combat planes: Brazilian-made EMB–326 Xavante light counterinsurgency aircraft (see table 12, Appendix). The composite squadron also had a few Cessna liaison aircraft and ten helicopters. Most of the composite squadron, including the Xavantes, were based at President Stroessner International Airport in Asunción. The second squadron performed transport missions and had a number of C–47s as well as a variety of other transports. Its assets were located both at President Stroessner International Airport and at Ñu Guazú (see fig. 7). The third squadron performed training missions out of Ñu Guazú and flew Chilean T–25 Universals, Brazilian T–23 Uirupurus, and United States T–6s acquired from Brazil. Primary flight training was on the Uirupurus; students then moved on to the Universals. There were additional airstrips located throughout the country, but although some of these were manned by air force detachments, none had flying units assigned to them.

The paratroop battalion consisted of about 500 personnel. It was based at Luque, outside the capital.

After completing the course at the military academy, air force officers transferred to the main base at Ñu Guazú for specialist and flight training. NCOs and enlisted personnel were trained at schools operated by the air force; most were located at Ñu Guazú.

Public Order and Internal Security

Public order was well established in the nation, and the government committed sufficient resources to law enforcement to maintain domestic order throughout the country. Urban and rural areas were generally safe, as was travel throughout the country. As a rule, citizens were able to conduct routine day-to-day affairs peaceably and without government interference. A major exception, however, was activity associated with opposition to the regime, to the Colorado Party, or to the interests of powerful and influential national and local figures. In these circumstances, individuals were likely to attract the negative attention of the police or other security personnel.

Security and Political Offenses

The tradition of authoritarian rule was deeply rooted in the national history and rigorously maintained by the Stroessner regime. The government tolerated only a narrow range of opposition to its policies and moved quickly and forcefully to put down any challenges that went beyond implicit but well-recognized limits, that threatened to be effective, or that were raised by groups not enjoying official recognition. The government pointed proudly to the stability that Stroessner's rule brought to Paraguay, which had been riven by years of political disruption. Noting that Paraguay escaped the instability, political violence, and upheaval that had troubled the rest of Latin America, government supporters dismissed charges by human rights groups that such stability often came at the cost of individual civil rights and political liberty.

The government relied on several pieces of security legislation to prosecute security and political offenses. Principal among these was the state-of-siege decree, provided for under Article 79 of the Constitution. With the exception of a very few short periods, a state of siege was in continuous effect from 1954 until April 1987. After 1970 the state of siege was technically restricted to Asunción. The restriction was virtually meaningless, however, because the judiciary ruled that authorities could bring to the capital those persons accused of security offenses elsewhere and charge them under the state-of-siege provisions. Under the law, the government could declare a state of siege lasting up to three months in the event of international war, foreign invasion, domestic disturbance, or the threat of any of these. Extensions had to be approved by the legislature, which routinely did so. Under the state of siege, public meetings and demonstrations could be prohibited. Persons could be arrested and detained indefinitely without charge.

The lapse of the state of siege in 1987 had little effect on the government's ability to contain political opposition as of late 1988. Other security legislation could be used to cover the same range of offenses. The most important of these provisions was Law 209, "In Defense of Public Peace and Liberty of Person." This law, passed in 1970, lists crimes against public peace and liberty, including the public incitement of violence or civil disobedience. It specifies the limits on freedom of expression set forth in Article 71 of the Constitution, which forbids the preaching of hatred between Paraguayans or of class struggle. Law 209 raises penalties set forth in earlier security legislation for involvement in groups that seek to replace the existing government with a communist regime or to use violence to overthrow the government. It makes it a criminal offense to be a member of such groups and to support them in any form, including subscribing to publications; attending meetings or rallies; and printing, storing, distributing, or selling print or video material that supports such groups. Law 209 also sets penalties for slandering public officials.

During the early 1980s, Law 209 was used to prosecute several individuals the government accused of taking part in conspiracies directed from abroad by Marxist-Leninist groups. Among these were a group of peasants who hijacked a bus to the capital in 1980 to protest being evicted from their land. In 1983 members of an independent research institute that published data on the economy and other matters were arrested after a journal published by the institute carried articles calling for the formation of a student-worker-peasant alliance. Human rights groups, critical of trial procedures and the evidence in the two cases, questioned the existence of a foreign-directed conspiracy, asserting instead that the cases represented carefully selected attempts to discourage organized opposition. During the mid-1980s, the government used Law 209 principally to charge political opponents with fomenting hatred, defaming government officials, or committing sedition.

The lapse of the state of siege also had little effect on the government's ability to handle security and political offenses because authorities routinely detained political activists and others without citing any legal justification at all. In these cases, suspects were held for periods of hours, days, or weeks, then released without ever being charged. In practice, persons subjected to arbitrary arrest and detention had no recourse to legal protection, and constitutional requirements for a judicial determination of the legality of detention and for charges to be filed within forty-eight hours were routinely ignored (see The Criminal Justice System, this ch.). According to the United States Department of State, 253 political opposition activists were detained at least overnight in 1987. Of these, thirty-nine were held for more than seven days, and formal charges were filed in only sixteen of the cases.

Many of those detained were taken to police stations, armed forces installations, or to the Department of Investigations at police headquarters in Asunción. There have been numerous well-documented allegations of beating in the arrest process and of torture during detention. The government has asserted that torture was not a common practice and that any abuses were investigated and their perpetrators prosecuted under the law. National newspapers have carried rare accounts of a few such investigations and trials, but continued allegations of torture suggested that the problem had not been brought under control as of the late 1980s.

The government also limited the expression of opposition views by denying permits for assemblies and refusing or cancelling printing or broadcasting licenses. In early 1987, an independent radio station suspended its broadcasts after the government refused to do anything about a months-long illegal jamming of its authorized frequencies. Meetings by the political opposition, students, and labor groups required prior authorization by police, who did not hesitate to block and repress assemblies that did not have prior approval, sometimes beating leaders and participants. The government has also restricted the travel of a few persons involved in the political opposition or in labor groups. Some foreign journalists and certain Paraguayans identified with the opposition were expelled. During 1987 two persons then in exile were allowed to return to Paraguay. The government claimed that a third, a poet, was also free to return.

The police and the military were the main means of enforcement of the regime. During the mid-1980s, however, armed vigilantes associated with the Colorado Party broke up opposition meetings and rallies, sometimes while police looked on. Such groups had been active since the 1947 civil war but had been used relatively infrequently after the 1960s. The principal group was a loosely organized militia known as the Urban Guards (Guardias Urbanas), whose members were linked with local party branches and worked closely with the police. A second group was led by the head of the Department of Investigations. The government did not appear concerned by the reemergence of such groups and may in fact have encouraged them. In September 1987, for example, vigilantes broke up a panel discussion of opposition and labor members that was being held in a Roman Catholic Church. The vigilantes used chains and clubs to attack panel members and a parish priest who tried to intervene. The minister of justice, who himself was the leader of an anticommunist association that maintained its own security group, later publicly commended the vigilantes.

Numerous sources of government opposition were targets of security forces during the 1980s. Activity by these groups as well as the violent suppression of such activity disturbed public order on numerous occasions.

Foremost among those groups officially viewed as a security threat was the Paraguayan Communist Party (Partido Comunista Paraguayo—PCP). Since its inception, the Stroessner government has justified the continuance of strict internal security policies, particularly the prolongation of the state of siege, as necessary measures to prevent a communist takeover. Thus, the PCP's efforts to establish and maintain a power base in Paraguay had been ineffective throughout the Stroessner regime. This anticommunist fervor did not abate during the 1980s, however, even though the PCP was completely isolated from the national population. As of mid-1988, the party was estimated to have some 4,000 members, most operating underground. Its leaders were either in exile or under arrest. The party claimed to have organized new cells during the 1980s, but their existence could not be confirmed. Excluded from the principal political opposition coalition, the PCP also claimed to have set up its own political front and labor front in exile. Both front organizations appeared, however, to exist only on paper, if at all.

The party was founded in 1928 and has been illegal since then, except for a short period in 1936 and again in the 1946–47 period before the PCP became involved in the 1947 civil war. The party's efforts to organize a general strike in 1959 were ineffective, as was

Guards at a military installation in Asunción
Courtesy Richard S. Sacks

its involvement in guerrilla attacks in the early 1960s. Both efforts drew harsh government reprisals. The party was believed to have two factions. The original one, the PCP, was loyal to the Soviet Union. A breakaway faction, the Paraguayan Communist Party—Marxist-Leninist (Partido Comunista Paraguayo—Marxista-Leninista) was formed in 1967; it was avowedly Maoist. In 1982 the government arrested several persons that it identified as being members of the pro-China wing of the PCP. Evidence in that case has been criticized by international human rights groups, however, and it was unclear as of late 1988 whether either wing of the PCP was active in the country at all. The party held its last conference in 1971.

Another illegal opposition group was the Political-Military Organization (Organización Político-Militar—OPM). The group was founded in 1974 by leftist Catholic students and drew some support from radical members of the clergy and Catholic peasant organizations. The government made extensive arrests of OPM members and sympathizers in 1976, after which operations of the movement declined. It was unclear whether the OPM still existed as of mid-1988, but the government continued to warn of its threat, claiming that it was under communist control.

The activities of illegal opposition parties—including the Colorado Popular Movement (Movimiento Popular Colorado—

Mopoco), the Authentic Radical Liberal Party (Partido Liberal Radical Auténtico—PLRA), and the Christian Democratic Party (Partido Demócrata Cristiano—PDC)—also drew official attention. Members of illegal parties were subject to regular police surveillance. They have alleged that their telephones were illegally tapped and their correspondence intercepted. The unrecognized opposition parties were routinely denied permits for meetings, so that any they held usually were broken up, often violently, by police, who cited them for illegally holding unauthorized assemblies. In 1979 these three parties joined with a legally recognized opposition party, the PRF, in a coalition known as the National Accord (Acuerdo Nacional). Leaders of this coalition, whether members of legal or illegal parties, were also subject to detentions and deportations (see Opposition Parties, ch. 4).

Independent labor unions were another object of surveillance by government security forces in the 1980s. Most labor unions belonged to the Paraguayan Confederation of Workers (Confederación Paraguaya de Trabajadores), which was allied with the government and carefully controlled by it (see Interest Groups, ch. 4). Although workers not sponsored by the official confederation were not authorized to organize freely, some independent labor unions had been given official recognition. Their activities, however, were closely monitored by the police, who sent representatives to all meetings. Despite tight controls—Paraguayan law made it virtually impossible to call a legal strike—a number of labor-related public disturbances took place in the mid-1980s. In April 1986, for instance, a peaceful protest by a medical workers' association in Asunción was forcibly broken up by police. Vigilante groups associated with the Colorado Party were also active in intimidating and assaulting the doctors, nurses, and technicians involved, as well as university students who joined in subsequent demonstrations supporting the medical workers. Hundreds of demonstrators organized by an independent workers' movement were clubbed and beaten in the capital in May 1986. Continued demonstrations in support of the jailed demonstrators and medical workers also drew police action.

In 1985 student demonstrations disturbed public order in the capital for the first time in twenty-five years. An estimated 2,000 students clashed with police in April of that year. After a student was shot to death in the clash, more demonstrations followed, and part of the National University was closed for several days. Since that time, students have been prominent in demonstrations organized by several other groups.

Land tenure issues were also apparent in outbreaks of public violence. Several incidents involved arrests by military and police personnel of militant landless peasants who were squatting on private or public land (see Land Tenure, ch. 3; Interest Groups, ch. 4). In 1986 three squatter incidents were publicized in the local press; after military involvement in the shooting deaths of two peasants was revealed, the military made efforts to leave action in similar cases to the police. Local community leaders chosen to represent peasants in negotiations with the government over land tenure issues have also been subject to harassment by local police and judicial officials. Reports have appeared in both the national and international press about abuses of the rights of the nation's small, unassimilated Indian population. Most frequently, abuses were alleged to occur in land disputes. The abuses appeared to result from the relative powerlessness of the Indian population vis-à-vis local landowners and the remoteness of tribal areas.

The government controlled most print media, both television channels, and most radio stations and tolerated only limited criticism from the press. Major media usually avoided criticizing the president, his family, the military, and key civilian leaders. Topics related to official corruption and national security were also generally avoided, and coverage of the political opposition was strictly limited. Violations of these rules were answered with force eventually—sometimes immediately—by the government (see The Media, ch. 4).

During the mid-1980s, the Roman Catholic Church emerged as a leader of antigovernment forces. The church was openly opposed to the Stroessner regime during the 1960s and early 1970s, until the government cracked down, sending troops into the private Catholic University on more than one occasion and eventually leaving it in shambles. The harsh government response was followed by several years of relative quiet from the church. During the mid-1980s, church officials offered to serve as a bridge for the reconciliation of the government and the opposition but were turned down by the government. Roman Catholic bishops also began to take a larger role in pressing for a transition to democracy and investigation of human rights abuses. The wave of antigovernment protests in 1986 and the government's forcible response, however, appeared to have inspired the church to take a more overt political stance. In May 1986, the archbishop of Asunción announced a series of protests that culminated in the ringing of church bells throughout the capital. Some 800 priests and members of religious orders, joined by members of the opposition parties and other people, led a march of silence in the capital in October 1987. The government permitted the crowd—estimated at 40,000—

to proceed peacefully. Provincial clergy, long active among the rural poor, also have been involved in land tenure disputes and in setting up peasant cooperative enterprises. Activities in both areas have been met with displeasure by local landowners and have resulted in clashes with the military and with local police. Following the government's closure in 1984 of *ABC Color,* the Roman Catholic Church's newspaper, *Sendero,* became an important source of information on opposition activities.

Crime

As a matter of policy, the government did not publish statistics on crime, so it was impossible to determine the incidence of crime, the frequency of particular crimes, or the direction of overall crime rates.

The nation had a relatively homogeneous population, however, and did not appear to be troubled by the high rates of ordinary crimes, such as murder, assault, and theft, that have been associated with ethnic tensions or class divisions found in other areas of Latin America. However, three special types of crimes—corruption, smuggling, and drug trafficking—attracted media attention both locally and internationally in the 1980s.

Official corruption has been a very sensitive issue throughout the Stroessner regime and remained so during the late 1980s. National standards of public conduct appeared to accommodate a certain amount of personal intervention on behalf of family members, friends, and business associates. It was widely agreed, however, both within the nation and outside it, that serious breaches of these standards by senior civilian and military officials were rarely investigated or prosecuted. Indeed, efforts by officials to generate wealth or to influence the outcome of legal or business decisions, either on their own behalf or on that of relatives, friends, or associates, were treated by the government as a perquisite of office and a reward for loyalty. Allegations of high-level corruption and graft in the local press were officially frowned upon, and displeasure was expressed overtly by confiscating publications and arresting journalists and publishers. Nonetheless, some investigations and arrests of alleged perpetrators have taken place and been reported. One example was the arrest in late 1985 of twenty-nine senior bureaucrats and businessmen on charges of embezzlement of an estimated US$100 million from the Central Bank.

Involvement or connivance in smuggling appeared to be a significant element of official corruption. Most observers have estimated that the volume of illegal foreign trade at the very least came close to matching that of legal commerce during the mid-1980s and possibly surpassed it (see External Trade, ch.3). In 1987 the leader of a business association of commercial and industrial interests estimated that contraband accounted for two-thirds of Paraguay's foreign trade. The avoidance of import duties represented a serious loss of revenue to the government. The flood of cheaper goods also harmed local producers, who could not compete with the artificially low prices of smuggled goods. The illegal commerce also had raised tensions with Brazil because it undercut Brazil's own economy (see Argentina and Brazil, ch. 4).

Smuggling has had a long history in Paraguay. During the 1950s, most operators worked on a small scale, but by the 1960s it was apparent that several persons had made fortunes in the trade. During the 1970s, smugglers moved into exports as well as imports. The trade began by focusing on such luxury items as whiskey and cigarettes, but by the 1980s, smuggled goods included electronic goods, appliances, and even commodities such as wheat. Logs taken from Eastern Paraguay and sold in Brazil were a major illegal export item. The growing disparity between official exchange rates and market exchange rates during the 1980s made the trade increasingly lucrative, because traders were able to buy goods outside the country at market rates and then sell them in Paraguay at a price that was below that of legally imported goods but still high enough to render a substantial profit. Movement of the heavy volume of illegal trade necessitated crossing river borders patrolled by the navy and crossing land borders and road checkpoints patrolled by the army and the police. Entry by air entailed transport through airports controlled by the air force. Despite these controls, few smugglers were arrested as the trade in illegal goods burgeoned and illegal markets thrived openly in the capital and other cities, especially Puerto Presidente Stroessner, which borders Brazil. The apparent tolerance of smuggling and the fact that several senior military and civilian officials had unaccounted-for sources of wealth contributed to a widely held local belief that there was official involvement in the trade.

An especially serious outgrowth of smuggling was the expansion into drug trafficking during the early 1980s, when Paraguay emerged as a transit point in the international drug trade. The nation was well situated for the role. It was located near Bolivia and Peru, which were major Latin American sources of illegal drugs. Moreover, Paraguay's sparsely populated and remote border areas presented difficulties for police surveillance. The nation had been used as a transit point during the 1960s, but international and local efforts had shut down the trade by the early 1970s. A series of seizures of drugs and of chemicals used to refine them during the 1984–87 period suggested that the problem had resurfaced, however. The problem first reached public attention in 1984 when a large quantity of chemicals used to refine coca paste into cocaine was seized by authorities in Paraguay. In 1986 and 1987, officials in Panama and Belgium discovered large amounts of cocaine that had been shipped from Paraguay. Again in 1987, evidence of Paraguayan involvement in drug trafficking surfaced after a plane carrying a major shipment of cocaine crashed in Argentina, having taken off in Paraguay. The Stroessner government denied charges by United States government officials that Paraguayan military and civilian officials were involved in the trade and vowed to take a tough stand against any drug traffickers. According to a United States Department of State official, Paraguay was also a major producer of marijuana for export.

The Police

The police had a long history in Paraguay. Francia maintained the nation's first police establishment, using it to enforce his complete control of the state. Under him, the police maintained a wide-reaching spy network that moved ruthlessly to suppress dissent and generated an atmosphere of fear. The police have remained a powerful and politicized institution ever since. Until the mid-1950s, the police often served as a counterweight to the armed forces, but after police officials were implicated in an abortive coup against Stroessner in late 1955, the force was purged, and police paramilitary units were sharply cut back. Since then, the police chief has almost always been a serving or retired army officer. Army officers have also held many key positions in the police hierarchy.

The Paraguayan police force was a centralized organization under the administration of the minister of interior. The force comprised two main elements, one for the capital and another for the rest of the nation. A separate highway police patrolled the nation's roads and was administered by the minister of public works and communication.

In 1988 police strength was estimated at 8,500 personnel; about 4,500 were assigned to the capital and the rest to the nation's 19 departments. The ratio of police to the rest of the population was one of the world's highest. Most rank-and-file police personnel were two-year conscripts who generally served outside their home area.

The capital police force was headed by a chief of police. Police personnel were assigned to headquarters or to one of twenty-three borough precincts. Police headquarters had three departments. The regular police, who dealt with ordinary crime, as well as having traffic-control, mounted, and motorized elements, came under the administration of the Department of Public Order. The Department of Investigations, an internal security organ, dealt with political and security offenses. The Department of Training and Operations handled police administration and planning and ran police training establishments. Several directorates at police headquarters specialized in particular areas; among these were surveillance and offenses, identification, alien registration, and politics. A separate directorate specializing in political intelligence—formerly the sole province of the army staff's intelligence section—was established in mid-1987. Police personnel also ran the capital's fire department.

A special unit of the capital police was the Security Guard, a 400-strong unit called up in cases of emergency and used in ceremonies and parades. About one-half of the unit, which had two rifle companies, was manned by conscripts.

Police in the interior were under the control of the government delegate heading the department in which police operated. For police functions, the delegate was in turn responsible to the minister of interior. Each delegate usually had a police chief who handled routine matters, an investigative section to process the identity cards carried by all citizens, and an additional person to supervise police arrests with a view to bringing charges. Departments were divided into districts in which a justice of the peace had several police conscripts assigned to him to carry out guard and patrol duties and other routine police functions.

All police training took place in Asunción. Basic training was given at the Police College, which offered a five-year course in modern police techniques. The Higher Police College offered specialized training. The police also operated a school for NCOs and an in-service training battalion.

The Criminal Justice System

In practice the criminal justice system was composed of two parallel structures. The first comprised the formal legal system set forth in the Constitution and in numerous statutes that provided for an independent judiciary and that specified legal procedures (see The Judiciary, ch. 4). The second system was one in which political and economic clout determined the outcome of conflict resolution. When the two structures clashed, the second was generally perceived to prevail. The widespread perception that the criminal justice system was susceptible to economic and political manipulation meant that few people were willing to confront police, military, or political authority.

The Penal Code

During the colonial period, criminal justice was administered in courts in what is now Paraguay according to provisions in several codes developed by the Spanish. Appeal in specific cases was referred to higher tribunals in the mother country. Many of those laws continued to be applied during the period following independence, except when Paraguayan rulers arbitrarily applied their own self-made law. In 1883 the nation adopted the Argentine penal code. This was replaced by a national code drawn up by Paraguayan jurists in 1890. This code was rewritten in 1910, and the new code proclaimed in 1914. The 1914 Penal Code, as amended, was still in force as of 1988.

The code is set forth in two books, each of which has two sections. The first section of Book I gives general provisions defining the application of the law and criminal liability, addressing such issues as mitigating circumstances, insanity, and multiple crimes. According to the code, active-duty members of the armed forces come under the jurisdiction of the Military Penal Code, as do perpetrators of purely military offenses. Section 2 of Book I establishes punishments and provides for the cancellation of legal actions and the exercise of prosecution functions. The death sentence was abolished in 1967, and the punishments provided for are imprisonment, jailing, exile, suspension, fines, and disqualification. Jailing, which like imprisonment can entail involuntary labor, is served by those persons convicted of less serious crimes in special institutions distinct from prisons, which house those convicted of serious crimes that draw long-term sentences. Disqualification can entail loss of public office or loss of public rights, including suffrage and pension benefits.

The first half of Book II of the code comprises a sixteen-chapter section that groups offenses into broad categories, defines specific types of violations, and sets penalties for each type. The major categories include crimes against the state, against public order and public authority, and against persons and property. The second half of Book II sets forth misdemeanor offenses and their punishments.

Criminal Procedure

Sources of procedural criminal law are the Constitution, special laws, the Penal Code, and the Code of Penal Procedure. These sources govern pleading and practices in all courts as well as admission to the practice of law.

The entire court system was under the control of the national government. In addition to the judiciary, which was a separate branch of government, the Ministry of Justice and Labor was also involved in the administration of justice. It was responsible for judicial officers attached to the attorney general's office. These officials were assigned to the various courts and represented the government in trial proceedings. The ministry was also responsible for the judiciary's budget and the operation of the penal system.

At the apex of the criminal court system was the Supreme Court of Justice, which was made up of five justices appointed by the president. Below the Supreme Court of Justice, which was responsible for the administration of the judiciary, was the criminal court of appeal. Both courts were located in Asunción. Courts of original jurisdiction were divided between the courts of the first instance, which heard serious cases, and justice of the peace courts, whose jurisdiction was limited to minor offenses. There were six courts of the first instance in the country during the 1980s. There were far more justice of the peace courts, but the exact number was not publicly available.

Although theoretically a coequal branch of government, the judiciary, along with the legislature, has traditionally been subordinate to the executive. Members of the judiciary were appointed by the president and served a five-year term coinciding with that of the president. In practice, the courts rarely challenged government actions. Under the law, the Supreme Court of Justice had jurisdiction over executive actions, but it continued not to accept jurisdiction in political cases as of mid-1988. The independence of the judiciary was also made problematic by the executive's complete control over the judiciary's budget. Moreover, during the Stroessner regime, membership in the Colorado Party was a virtual requirement for appointment to the judiciary; in 1985 all but two judges were members. Many justices of the peace, in particular, were appointed by virtue of their influence in their local communities. During the mid-1980s, the government made an effort to improve the public image of judges, suspending a small number for corruption. It appeared, however, that more would be necessary to promote public confidence in judicial independence.

The Constitution theoretically guarantees every citizen the rights of due process, presumption of innocence, prohibition against self-incrimination, and speedy trial. It protects the accused from ex post facto enactments, unreasonable search and seizure, and cruel and unusual punishment. Habeas corpus protection is extended to all citizens.

Criminal actions can be initiated by the offended party or by the police acting under the direction of a judicial official. According to the law, police had to secure warrants to arrest suspects or to conduct searches unless a crime was in progress while the police were present. Police could detain suspects for only twenty-four hours without pressing charges. Within forty-eight hours, a justice of the peace had to be informed of the detention. Upon receiving the charges of the police and determining that there were grounds for those charges, the justice of the peace then took action according to the gravity of the offense charged. In the case of misdemeanors, the justice of the peace was empowered to try the suspect and to pass sentences of up to thirty days in jail or an equivalent fine. In the case of felonies, a justice of the peace, although not possessing authority to try the case, performed several important functions. If upon hearing the charges, the justice of the peace determined that there were grounds to suspect the individual charged, he informed the suspect of charges against him or her, fixed a time within twenty-four hours to permit the suspect to present an unsworn statement, established a time for witnesses to make sworn statements, and determined a time for inspecting the scene of the crime.

After investigation and the receipt of the suspect's unsworn statement, the justice of the peace could order the suspect to be held in preventive detention, if necessary for up to three days incommunicado. This period was renewable for additional three-day periods and was intended to prevent the suspect from communicating with coconspirators still at large. Justices of the peace could also order impoundment of a suspect's goods, except those needed by his or her family.

Finally, the justice of the peace prepared the case for trial in the criminal court of the first instance. This preparation was done by assembling the evidence into a document known as the summary and sending it to the higher court along with supporting documents such as statements of witnesses. The investigative stage of criminal proceedings was limited by law to two months—subject to a formal petition for extension.

Despite these important responsibilities, many justices of the peace were not qualified lawyers. Therefore, in several of the larger cities, a special official, known as a proceedings judge, took over the most difficult cases before sending the information to Asunción for trial. These judges were empowered to release suspects on bail—something a justice of the peace could not do.

Trials were conducted almost exclusively by the presentation of written documents to a judge who then rendered a decision. As was true for most Latin American nations, Paraguay did not have trial by jury. Verdicts were automatically referred to the appellate court and in some cases could be appealed further to the Supreme Court of Justice. A portion of the trial was usually open to the public.

The safeguards set forth in the Constitution and in legal statutes often were not honored in practice. The police frequently ignored requirements for warrants for arrest and for search and seizure. Legal provisions governing speedy trial were ineffective, and delays were legendary. Most accused persons were released before trial proceedings were complete because they had already been detained for the length of time prescribed for their alleged offense. A 1983 United Nations study found that Paraguay had the highest rate of unsentenced prisoners in the Western Hemisphere. Moreover, defense lawyers, particularly in security and political cases, were subjected to police harassment and sometimes to arrest.

The Prison System

In 1988 the operation of prisons was under the General Directorate of Penal Institutions, controlled by the Ministry of Justice and Labor. According to Article 65 of the Constitution, penal institutions are required to be healthful and clean and to be dedicated to rehabilitating offenders. Economic constraints made conditions in prisons austere, however, and overcrowding was a serious problem. A report by an independent bar association in the early 1980s criticized the prison system for failing to provide treatment for convicts.

The National Penitentiary in Asunción was the country's principal correctional institution. Observers believed that the total population of the institution averaged about 2,000, including political prisoners. Another prison for adult males was the Tacumbu Penitentiary located in Villa Hayes, near Asunción.

Women and juveniles were held in separate institutions. Females were incarcerated in the Women's Correctional Institute under the supervision of the Sisters of the Good Shepherd. The institution offered courses in domestic science. A correctional institute for minors was located in Emboscada, which was also near the capital. It stressed rehabilitating inmates and providing them with skills that would help them secure employment when their sentences were completed.

In addition to the penal institutions in the Central Department, each of the other departments maintained a prison or jail in its capital. Many smaller communities did not have adequate facilities even for temporary incarceration, however. A suspect receiving a sentence of more than one year usually was transferred to a national penitentiary.

* * *

As of late 1988, no definitive studies that deal comprehensively with national security matters in contemporary Paraguay had been published. A general treatment of modern Paraguayan political life, touching on the military and its place in the national life, can be found in two works by Paul H. Lewis: *Paraguay Under Stroessner* and *Socialism, Liberalism, and Dictatorship in Paraguay.* The most complete coverage of the history and development of the armed forces is contained in the section, ''Paraguay,'' in Adrian J. English's *Armed Forces of Latin America.* For developments since 1980, the reader must search through issues of the *Latin American Weekly Report* [London], the *Latin America Report* prepared by the Joint Publications Research Service, and the *Daily Report: Latin America* put out by the Foreign Broadcast Information Service. Current order-of-battle data are available in the International Institute of Strategic Studies' excellent annual, *The Military Balance.* The best overview of conditions of public order is contained in the section on Paraguay in *Country Reports on Human Rights Practices,* a report submitted annually by the United States Department of State to the United States Congress. Two reports by the Americas Watch Committee—*Paraguay: Latin America's Oldest Dictatorship Under Pressure* and *Rule by Fear: Paraguay After Thirty Years Under Stroessner*—also provide data on the treatment of political and security offenses under the criminal justice system as well as the government's observance of human rights. (For further information and complete citations, see Bibliography.)

Appendix

Table

Table 1. Metric Conversion Coefficients and Factors

When you know	Multiply by	To find
Millimeters	0.04	inches
Centimeters	0.39	inches
Meters	3.3	feet
Kilometers	0.62	miles
Hectares (10,000 m²)	2.47	acres
Square kilometers	0.39	square miles
Cubic meters	35.3	cubic feet
Liters	0.26	gallons
Kilograms	2.2	pounds
Metric tons	0.98	long tons
....	1.1	short tons
....	2,204	pounds
Degrees Celsius	9	degrees Fahrenheit
(Centigrade)	divide by 5 and add 32	

Table 2. Population Growth, Selected Years, 1886–1982

Census Year	Total Population	Annual Intercensal Growth Rate (in percentage)
1886–87	329,645	
1914	650,451	2.5
1924	828,968	2.5
1936	992,420	1.5
1950	1,343,100	2.2
1962	1,854,400	2.7
1972	2,357,955	2.7
1982	3,026,165	2.5

Source: Based on information from Paraguay, Dirección General de Estadística y Censos, *Censo nacional de población y viviendas, 1982: Cifras provisionales,* Asunción, December 1982, 30.

Table 3. Population and Intercensal Growth Rates, 1950–82

	Total Population				Annual Growth Rate (in percentage)		
	1950	1962	1972	1982	1950–62	1962–72	1972–82
Asunción Metropolitan Area	271,901	409,273	579,014	794,165	3.5	3.6	3.2
Central Asunción	206,634	288,822	388,958	455,517	2.8	3.1	1.6
Paraguay Total	1,328,452	1,819,103	2,357,955	3,026,165	2.7	2.7	2.5

Source: Based on information from Paraguay, Dirección General de Estadística y Censos, *Censo nacional de población y viviendas, 1982: Cifras provisionales*, Asunción, December 1982, 21–2.

Table 4. Educational Enrollment by Age-group, 1965 and 1985
(in percentage)

Level	Sex	1965	1985
Primary	Male	109 *	104 *
	Female	96	98
	Total	102 *	101 *
Secondary	Male	13	31
	Female	13	30
	Total	13	31
Tertiary	Total	4	10

* Gross enrollment sometimes exceeded 100 percent, because some pupils might be younger or older than the standard primary-school age.

Source: Based on information from World Bank, *World Development Report: 1988,* New York, 1988.

Table 5. Inoculation of Children Under One Year of Age, 1981–84
(in percentage)

Vaccine	1981	1982	1983	1984
Tuberculosis	42	47	55	80
DPT *	28	34	45	67
Poliomyelitis	26	39	47	68
Measles	16	27	37	62

* Diphtheria, pertussis, and tetanus.

Source: Based on information from Pan American Health Organization, *Health Conditions in the Americas, 1981-1984,* II, Washington, 1986, 188.

Table 6. Deaths by Age-group, 1981–84

Age-Group	Percentage of all Deaths				Rate per 1,000 Inhabitants			
	1981	1982	1983	1984	1981	1982	1983	1984
Less than 1	21	21	20	20	59.0	51.2	51.0	49.8
1-4	7	7	7	8	4.2	3.8	4.1	4.1
5-14	3	3	3	3	0.6	0.7	0.7	0.7
15 and over	69	69	70	69	7.5	7.7	8.1	8.0
TOTAL	100	100	100	100	6.9	6.4	6.7	6.6

Source: Based on information from Pan American Health Organization, *Health Conditions in the Americas, 1981-1984,* II, Washington, 1986, 185.

Table 7. Balance of Payments, Selected Years, 1980–86
(in millions of United States dollars)

	1980	1982	1984	1986
Merchandise				
Exports (f.o.b.) *				
Registered exports	311.0	329.9	334.5	232.5
Unregistered exports	271.9	162.1	143.4	138.4
Total exports	582.9	492.0	477.9	370.9
Imports (f.o.b.) *				
Registered imports	675.3	723.4	661.0	518.1
Unregistered imports	379.0	124.5	99.5	379.7
Total imports	1054.3	847.9	760.5	897.8
Trade Balance	−471.4	−355.9	−282.6	−526.9
Services				
Credits	118.1	177.5	103.6	174.4
Debits	260.0	360.9	194.9	264.9
Net services	−141.9	−183.4	−91.3	−90.5
Income				
Receipts	80.2	122.9	70.7	62.0
Payments	84.5	91.3	91.6	106.0
Net income	−4.3	31.6	−20.9	−44.0
Transfers				
Official	4.8	3.5	6.8	12.5
Private	−0.3	1.5	2.5	0.6
Net transfers	4.5	5.0	9.3	13.1
Current account balance	−613.1	−502.7	−385.5	−648.3
Net Direct foreign investment	29.8	33.7	0.5	31.0
Long-term loans				
Official sources	36.4	106.1	136.5	96.5
Private sources	89.1	137.7	25.7	1.0
Net long-term loans	125.5	243.8	162.2	97.5
Other capital				
Net short-term loans	0.0	−82.0	−35.0	−44.7
Errors and omissions	203.6	−168.7	−51.7	375.1
Net other capital	203.6	−250.7	−86.7	330.4
Overall balance				
excluding Itaipú hydroelectric plant ..	−254.2	−475.9	−309.5	−189.4
Net inflows related to				
Itaipú hydroelectric plant	405.1	345.7	213.2	110.0
Overall balance	150.9	−130.2	−96.3	−79.4
Changes in reserves				
(−means increase)	−150.9	130.2	96.3	79.4

* Free on board.

Table 8. Presidential Election Results, 1954-88
(as reported by the government)

Year	Total Votes	Colorado Party	Radical Liberal Party	Liberal Party	Febrerista Revolutionary Party	Blank/ Annulled Votes
1954	239,978	236,191 (98.4%)	—	—	—	3,787 (1.6%)
1958	303,478	295,414 (97.3%)	—	—	—	8,064 (2.7%)
1963	628,615	569,551 (90.6%)	—	47,750 [1] (7.6%)	—	11,314 (1.8%)
1968	656,414	465,535 (70.9%) [2]	139,622 (21.3%)	27,965 (4.3%)	16,871 (2.6%)	6,421 (1.0%)
1973	814,610	681,306 (83.6%)	98,096 (12%)	24,611 (3%)	—	10,597 (1.3%)
1978	1,091,994	990,774 (90.7%)	54,984 (5%)	37,059 (3.4%)	—	9,177 (.8%)
1983	1,048,886	944,637 (90.1%)	59,094 (5.6%)	34,010 (3.2%)	—	11,145 (1.1%)
1988	1,339,003	1,187,738 (88.7%)	95,500 (7.1%)	42,442 (3.2%)	—	13,323 (1%)

— Means did not participate.
[1] Participated as the Renovation Movement.
[2] Percentages for some elections do not add to 100 because of rounding.

Source: Based on information from *El Diario de noticias* [Asunción], February 14, 1988; and Foreign Broadcast Information Service, *Daily Report: Latin America.* (FBIS-LAT-88-033A.) Washington, February 19, 1988, 38.

Table 9. *Composition of the Paraguayan Army, 1988*

Type of Unit	Number
Presidential Escort Regiment	1 *
Corps headquarters	3
Infantry divisions	8
Cavalry division	1
Artillery battalions	3
Engineer battalions	6
Signals and transport battalion	1
TOTAL STRENGTH	12,500

* Administered independently.

Table 10. *Major Equipment of the Paraguayan Army, 1988*

Equipment	Number	Source
M–4A3 Sherman and Sherman Firefly medium tanks	12	Argentina (United States-made)
M–3A1 light tanks	12	Brazil (United States-made)
M–8 and M–3 armored cars	12	Brazil (United States-made)
EE–9 Cascavel armored cars	20	Brazil
M–2 modified half-track armored personnel carriers	3	Brazil (United States-made)
EE–11 Urutu armored personnel carriers	10	Brazil
152mm Vickers Mk V coastal guns	6	Britain
75mm Bofors Model 1927/34 howitzers	25	Argentina (Swedish-made)
105mm M–101 howitzers	48	France
81mm mortars	n.a.	France
107 mortars	n.a.	United States
75mm antitank guns	n.a.	United States
20mm air defense guns	20	n.a.
40mm M–1A1 air defense guns	10	United States
Army Aviation		
Fokker S–11 aircraft	8	Brazil (United States-made)
Bell 47G helicopters	3	Brazil (United States-made)

n.a.—not available.

Table 11. Major Equipment of the Paraguayan Navy, 1988

Type of Vessel	Number	Source	Size
Roraima-class gunboat with helicopter deck	1	1983 Brazil	220 tons
Bouchard ex-minesweepers	3	1937-38 Argentina	450 tons
Paraguay class	2	1931 Italy	636 tons
701-class small patrol craft	6	1940s United States	15 tons
Large patrol craft	1	1907 Netherlands	180 tons
LSM 1-class with helicopter deck	1	1944 United States	n.a.
LCU 501-class	2	1945 United States	143 tons
Freighter	1	1968 Spain	1,150 tons
River transport	1	1901 Belgium	n.a.
Floating dock	1	1944 United States	n.a.
Floating workshop	1	1942 United States	n.a.
Floating crane	1	1907 Netherlands	n.a.
Tugs	2	1945 United States	84 tons
Marine battalion	1		
Naval aviation			
Douglas C-47 transport aircraft	1	United States	n.a.
Cessna 150M and 206 aircraft	9	United States	n.a.
T-6G Texan armed training aircraft	2	United States	n.a.
OH-13 Sioux helicopters	3	United States	n.a.
Hiller UH-12E helicopters	2	United States	n.a.
On Order			
HB-35OB Esquilo helicopters	2	Brazil	n.a.
Total strength	3,150		

n.a.—not available.

Table 12. Major Equipment of the Paraguayan Air Force, 1988

Type of Aircraft	Number
Composite Squadron	
EMB-326 Xavante light counterinsurgency aircraft	8
Cessna aircraft (337, 402, 185 Skywagon)	7
Bell OH-13A helicopters	8
Hiller UH-12 helicopters	2
Transport Squadron	
Douglas DC-6B	3
Douglas C-54 transport aircraft	2
Douglas C-47 transport aircraft	11
DeHavilland Canada DHC-6 Twin Otter	1
DeHavilland Canada DHC-3 Otter	1
CASA C-212 Aviocar	4
Convair PBY-5A Catalina amphibious aircraft	1
Training Squadron	
Neiva T-25 Universal	10
Aerotec T-23 Uirupuru	8
North American T-6 Texan armed trainers	7

Bibliography

Chapter 1

Abente, Diego. "Constraints and Opportunities: External Factors, Authoritarianism, and Prospects for Democratization in Paraguay," *Journal of Interamerican Studies and World Affairs*, 30, No. 1, Spring 1988, 73–104.

Agee, Philip. *Inside the Company: CIA Diary*. London: Penguin Books, 1975.

Arens, Richard (ed.). *Genocide in Paraguay*. Philadelphia: Temple University Press, 1976.

Arnold, Adlai F. *Foundations of an Agricultural Policy in Paraguay*. (Praeger Special Studies in International Economics and Development.) New York: Praeger, 1971.

Baer, Werner, and Luis Breuer. "From Inward to Outward Oriented Growth: Paraguay in the 1980s," *Journal of Interamerican Studies and World Affairs*, 28, No. 3, Fall 1986, 125–49.

Barrett, William E. *Woman on Horseback*. New York: Frederick A. Stokes, 1938.

Benítez, Luis G. *Historia del Paraguay: época colonial*. Asunción: Imprenta Comuneros, 1985.

Bourne, Richard. *Political Leaders of Latin America*. Harmondsworth, Middlesex, United Kingdom: Penguin Books, 1969.

Box, Pelham Horton. *The Origins of the Paraguayan War*. New York: Russell and Russell, 1967.

Britos de Villafañe, Margarita. *Las épocas históricas del Paraguay*. Asunción: N. pub., 1982.

Caraman, Philip. *The Lost Paradise: An Account of the Jesuits in Paraguay, 1607–1768*. London: Sidgwick and Jackson, 1975.

Cardozo, Efraím. *Breve historia del Paraguay*. Buenos Aires: Editorial Universitaria de Buenos Aires, 1965.

———. *Vísperas de la guerra del Paraguay*. Buenos Aires: El Ateneo, 1954.

Chaves, Julio César. *El supremo dictador*. Madrid: Ediciones Atlas, 1964.

Chaves, Osvaldo. *La formación del pueblo Paraguayo*. Buenos Aires: Ediciones Amerindia, 1976.

Estigarribia, José Félix. *The Epic of the Chaco: Marshall Estigarribia's Memoirs of the Chaco War, 1932–1935*. New York: Greenwood Press, 1969.

Ferguson, J. Halcro. *The River Plate Republics: Argentina, Paraguay, Uruguay.* New York: Time-Life, 1965.

Graham, R.B. Cunninghame. *Portrait of a Dictator.* London: William Heinemann, 1933.

_____. *A Vanished Arcadia: Being Some Account of the Jesuits in Paraguay, 1607–1767.* New York: Dial Press, 1924.

Grow, Michael. *The Good Neighbor Policy and Authoritarianism in Paraguay.* Lawrence: Regents Press of Kansas, 1981.

Hicks, Frederic. "Interpersonal Relationships and *Caudillismo* in Paraguay," *Journal of Inter-American Studies and World Affairs,* 13, No. 1, January 1971, 89–111.

Kolinski, Charles J. *Independence or Death! The Story of the Paraguayan War.* Gainesville: University of Florida Press, 1965.

Lewis, Paul H. *Paraguay Under Stroessner.* Chapel Hill: University of North Carolina Press, 1980.

_____. *The Politics of Exile: Paraguay's Febrerista Party.* Chapel Hill: University of North Carolina Press, 1965.

_____. *Socialism, Liberalism, and Dictatorship in Paraguay.* (Politics in Latin America Series.) New York: Praeger, 1982.

Lieuwen, Edwin. *Arms and Politics in Latin America.* New York: Frederick A. Praeger, 1960.

López, Adalberto. *The Revolt of the Comuneros, 1721–1735.* Cambridge, Massachusetts: Schenkman, 1976.

Lott, Leo B. *Venezuela and Paraguay: Political Modernity and Tradition in Conflict.* New York: Holt, Rinehart, and Winston, 1972.

McNaspy, Clement J. *Conquistador Without Sword: The Life of Roque González, S.J..* Chicago: Loyola University Press, 1984.

Méndez, Epifanio. *Diagnosis Paraguaya.* Montevideo: Talleres Prometeo, 1965.

Meyer, Gordon. *The River and the People.* London: Methuen, 1965.

Nichols, Byron Albert. "The Role and Function of Political Parties in Paraguay." (Unpublished Ph.D. dissertation.) Johns Hopkins University, 1969.

Nickson, R. Andrew. "Tyranny and Longevity: Stroessner's Paraguay," *Third World Quarterly,* 10, No. 1, January 1988, 237–59.

Pendle, George. *Paraguay: A Riverside Nation.* (3d ed.) London: Oxford University Press, 1967.

Phelps, Gilbert. *Tragedy of Paraguay.* New York: St. Martin's Press, 1975.

Pincus, Joseph. *The Economy of Paraguay.* New York: Frederick A. Praeger, 1968.

Poppino, Rollie. *International Communism in Latin America.* Toronto: Free Press at Glencoe, 1964.

_____. "Paraguay." Pages 355-56 in Witold S. Sworakowski (ed.), *World Communism: A Handbook, 1918-1965.* Stanford: Hoover Institution Press, 1973.

Raine, Philip. *Paraguay.* New Brunswick, New Jersey: Scarecrow Press, 1956.

Rengger, Johann Rudolph, and Marcel Longchamps. *The Reign of Doctor Joseph Gaspar Roderick de Francia in Paraguay: Being an Account of a Six Years' Residence in that Republic, from July, 1819 to May, 1825.* (Series in Latin American History and Culture.) Port Washington, New York: Kennikat Press, 1971.

Roett, Riordan, and Amparo Menéndez-Carrión. "Authoritarian Paraguay: The Personalist Tradition." Pages 341-61 in Howard J. Wiarda and Harvey F. Kline (eds.), *Latin American Politics and Development.* (2d ed.) Boulder, Colorado: Westview Press, 1985.

_____. "Paraguay." Pages 595-606 in Gerald Michael Greenfield and Sheldon Maram (eds.), *Latin American Labor Organizations.* Westport, Connecticut: Greenwood Press, 1987.

Rout, Leslie. *Politics of the Chaco Peace Conference, 1935-1939.* Austin: University of Texas Press, 1970.

Seiferheld, Alfredo M. (ed.). *La caída de Federico Chaves: Una visión documental norteamericana.* Asunción: Editorial Histórica, 1987.

Service, Elman R. *Spanish-Guaraní Relations in Early Colonial Paraguay.* Westport, Connecticut: Greenwood Press, 1971.

Service, Elman R., and Helen S. Service. *Tobatí: Paraguayan Town.* Chicago: University of Chicago Press, 1954.

Warren, Harris Gaylord. *Paraguay: An Informal History.* Norman: University of Oklahoma Press, 1946.

_____. *Paraguay and the Triple Alliance: The Postwar Decade, 1869-1878.* Austin: University of Texas Press, 1978.

_____. "Political Aspects of the Paraguayan Revolution, 1936-1940," *Hispanic American Historical Review,* 30, No. 1, February 1950, 2-25.

_____. *Rebirth of the Paraguayan Republic: The First Colorado Era, 1878-1904.* Pittsburgh: University of Pittsburgh Press, 1985.

Washburn, Charles A. *The History of Paraguay, with Notes of Personal Observations, and Reminiscences of Diplomacy under Difficulties.* (2 Vols.). New York: AMS Press, 1973.

White, Richard Alan. *Paraguay's Autonomous Revolution, 1810-1840.* Albuquerque: University of New Mexico Press, 1978.

Wilgus, A. Curtis. *Historical Atlas of Latin America: Political, Geographic, Economic, Cultural.* New York: Cooper Square, 1967.

Williams, John Hoyt. "Governor Velasco, the Portuguese, and the Paraguayan Revolution of 1811: A New Look," *The Americas,* 28, No. 4, April 1972, 441-49.

_____. "Paraguay's Stroessner: Losing Control?," *Current History*, 86, No. 516, January 1987, 25–8.

_____. *The Rise and Fall of the Paraguayan Republic, 1800–1870.* (Institute of Latin American Studies, Latin American Monographs, No. 48.) Austin: University of Texas Press, 1979.

Wood, Bryce. *The United States and Latin American Wars, 1932–1942.* New York: Columbia University Press, 1966.

Zook, David H., Jr. *The Conduct of the Chaco War.* New Haven: Bookman Associates, 1960.

Chapter 2

Arens, Richard (ed.). *Genocide in Paraguay.* Philadelphia: Temple University Press, 1976.

Arnold, Adlai F. *Foundations of an Agricultural Policy in Paraguay.* (Praeger Special Studies in International Economics and Development.) New York: Praeger, 1971.

Baer, Werner, and Melissa Birch. "The International Economic Relations of a Small Country: The Case of Paraguay," *Economic Development and Cultural Change*, 35, No. 3, April 1987, 601–27.

Benítez, Luis G. *Historia de la educación paraguaya.* Asunción: Industrial Gráfica Comuneros, 1981.

Caraman, Philip. *The Lost Paradise: An Account of the Jesuits in Paraguay, 1607–1768.* London: Sidgwick and Jackson, 1975.

Chase-Sardi, Miguel. "La antropología aplicada en el Chaco paraguayo," *Suplemento antropológico* [Asunción], 16, No. 2, 1981, 157–66.

Chase-Sardi, Miguel, and Marcos Martínez Almada. "Encuesta para detectar la actitud de la sociedad ante el indígena," *Ateneo paraguayo: Suplemento antropológico* [Asunción], 7, Nos. 1–2, 1973, 163–70.

Corvalán, Grazziella. "Paraguay: System of Education." Pages 3765–68 in Torsten Husen and T. Neville Postlethwaite (eds.), *The International Encyclopedia of Education.* Oxford: Pergamon Press, 1985.

Engelbrecht, Guillermina, and Leroy Ortiz. "Guaraní Literacy in Paraguay," *International Journal of Sociology of Language*, 42, 1983, 53–67.

Ferreira Gubetich, Hugo. *Geografía del Paraguay.* (12th ed.) Asunción: Orbis, 1975.

Frutos, Juan Manuel. *Con el hombre y la tierra hacia el Bienestar Rural.* Asunción: Cuadernos Republicanos, 1982.

Gillespie, Fran. "Comprehending the Slow Pace of Urbanization in Paraguay Between 1950 and 1972," *Economic Development and Cultural Change,* 31, No. 2, January 1983, 355-76.

Gillespie, Fran, and Harley Browning. "The Effect of Emigration upon Socioeconomic Structure: The Case of Paraguay," *International Migration Review,* 13, No. 3, Fall 1979, 502-18.

González, Carlos Alberto. "Algunas consideraciones sobre la reglamentación de la ley 904 en cuanto a la propiedad de la tierra," *Suplemento antropológico* [Asunción], 17, No. 2, 1982, 213-19.

Graham, R.B. Cunninghame. *A Vanished Arcadia: Being Some Account of the Jesuits in Paraguay, 1607-1767.* New York: Dial Press, 1924.

Hill, Kim, et al. "Men's Time Allocation to Subsistence Work among the Aché of Eastern Paraguay," *Human Ecology,* 13, No. 1, 1985, 29-47.

_____. "Seasonal Variance in the Diet of Aché Hunter-Gatherers in Eastern Paraguay," *Human Ecology,* 12, No. 2, 1984, 101-32.

Hopkins, Edward, Raymond Crist, and William Snow. *Paraguay: 1852 and 1968.* (Occasional Publication No. 2.) New York: American Geographical Society, 1968.

Kaplan, Hillard, and Heather Dove. "Infant Development among the Aché of Eastern Paraguay," *Developmental Psychology,* 23, No. 2, 1987, 190-8.

Kaplan, Hillard, and Kim Hill. "Food Sharing among Aché Foragers: Tests of Explanatory Hypotheses," *Current Anthropology,* 26, No. 2, April 1985, 223-46.

_____. "Hunting Ability and Reproductive Success among Male Aché Foragers: Preliminary Results," *Current Anthropology,* 26, No. 1, February 1985, 131-35.

Klein, Harriet Manelis, and Louisa R. Stark. "Indian Languages of the Paraguayan Chaco," *Anthropological Linguistics,* 19, No. 8, November 1977, 378-401.

Lernoux, Penny. *1984 Revisited: Welcome to Paraguay.* New York: Alicia Patterson Foundation, 1976.

Lewis, Paul H. *Paraguay Under Stroessner.* Chapel Hill: University of North Carolina Press, 1980.

_____. *Socialism, Liberalism, and Dictatorship in Paraguay.* (Politics in Latin America Series.) New York: Praeger, 1982.

Martínez Díaz, Nicasio. *La reforma agraria.* Buenos Aires: Colección Economía Paraguaya, 1963.

Maybury-Lewis, David, and James Howe. *The Indian Peoples of Paraguay: Their Plight and Their Prospects.* (Special Report No. 2.) Cambridge, Massachusetts: Cultural Survival, 1980.

Metraux, Alfread. "The Guaraní." Pages 69–94 in Julian H. Steward (ed.), *Handbook of South American Indians,* III. Washington: GPO, 1948.

Mickelwait, Donald R., Mary Ann Riegelman, and Charles F. Sweet. *Women in Rural Development: A Survey of the Roles of Women in Ghana, Lesotho, Kenya, Nigeria, Bolivia, Paraguay, and Peru.* (Westview Special Studies in Social, Political, and Economic Development.) Boulder, Colorado: Westview Press, 1976.

Miranda, Aníbal. *Desarrollo y pobreza en Paraguay.* Asunción: El Gráfico, 1982.

Morínigo A., and José Nicolás. "El incipiente proceso de asentamiento de los núcleos de población en el Bajo Chaco paraguayo." Pages 263–306 in *Ciudad y vivenda en el Paraguay.* Asunción: Sociedad de Análisis, Estudios, y Proyectos, 1984.

Morínigo A., José Nicolás, and Roberto Luis Céspedes. "El proceso de urbanización en el Paraguay: de la quietud al dinamismo (1870–1982)." Pages 186–262 in *Ciudad y vivienda en el Paraguay.* Asunción: Sociedad de Análisis, Estudios, y Proyectos, 1984.

Morss, Elliott R., et al. *Strategies for Small Farmers Development, II: Case Studies.* (Westview Special Studies in Social, Political, and Economic Development.) Boulder, Colorado: Westview Press, 1976.

Nickson, R. Andrew. "Brazilian Colonization of the Eastern Border Region of Paraguay," *Journal of Latin American Studies,* 13, No. 1, May 1981, 111–31.

Obelar, Alejo. "La problemática indígena en el Paraguay," *Suplemento antropológico* [Asunción], 16, No. 2, 1981, 7–18.

Pan American Health Organization. *Evaluation of the Strategy for Health for All by the Year 2000.* Washington: 1986.

———. *Health Conditions in the Americas, 1981–1984,* II. Washington: 1986.

Paraguay. Dirección General de Estadística y Censos. *Anuario estadístico del Paraguay, 1982.* Asunción: December 1983.

———. *Censo nacional de población y viviendas, 1982: Cifras provisionales.* Asunción: December 1982.

———. *Censo nacional de población y viviendas, 1982: Muestra del 10%.* Asunción: September 1984.

Paraguay. Instituto Paraguayo del Indígena. *Censo y estudio de la población indígena del Paraguay, 1981.* Asunción: 1982.

Paraguay. Presidencia de la República. Secretaría Técnica de Planificación. División de Programación de Población y Recursos Humanos. *Paraguay: Proyección de la población urbana y rural, regional y departamental por sexo y grupos de edades. Período 1970–2000.* Asunción: 1981.

Pendle, George. *Paraguay: A Riverside Nation.* (3d ed.) London: Oxford University Press, 1967.

Plett, Rudolf. *Presencia Menonita en el Paraguay.* Asunción: Instituto Bíblico Asunción, 1979.

Ramírez, Miguel Angel. "Comunidades indígenas y reforma agraria," *Suplemento antropológico* [Asunción], 17, No. 2, 1982, 203–11.

Raine, Philip. *Paraguay.* New Brunswick, New Jersey: Scarecrow Press, 1956.

Redekop, Calvin. *Strangers Become Neighbors: Mennonite and Indigenous Relations in the Paraguayan Chaco.* (Studies in Anabaptist and Mennonite History, No. 22.) Scottdale, Pennsylvania: Herald Press, 1980.

Rivarola, Domingo, and G. Heisecke (eds.). *Población, urbanización, y recursos humanos en el Paraguay.* Asunción: Centro Paraguayo de Estudios Sociológicos, 1969.

Rubin, Joan. *National Bilingualism in Paraguay.* The Hague: Mouton, 1968.

Sanders, Thomas G. *Education and Authoritarianism in the Southern Cone.* (American Universities Field Staff. Fieldstaff Reports. South America Series, No. 12.) Hanover, New Hampshire: AUFS, 1981.

––––––. *Paraguay: Population and the Economy.* (Universities Field Staff International. UFSI Reports. Latin America, No. 36, TGS-7-86.) Indianapolis: UFSI, 1986.

Sautu, Ruth. "The Female Labor Force in Argentina, Bolivia, and Paraguay," *Latin American Research Review,* 15, No. 2, 1980, 152–61.

Service, Elman R., and Helen S. Service. *Tobatí: Paraguayan Town.* Chicago: University of Chicago Press, 1954.

Shoemaker, Juan F. *Evaluación de la encuesta nacional de fecundidad del Paraguay de 1979.* (World Fertility Survey Scientific Reports, No. 62.) Voorburg, Netherlands: International Statistical Institute, 1984.

Steward, Julian H., and Louis C. Faron. *Native Peoples of South America.* New York: McGraw-Hill, 1959.

Stewart, Norman R. *Japanese Colonization in Eastern Paraguay.* (National Academy of Sciences, Publication No. 1490.) Washington: National Research Council, 1967.

United States. Department of Health and Human Services. Social Security Administration. Office of Policy. Office of Research, Statistics, and International Policy. *Social Security Programs Throughout the World—1985.* (Research Report No. 60.) Washington: GPO, 1986.

Vásquez Li, Mirna. "Historia de la legislación indigenista paraguaya," *Suplemento antropológico* [Asunción], 16, No. 2, 1981, 93–103.

Viedma, Pablo Franco. *El Paraguay: Su geografía general.* Asunción: Imprenta Comuneros, 1972.

Wainerman, Catalina H., Zulma Recchini de Lattes, and Ruth Sautu. "The Participation of Women in Economic Activity in Argentina, Bolivia, and Paraguay: A Comparative Study," *Latin American Research Review*, 15, No. 2, 1980, 143–51.

World Bank. *World Development Report: 1988.* New York: Oxford University Press, 1988.

Chapter 3

Arnold, Adlai F. *Foundations of an Agricultural Policy in Paraguay.* (Praeger Special Studies in International Economics and Development.) New York: Praeger, 1971.

Baer, Werner, and Melissa Birch. "Expansion of the Economic Frontier: Paraguayan Growth in the 1970s," *World Development,* 12, No. 8, August 1984, 783–98.

———. "The International Economic Relations of a Small Country: The Case of Paraguay," *Economic Development and Cultural Change,* 35, No. 3, April 1987, 601–27.

Bair, Frank E. (ed.). *International Marketing Handbook,* II. (3d ed.) Detroit: Gale Research, 1985.

Bray, David, and Dionisio Borda. "Small Farmer Organizations and the Crisis in Cotton: Paraguayans and Brazilians in Eastern Paraguay." (Paper presented at the Latin American Studies Association Conference.) New Orleans: March 16–19, 1988.

Brooks, John (ed.). *1988 South America Handbook.* (64th ed.) Bath, Avon, United Kingdom: Trade and Travel, 1987.

Canese, Ricardo, and Luis Alberto Mauro. *Itaipú: Dependencia o desarrollo.* Asunción: Editorial Aravera, 1985.

Centro Paraguayo de Estudios Sociológicos. *Economía del Paraguay contemporáneo.* Asunción: 1984.

———. *Economía paraguaya 1986, I: Análisis/Debates.* Asunción: 1987.

———. *Economía paraguaya 1986, II: Documentos.* Asunción: 1987.

———. *Economía paraguaya 1986, III: Estadísticas.* Asunción: 1987.

"Crece 150% la red carretera y caminera," *Progreso* [Mexico City], March 1988, 16–17.

La Crisis económica paraguaya, 1986-1987. Asunción: El Lector, 1987.

da Rosa, J. Eliseo. "Economics, Politics, and Hydroelectric Power:

The Paraná River Basin," *Latin American Research Review,* 17, No. 3, 1983, 77-108.

Economist Intelligence Unit. *Country Report: Uruguay, Paraguay* [London], No. 1, 1987.

_____. *Country Report: Uruguay, Paraguay* [London], No. 3, 1987.

_____. *Country Report: Uruguay, Paraguay* [London], No. 1, 1988.

"Energía," *Paraguayo económico* [Asunción], 1, No. 10, October 1982, 9-12.

Gutiérrez, Jonas. "Paraguay-Agribusiness vs. Peasants," *Nacla Report on the Americas,* 14, No. 3, May-June 1980, 38-41.

Hill, A.W. "En torno a la problemática del desarrollo paraguayo," *Revista paraguaya de sociología* [Asunción], 18, No. 41, June-September 1981, 129-48.

Institute for International Finance. *Paraguay: Country Update.* Washington: 1987.

Inter-American Development Bank. *Social and Economic Progress in Latin America, 1987 Report.* Washington: 1987.

_____. *Social and Economic Progress in Latin America, 1988 Report.* Washington: 1988.

International Monetary Fund. *Direction of Trade Statistics.* Washington: 1988.

_____. *Exchange Rate Agreements.* Washington: October 1987.

Kurian, George Thomas. *Encyclopedia of the Third World,* II. (Rev. ed.). New York: Facts on File, 1982.

_____. *Encyclopedia of the Third World,* II. (3d ed.). New York: Facts on File, 1987.

Lewis, Paul H. *Paraguay Under Stroessner.* Chapel Hill: University of North Carolina Press, 1980.

_____. *Socialism, Liberalism, and Dictatorship in Paraguay.* (Politics in Latin America Series.) New York: Praeger, 1982.

MacDonald, Ronald. "The Emerging New Politics in Paraguay," *Inter-American Economic Affairs,* 35, No. 1, Summer 1981, 25-44.

Masi, Fernando. "Contribución al estudio de la evolución socio-económica del Paraguay," *Revista paraguaya de sociología* [Asunción], 19, No. 52, January-April 1983, 33-64.

Miranda, Aníbal. *Desarrollo y pobreza en Paraguay.* Asunción: El Gráfico, 1982.

Organization of American States. *Statistical Bulletin of the OAS,* 8, Nos. 3-4, July-December 1986, 94-6.

_____. *Desarrollo regional integrado del Chaco paraguayo.* Asunción: 1983.

Pan American Development Foundation and Distributive Education Clubs of America. *The Way Up from Poverty: Microentrepreneurship in Latin America and the Caribbean.* Washington: Distributive Education Clubs of America, 1988.

"Paraguay: Ayer y hoy," *Visión* [Mexico City], 69, No. 5, September 7, 1987, 8-10.

Paraguay. Banco Central del Paraguay. Departamento de Estudios Económicos. *Boletín estadístico* [Asunción], No. 354, January 1988.

_____. *Cuentas nacionales, 1976-1985.* Asunción: 1985.

Peroni, Guillermo F., and Martin Burt. *Paraguay: Laws and Economy.* Asunción: Editora Litocolor, 1985.

Price, Waterhouse, and Company. *Doing Business in Paraguay.* New York: Price Waterhouse Center for Transnational Taxation, 1976.

"Las Primeras 500 empresas en américa latina," *Progreso* [Mexico City], December 1986, 15-36.

Raine, Philip. *Paraguay.* New Brunswick, New Jersey: Scarecrow Press, 1956.

Reissner, Marc, and Ronald MacDonald. "The High Costs of High Dams." Pages 270-307 in Andrew Maguire and Janet Welsh Brown (eds.), *Bordering on Trouble: Resources and Politics in Latin America.* Bethesda, Maryland: Adler and Adler, 1986.

Rodríguez Silvero, Ricardo. *La deformación estructural: Reflexiones sobre el desarrollo socio-económico en el Paraguay contemporáneo.* Asunción: Arte Nuevo Editores, 1985.

_____. "Paraguay: El Endeudamiento externo," *Revista paraguaya de sociología* [Asunción], 17, No. 50, January-May 1980, 65-87.

Roett, Riordan, and Amparo Menéndez-Carrión. "Authoritarian Paraguay: The Personalist Tradition." Pages 341-61 in Howard J. Wiarda and Harvey F. Kline (eds.), *Latin American Politics and Development.* (2d ed.) Boulder, Colorado: Westview Press, 1985.

Sanders, Thomas G. *Paraguay: Population and the Economy.* (Universities Field Staff International. UFSI Reports. Latin America, No. 36, TGS-7-86.) Indianapolis: UFSI, 1986.

_____. *Prospects for Political Change in Paraguay.* (Universities Field Staff International. UFSI Reports. Latin America, No. 37, TGS-8-86.) Indianapolis: UFSI, 1986.

Sewell, John, and Stuart K. Tucker. *Growth, Exports, and Jobs in a Changing World Economy: Agenda 1988.* New Brunswick, New Jersey: Transaction, 1988.

Storrs, K. Larry. "US Bilateral Economic and Military Assistance to Latin America and the Caribbean, FY 1946 to 1987." (Library of Congress. Congressional Research Service, Issue Brief.) July 31, 1987.

Ugarte Centurión, Delfín. *Evolución histórica de la economía paraguaya.* Asunción: Graphis, 1983.

_____. *Política económica y realizaciones del gobierno del Presidente Stroessner.* Asunción: El Gráfico, 1981.

United Nations. Comisión económica para américa latina. *Las Empresas transnacionales en la economía del Paraguay.* Santiago, Chile: 1987.

_____. *Paraguay.* Santiago, Chile: 1986.

_____. *Paraguay.* Santiago, Chile: 1987.

United States. Agency for International Development. *Annual Budget Submission FY 1986: Paraguay.* Washington: GPO, May 1984.

_____. Agency for International Development. *Congressional Presentation FY 1984, Annex II, Latin America and the Caribbean.* Washington: GPO, 1983.

_____. Agency for International Development. *Congressional Presentation FY 1987, Annex II, Latin America and the Caribbean.* Washington: GPO, 1986.

_____. Congress. 99th, 2d Session. House of Representatives. Committee on Armed Services. *Report of the Delegation to Latin America, November 30–December 7, 1986.* Washington: GPO, 1987.

_____. Department of Agriculture. Foreign Agriculture Service. *Paraguay: Agricultural Situation, 1987.* (Report PA–88–24A.) Washington: March 30, 1988.

_____. Department of Commerce. International Trade Administration. *Foreign Economic Trends and Their Implications for the United States: Paraguay.* (International Marketing Information Series. FET 87–76.) Washington: GPO, September 1987.

Wilkie, James W., David E. Lorey, and Enrique Ochoa (eds.). *Statistical Abstract of Latin America,* XXVI. Los Angeles: UCLA Latin American Center, 1988.

Williams, John Hoyt. "Paraguay's Stroessner: Losing Control?," *Current History,* 86, No. 516, January 1987, 25–8.

Winrock International. *Agricultural Development Indicators.* (4th ed.) Morrilton, Arkansas: 1987.

World Bank. *World Debt Tables: External Debt of Developing Countries.* Washington: 1987.

Young, Gordon. "Paraguay: Paradox of South America," *National Geographic,* 162, No. 2, August 1982, 240–69.

Chapter 4

Americas Watch Committee. *Paraguay: Latin America's Oldest Dictatorship Under Pressure.* New York: 1986.

_____. *Paraguay: Repression in the Countryside.* New York: 1988.

_____. *Rule by Fear: Paraguay After Thirty Years Under Stroessner.* New York: 1985.

Anuario Paraguay, 1987. (2 vols.). Asunción: Ediciones Ñandutí Vive, 1988.

Baer, Werner, and Luis Breuer. "From Inward to Outward Oriented Growth: Paraguay in the 1980s," *Journal of Interamerican Studies and World Affairs,* 28, No. 3, Fall 1986, 125–49.

Baer, Werner, and Melissa Birch. "Expansion of the Economic Frontier: Paraguayan Growth in the 1970s," *World Development,* 12, No. 8, August 1984, 783–98.

Blanch, José. "La Influencia de la iglesia en el cambio de la sociedad." (Paper presented at the Conference on Church and Politics in Latin America.) San Diego: Institute of the Americas, May 1987.

Bryce, Inigo García. "Signs of Change in Paraguay," *Harvard International Review,* 6, No. 6, May–June 1986, 30–1.

Conferencia Episcopal Paraguaya. *Anuario 1987: Sendero.* Asunción: December 22, 1987.

da Rosa, J. Eliseo. "Paraguay." Pages B143–67 in Abraham F. Lowenthal (ed.), *Latin America and Caribbean Contemporary Record, V: 1985–1986.* New York: Holmes and Meier, 1988.

Griesgraber, Jo Marie. "Transitions Do Not Lead Inevitably Toward Democracy: Post-Stroessner Paraguay." (Paper presented at the Latin American Studies Association Conference.) New Orleans: March 16–19, 1988.

Human Rights Watch and Lawyers Committee for Human Rights. *Critique: Review of the Department of State's Reports on Human Rights Practices for 1987.* New York: June 1988.

Lewis, Paul H. *Paraguay Under Stroessner.* Chapel Hill: University of North Carolina Press, 1980.

――――. *The Politics of Exile: Paraguay's Febrerista Party.* Chapel Hill: University of North Carolina Press, 1965.

Menezes, Alfredo da Mota. "The Stroessner Heritage: A History of Brazilian-Paraguayan Relations, 1955–1980." (Unpublished Ph.D. dissertation.) New Orleans: Department of History, Tulane University, 1984.

Miranda, Carlos R. "Obstacles to Redemocratization in Latin America: The Case of Paraguay." (Paper presented at the Latin American Studies Association Conference.) New Orleans: March 16–19, 1988.

Nickson, R. Andrew. "Tyranny and Longevity: Stroessner's Paraguay." *Third World Quarterly,* 10, No. 1, January 1988, 237–59.

Paraguay. *Constitution of the Republic of Paraguay 1967.* Washington: Organization of American States, 1969.

"Paraguay." Pages 342–65 in Adrian J. English, *Armed Forces of Latin America: Their Histories, Development, Present Strength, and Military Potential.* London: Jane's, 1984.

Roett, Riordan, and Amparo Menéndez-Carrión. "Authoritarian Paraguay: The Personalist Tradition." Pages 341–61 in Howard J. Wiarda and Harvey F. Kline (eds.), *Latin American Politics and Development.* (2d ed.) Boulder, Colorado: Westview Press, 1985.

Sanders, Thomas G. *Education and Authoritarianism in the Southern Cone.* (American Universities Field Staff. Fieldstaff Reports. South America Series, No. 12.) Hanover, New Hampshire: AUFS, 1981.

———. *Paraguay: Population and the Economy.* (Universities Field Staff International. UFSI Reports. Latin America, No. 36, TGS-7-86.) Indianapolis: UFSI, 1986.

———. *Prospects for Political Change in Paraguay.* (Universities Field Staff International. UFSI Reports. Latin America, No. 37, TGS-8-86.) Indianapolis: UFSI, 1986.

Secretariado internacional de juristas por la amnistía y la democracia en Paraguay. *Paraguay: Un Desafío a la responsabilidad internacional.* Montevideo: Ediciones de la Banda Oriental, 1986.

United States. Congress. 98th, 1st Session. House of Representatives. Committee on Foreign Affairs. Subcommittee on Human Rights and International Organizations. Subcommittee on Western Hemisphere Affairs. *Human Rights in Argentina, Chile, Paraguay, and Uruguay.* Washington: GPO, 1984.

———. Congress. 99th, 2d Session. House of Representatives. Committee on Armed Services. *Report of the Delegation to Latin America, November 30–December 7, 1986.* Washington: GPO, 1987.

———. Congress. 100th, 2d Session. House of Representatives. Committee on Banking, Finance, and Urban Affairs. Subcommittee on International Development Institutions and Finance. *Decertification Resolutions.* Washington: GPO, 1988.

———. Department of State. Bureau of Public Affairs. Office of Public Communication. *Background Notes: Paraguay.* Washington: GPO, June 1987.

———. Department of State. *Country Reports on Human Rights Practices for 1987.* (Report submitted to United States Congress, 101st, 1st Session, House of Representatives, Committee on Foreign Affairs, and Senate, Committee on Foreign Relations.) Washington: GPO, 1988.

Vinocur, John. "A Republic of Fear," *New York Times Magazine,* September 23, 1984, 21–3.

Williams, John Hoyt. "Paraguay." Pages 365–73 in Jack W. Hopkins (ed.), *Latin America and Caribbean Contemporary Record, IV, 1984–1985.* New York: Holmes and Meier, 1986.

———. "Paraguay's Stroessner: Losing Control?" *Current History,* 86, No. 516, January 1987, 25–8.

———. "Social Issues in Post-Stroessner Paraguay." (Paper presented at the Latin American Studies Association Conference.) New Orleans: March 16–19, 1988.

———. "Stroessner's Paraguay," *Current History,* 82, No. 469, February 1983, 66–8.

Yearbook on International Communist Affairs 1986. Stanford, California: Hoover Institution Press, 1986.

(Various issues of the following publications were also used in the preparation of this chapter: *Christian Science Monitor; El Diario de Noticias* [Asunción]; *Economist* [London]; Foreign Broadcast Information Service, *Daily Report: Latin America;* Joint Publications Research Service, *Latin America Report; Latinamerica Press* [Lima]; *Latin American Monitor* [London]; *Latin American Weekly Report* [London]; *Los Angeles Times; New York Times; Sendero* [Asunción]; *Veja* [Rio de Janeiro]; and *Washington Post.*)

Chapter 5

Air Forces of the World. Geneva: Interavia, 1986.

Americas Watch Committee. *Paraguay: Latin America's Oldest Dictatorship Under Pressure.* New York: 1986.

———. *Rule by Fear: Paraguay After Thirty Years Under Stroessner.* New York: 1985.

Amnesty International. *Amnesty International Report 1986.* London: 1986.

Andrade, John. *World Police and Paramilitary Forces.* New York: Stockton Press, 1985.

Brindley, John F. (ed.). *Globemac: The Global Military Airpower Census.* Geneva: Aeroreference, 1984.

Combat Fleets of the World 1986–87. (Ed., Jean Labayle Couhat.) Annapolis, Maryland: Naval Institute Press, 1986.

Copley, Gregory R. *Defense and Foreign Affairs Handbook.* Washington: Perth, 1987.

Gunston, Bill (ed.). *Encyclopedia of World Air Power.* New York: Crescent Books, 1980.

Hobday, Charles. *Communist and Marxist Parties of the World.* Burnt Mill Hollow, Essex, United Kingdom: Longman, 1986.

Huskey, James L. (ed.). *Lambert's Worldwide Directory of Defense Authorities with International Defense Organizations and Treaties.* Washington: Lambert, 1983.

International Institute of Strategic Studies. *The Military Balance 1987–88.* London: 1987.

International Monetary Fund. *Government Finance Statistics Yearbook,* X. Washington: 1986.

_____. *International Financial Statistics Supplement 1986.* Washington: 1986.

_____. *International Financial Statistics Yearbook 1987,* XL. Washington: 1987.

International Yearbook and Statesmen's Who's Who 1986. East Grinstead, West Sussex, United Kingdom: Thomas Skinner Directories, 1986.

Jane's All the World's Aircraft 1987-88. (Ed., John W.R. Taylor.) London: Jane's, 1987.

Jane's Armour and Artillery 1987-88. (Ed., Christopher F. Foss.). London: Jane's, 1987.

Jane's Fighting Ships 1987-88. (Ed., John Moore.) London: Jane's, 1987.

Keegan, John (ed.). *World Armies.* New York: Facts on File, 1984.

Kolinski, Charles J. *Historical Dictionary of Paraguay.* Metuchen, New Jersey: Scarecrow Press, 1973.

Kurian, George Thomas. *Encyclopedia of the Third World,* II. (Rev. ed.). New York: Facts on File, 1982.

Lewis, Paul H. *Paraguay Under Stroessner.* Chapel Hill: University of North Carolina Press, 1980.

_____. *The Politics of Exile: Paraguay's Febrerista Party.* Chapel Hill: University of North Carolina, 1965.

_____. *Socialism, Liberalism, and Dictatorship in Paraguay.* (Politics in Latin America Series). New York: Praeger, 1982.

Organization of American States. *Report on the Situation of Human Rights in Paraguay.* Washington: Inter-American Commission on Human Rights, 1978.

Paraguay. *Código penal del Paraguay y leyes complementarias actualizadas.* Asunción: Ediciones Comuneros, 1981.

Paraguay. *Constitution of the Republic of Paraguay 1967.* Washington: Organization of American States, 1969.

"Paraguay." Pages 342-65 in Adrian J. English, *Armed Forces of Latin America: Their Histories, Development, Present Strength, and Military Potential.* London: Jane's, 1984.

Sivard, Ruth Leger. *World Military and Social Expenditures 1987-88.* Leesburg, Virginia: World Priorities, 1987.

United States. Arms Control and Disarmament Agency. *World Military Expenditures and Arms Transfers, 1967-76.* Washington: 1978.

_____. Arms Control and Disarmament Agency. *World Military Expenditures and Arms Transfers, 1972-82.* Washington: 1984.

_____. Arms Control and Disarmament Agency. *World Military Expenditures and Arms Transfers, 1978-87.* Washington: 1988.

————. Congress. 98th, 1st Session. House of Representatives. Committee on Foreign Affairs. *Hearings Before the Subcommittees on Human Rights and International Organizations and on Western Hemisphere Affairs.* Washington: GPO, 1984.

————. Department of Defense. Security Assistance Agency. *Congressional Presentation for Security Assistance Programs, Fiscal Year 1988.* Washington: GPO, 1988.

————. Department of State. *Country Reports on Human Rights Practices for 1985.* (Report submitted to United States Congress, 100th, 1st Session, House of Representatives, Committee on Foreign Affairs, and Senate, Committee on Foreign Relations.) Washington: GPO, 1986.

————. Department of State. *Country Reports on Human Rights Practices for 1986.* (Report submitted to United States Congress, 100th, 2d Session, House of Representatives, Committee on Foreign Affairs, and Senate, Committee on Foreign Relations.) Washington: GPO, 1987.

————. Department of State. *Country Reports on Human Rights Practices for 1987.* (Report submitted to United States Congress, 101st, 1st Session, House of Representatives, Committee on Foreign Affairs, and Senate, Committee on Foreign Relations.) Washington: GPO, 1988.

Williams, John Hoyt. "Paraguay's Stroessner: Losing Control?" *Current History,* 86, No. 516, January 1987, 25-8.

————. "Stroessner's Paraguay," *Current History,* 82, No. 469, February 1983, 66-8.

Yearbook on International Communist Affairs 1976. (Ed., Richard F. Staar.) Stanford: Hoover Institution Press, 1976.

Yearbook on International Communist Affairs 1987. (Ed. Richard F. Staar.) Stanford: Hoover Institution Press, 1987.

Yearbook on International Communist Affairs 1988. (Ed. Richard F. Staar.) Stanford: Hoover Institution Press, 1988.

(Various issues of the following publications were also used in the preparation of this chapter: Economist Intelligence Unit, *Country Report: Uruguay, Paraguay* [London]; Foreign Broadcast Information Service, *Daily Report: Latin America;* Joint Publications Research Service, *Latin America Report; Latin American Weekly Report* [London]; *New York Times; Nuestro Tiempo* [Asunción]; and *Washington Post.*)

Glossary

desarrollismo—A post-World War II school of thought in Latin America emphasizing rapid economic development through import substitution and industrialization.

fiscal year (FY)—Calendar year.

GDP—gross domestic product. A measure of the total value of goods and services produced by the domestic economy during a given period, usually one year. Obtained by adding the value contributed by each sector of the economy in the form of profits, compensation to employees, and depreciation (consumption of capital). The income arising from investments and possessions owned abroad is not included, only domestic production. Hence, the use of the word "domestic" to distinguish GDP from GNP (*q.v.*).

GNP—gross national product. Total market value of all final goods and services produced by an economy during a year. Obtained by adding GDP (*q.v.*) and the income received from abroad by residents less payments remitted abroad to nonresidents.

guaraní (₲)—The national currency. From 1960 to 1982 the guaraní remained pegged to the United States dollar at ₲126=US$1. Responding to the completion of construction of the Itaipú hydroelectric plant and lower commodity prices for soybeans and cotton, in July 1982 the Central Bank established a multitiered exchange rate system. The most favorable rate was reserved for the imports of certain state-owned enterprises and for external debt-service payments. Three other controlled rates were applied to imports of petroleum and petroleum derivatives; disbursements of loans to the public sector; and agricultural imports and most exports. Commercial banks set a fifth, free-market rate that governed most of the private sector's nonoil imports. In early 1988, these five rates were ₲240=US$1, ₲320=US$1, ₲400=US$1, ₲550=US$1, and approximately ₲900=US$1, respectively. The multitiered system constituted a massive subsidy to state-owned enterprises. Central Bank losses in controlled exchange rate transactions accounted for nearly half of public-sector deficit in 1986. In July 1988, the Central Bank eliminated the two most favorable exchange rates; set ₲400=US$1 as the rate for imports of state-owned enterprises, external debt-service payments, and petroleum imports; and established ₲550=US$1 as the rate for disbursements of loans to the public sector, agricultural imports, and most exports. In January 1989, the Central Bank further devalued the guaraní by setting the controlled rates at ₲600=US$1 and ₲750=US$1 and also required petroleum imports to be paid at the higher rate. In early 1989, the free-market rate exceeded ₲1,000=US$1.

IMF—International Monetary Fund. Established along with the World Bank (*q.v.*) in 1945, the IMF is a specialized agency affiliated with the United Nations that takes responsibility for stabilizing international exchange rates and payments. The main business of the IMF is the provision of loans to its members when they experience balance-of-payments difficulties. These loans often carry conditions that require substantial internal economic adjustments by the recipients.

informal sector—The sector of the economy beyond government regulation and taxation. Most active in urban areas among those involved in simple manufacturing and commercial and other services.

Southern Cone—name for area of South America consisting of Argentina, Chile, Paraguay, and Uruguay.

World Bank—Informal name used to designate a group of three affiliated international institutions: the International Bank for Reconstruction and Development (IBRD), the International Development Association (IDA), and the International Finance Corporation (IFC). The IBRD, established in 1945, has the primary purpose of providing loans to developing countries for productive projects. The IDA, a legally separate loan fund administered by the staff of the IBRD, was set up in 1960 to furnish credits to the poorest developing countries on much easier terms than those of conventional IBRD loans. The IFC, founded in 1956, supplements the activities of the IBRD through loans and assistance designed specifically to encourage the growth of productive private enterprises in less developed countries. The president and certain senior officers of the IBRD hold the same positions in the IFC. The three institutions are owned by the governments of the countries that subscribe their capital. To participate in the World Bank group, member states must first belong to the IMF (*q.v.*).

Index

273

Published Country Studies

(Area Handbook Series)

550-65	Afghanistan		550-153	Ghana
550-98	Albania		550-87	Greece
550-44	Algeria		550-78	Guatemala
550-59	Angola		550-174	Guinea
550-73	Argentina		550-82	Guyana
550-169	Australia		550-151	Honduras
550-176	Austria		550-165	Hungary
550-175	Bangladesh		550-21	India
550-170	Belgium		550-154	Indian Ocean
550-66	Bolivia		550-39	Indonesia
550-20	Brazil		550-68	Iran
550-168	Bulgaria		550-31	Iraq
550-61	Burma		550-25	Israel
550-37	Burundi/Rwanda		550-182	Italy
550-50	Cambodia		550-30	Japan
550-166	Cameroon		550-34	Jordan
550-159	Chad		550-56	Kenya
550-77	Chile		550-81	Korea, North
550-60	China		550-41	Korea, South
550-26	Colombia		550-58	Laos
550-33	Commonwealth Caribbean, Islands of the		550-24	Lebanon
550-91	Congo		550-38	Liberia
550-90	Costa Rica		550-85	Libya
550-69	Côte d'Ivoire (Ivory Coast)		550-172	Malawi
550-152	Cuba		550-45	Malaysia
550-22	Cyprus		550-161	Mauritania
550-158	Czechoslovakia		550-79	Mexico
550-36	Dominican Republic/Haiti		550-76	Mongolia
550-52	Ecuador		550-49	Morocco
550-43	Egypt		550-64	Mozambique
550-150	El Salvador		550-88	Nicaragua
550-28	Ethiopia		550-157	Nigeria
550-167	Finland		550-94	Oceania
550-155	Germany, East		550-48	Pakistan
550-173	Germany, Fed. Rep. of		550-46	Panama

287

550-156	Paraguay	550-89	Tunisia
550-185	Persian Gulf States	550-80	Turkey
550-42	Peru	550-74	Uganda
550-72	Philippines	550-97	Uruguay
550-162	Poland	550-71	Venezuela
550-181	Portugal	550-32	Vietnam
550-160	Romania	550-183	Yemens, The
550-51	Saudi Arabia	550-99	Yugloslavia
550-70	Senegal	550-67	Zaire
550-180	Sierra Leone	550-75	Zambia
550-184	Singapore	550-171	Zimbabwe
550-86	Somalia		
550-93	South Africa		
550-95	Soviet Union		
550-179	Spain		
500-96	Sri Lanka		
550-27	Sudan		
550-47	Syria		
550-62	Tanzania		
550-53	Thailand